THE GUEST HOUSE

The
Guest House

A Nuremberg Memoir of Countess Kalnoky

with

Ilona Herisko

The Bobbs-Merrill Company, Inc.

Indianapolis/New York

ISBN 0-672-51827-9
Library of Congress catalog card number 73-22674
Designed by Jacques Chazaud
Manufactured in the United States of America

First printing

To my late husband and my children,
who shared these experiences with me

A GUEST BOOK SHOULD have a handsome cover; leather perhaps, or linen. But mine is only a small, by now rather dog-eared, notebook, the kind children might use to do their homework, or housewives to copy recipes. The signatures on its pages do not witness any memorable event in my family's life, but a black year in the life of my nation, for although I married a Hungarian and lived in Hungary for the first ten years of my marriage, I was born a German.

In the Germany to which I returned in 1945, even such a modest notebook as was to become my guest book could be found only at an American Post Exchange. But the lack of this particular commodity was less than serious. Those schools that were still standing had become barracks for the occupation forces; instead of doing homework, children kept busy begging leftover food from American field kitchens, and housewives needed no recipes to prepare the meager rations of potatoes and bread.

Perhaps, in a different, saner time, this notebook might have contained one of my children's lessons from which I would have helped him to study his vocabulary in French or English, while the signatures that now fill these pages would still be on diplomatic treaties or ministerial memoranda. But people cannot choose their time; they are caught in it, and it can break over them with all the violence of a tidal wave. Perhaps there are inevitable catastrophes in human history that parallel those in the natural world, forces gathering at some unmeasured depth to erupt and destroy. Like the stunned survivors of such a catastrophe, my "guests" and I met in Nuremberg in the shadow of the great war crimes trial that was to measure the limits of human justice against the boundless dimensions of evil itself.

1

I ARRIVED IN NUREMBERG in August 1945, nine months pregnant and alone. Seven months earlier in a small village in West Hungary I had kissed my husband goodbye and with my three children and Cuci, their nurse, joined the westward trek of refugees fleeing from the Russian advance. The decision to leave and so break up the family was made by us with great reluctance. Until we had talked to some eyewitnesses who had fled from behind the Russian lines, we had dismissed the rumors of Russian atrocities as German propaganda. After hearing their reports, however, my husband decided that it would be best for us to seek safety farther west. Because of a Gestapo warrant for his arrest, he could not accompany us; the refugee-clogged roads leading toward the Austrian border were too closely watched. He had earned his place on the Gestapo wanted list with a series of articles for his Budapest newspaper, the *Pesterlloyd*. Praising Churchill and criticizing German poli-

1

cies, some parts of these articles were picked up for broadcast by the BBC. Friends in the underground warned us of his impending arrest, and we were able to flee Budapest just hours before the Gestapo raided our home.

After weeks of flight through the villages of West Hungary, never daring to stay more than a day or two in one place, we found refuge with Baron Vilmos Apor, bishop of Gyoer, who had given shelter to a number of other political refugees, among them Professor Julius Szekfue, who later was to become Hungary's ambassador to Russia. By permitting my husband to pose as a member of his staff, the bishop almost certainly saved his life.

For several months we found a haven with that kind and generous man. But the front was moving ever closer, and by January the area around Gyoer was on the verge of becoming a combat zone. The bishop knew that I was expecting another child; his advice to us to leave and try to reach Austria while the roads were still open helped us reach the final decision. On a bitter cold night in January, with the sound of Russian artillery in our ears, we said goodbye. In my husband's eyes I could see my own fears, but we talked only about our hopes—that it wasn't far to the Austrian border, that the war couldn't last much longer, that we would soon be reunited. He had held on to the children in a last goodbye. When the carriage moved away I could not see his face as he receded into the dark, standing alone, as if forsaken, with one arm half-raised in a melancholy wave.

The following morning Cuci, the children, and I crossed the border into Austria. Only then, while standing on the refugee-crowded platform of a small railway station, did the full impact of our situation strike me. We too were homeless, uprooted, and dispossessed. I had not felt that bitter certainty while we were still in Hungary. Somehow there had always remained the hope that eventually we would be able to return home. We had concentrated on surviving one enemy, forgetting that for us there were two. The Germans were almost beaten, but the Russians came as victors.

2

The bullet-scarred train that came hours later took us to Vienna, where we found that the relatives with whom we had hoped to find shelter had moved away. A number of air raids and another perilous train journey later (we were attacked by American fighter planes), we arrived in Czechoslovakia, where, in the vicinity of Pilsen, my husband had relatives. There, for a time, we found shelter.

But the specter that had driven us from Gyoer was to force us into exile again. Within a few weeks of the German surrender the Czech authorities issued an order for the deportation of all aliens back to their countries of origin. Departure times and locations were broadcast over public address systems and posted on bulletin boards; heavy penalties were threatened for failure to comply. Hungary, of course, was solidly in Russian hands. Only a few days earlier I had been told by another refugee that Baron Apor had been shot by Russian soldiers. My husband, I was told, had been with the bishop but had not been harmed. That was the only piece of information I had had of my husband since our separation. But there was other information of which I had had more than enough. By now the scattered reports of Russian atrocities that had reached us in Gyoer had multiplied a thousandfold. I knew that I could not return. To defy the order or try to circumvent it seemed a lot less frightening than to comply with it. I was sick with worry about my husband. According to all reports, members of the gentry, if they could not manage to hide their identity, were subjected to particularly cruel treatment. I was certain that he would want me to try all in my power to prevent our return; this I resolved to do.

It was summer and I was by now close to term. If I had tried to be admitted to a Czech hospital I certainly would have been immediately deported. I wanted to get into Germany or Austria before it was too late. In my desperation I turned to the Americans who since May had been occupying this area of Czechoslovakia. I did not have to go far. The castle of Prince Trautmansdorff, my host for the past six months, had been taken over as a regimental headquarters. I found a major in one of the offices to whom I told my plight, while he listened expression-lessly with his feet on his desk, glancing at me now and then over the tips of his boots. I grew increasingly uncomfortable, because it suddenly occurred to me that there was nothing to prevent him from turning me over to the Czechs. In the midst of all this suffering, want, and chaos, why should he want to help me? I looked at my bony arms and brittle nails and noted the familiar gnawing in my stomach. The combination of hunger and pregnancy had taken its toll; my hair was falling out and my teeth were loose. I had been considered attractive, but my face bore the marks of the past year, reflecting the state of my body and mind. Before that silent major I felt suddenly ugly and alone and ashamed of my misery. I pitied myself and my unborn child—and yet, what was the weight of my misery within the sum of the whole? Why should this stranger be concerned for me? Quite literally overcome by an intense feeling of hopelessness, I fainted.

When I came to, I was lying on a sofa. Two American officers were looking down at me, one of them the heretofore straight-faced major, who shook his head and smiled. "You had me worried. I thought you were going to have the baby right here."

I felt too weak to be embarrassed.

"You'll be all right for now, but you don't seem to have much time left," said the other, a captain. "Do you have a place in a hospital?"

Because I didn't want to cry, I only shook my head. The major then told my story to the captain, who was a medical officer. Two hours later I had a pass authorizing me to travel into Germany with an armored unit of the U.S. Army that was to leave the following day. I was to be taken to Nuremberg, where the American doctor knew a German hospital to be in operation. The papers he gave me would help me gain admission.

I could not take the children. The decision to leave them behind was the most painful and difficult I had ever made. I

4

knew that for the time being they would be all right with Cuci. Although the threat of deportation hung over them as well, that was the lesser of my worries, since they could remain inconspicuous at the castle. In the overall confusion of sorting out all the uprooted humanity scattered like so much flotsam across Europe, it would be some time before they were found out. The secret was not to be noticed, not to be at the mercy of any of the relief agencies, or in need—as I was—of any other help. My greatest fear in leaving the children was the fact of separation in these times. Although the distance between Pilsen and Nuremberg could not have been more than two hundred kilometers, it might as well have been two thousand; besides, that little two hundred kilometers had a border running through it. All over, the bloody real estate of Europe was jigsawed into pieces, and the cuts never healed. Now our family was about to be cut in three.

Cuci and I spent a sleepless night considering alternatives, but there seemed to be none. Neither of us wanted to risk deportation. My going to Nuremberg gave us at least a chance to circumvent it; my remaining in Pilsen made it certain to happen. How, when, or where we would be reunited we did not know; with the thousands of other broken families, we would have to take our chances. When, after tearful goodbyes, I took my place in the jeep under the astonished stares of the soldiers and the somewhat worried looks of a Captain Yee, I had the feeling that I was about to travel into a void. I should have been grateful, but I felt only numb.

The road was rough, ripped by shells and littered with the burned-out hulls of armored vehicles. Captain Yee, a Chinese-American who turned out to be a medical officer, was solicitous, but nervous, and repeatedly reminded the driver to "take it easy." He was obviously relieved when we reached Nuremberg with me and the baby still in one piece. At the first house that still stood with its four walls intact and holding up a roof, Captain Yee, and with him the entire armored column, stopped. Smiling at me encouragingly, he knocked at the door and then turned me, my little bag, and half a dozen boxes of K-rations over to the bewildered inhabitants. Since they did not understand English the explanations were left to me. Captain Yee wished me good luck, sprinted back to his jeep, and waved as the column drove away down the rubble-lined street, while I looked after them miserably, feeling envious of all the smoking, gum-chewing, laughing, generous soldiers who had no bonds to these ruins.

The house was ancient and narrow, sagging, it seemed, under too great a burden. The only one remaining on its block, it appeared to balance itself unsteadily by hanging on to the remnants of its erstwhile neighbors. To say that the inhabitants—of which there were entirely too many—were reluctant to take me in is somewhat of an understatement. But my condition, added to the peculiar manner of my arrival, apparently convinced the lady of the house that it would be both inhumane and imprudent to turn me back out into the street. I was installed in an attic room containing only a glassless skylight and some debris. When I was an art student in Munich, a friend and I had shared a loft that had a northern skylight. It seemed a very long time ago now, almost as if it belonged to someone else's memory. This Nuremberg skylight was covered with cardboard. I wondered if it faced north. A man brought up a folding bed for me. It was his own, but he said he didn't mind for a few days, and he smiled at me kindly when I stammered my thanks.

As my loft grew dark it became more bearable. I removed the cardboard from the skylight and concentrated on the patch of summer sky, on the glow that made the darkness shimmer and richly patterned the room with shadows. Shades of darkness on the night's canvas: I suddenly remembered El Greco's sky above Toledo, though it wasn't at all like this Nuremberg sky glowing and serene with summer. Those restless clouds brooding over the gaunt city, gathering in densest darkness above the spire of the cathedral like smoke from inquisitional pyres—a worthy sky to look upon a tortured town. This sky above the window was wrong; it did not fit the picture's mood —and yet, I would paint it that way. If I had had a canvas I would have painted those shadows, those shades of darkness in patterns of debris beneath this patch of clear, bright night, a sky without El Greco's god brooding over the unhappy town to share its mortal pain; a twentieth-century sky.

I spent a little more than a week in my attic. The lady of the house helped me to find a German doctor who, with the help of my American papers, made the necessary arrangements to have me admitted to the hospital when my time came. When I went to the German authorities to apply for identification papers and ration coupons, the American documents proved equally effective. There was one other area in which I thought it advisable to turn once more to the Americans for assistance. The hospital was in another part of the city, and although streetcars were operating, they ran infrequently and slowly; in my condition it would have been quite risky to depend on them. I went to the nearest building I found occupied by Americans, gaining admission with my travel orders from Pilsen, which included a general appeal to army personnel to render assistance if needed. It was in this manner that I met Captain Kerr, a medical officer whose help was to mean considerably more to me than a jeep ride to the hospital. At that first meeting, though, he merely promised me the transportation I asked for and offered me a cigarette, and when he saw me draw on it greedily, he gave me the whole package. The house where I was staying was not far away. I arranged that I would send someone with the message when my time came.

Up to this point, my future was planned. What I would do after the baby's birth I had as yet no idea. Attempts to get in touch with relatives remained fruitless. My parents, if they had survived, were in the Russian zone; my sisters and brother were scattered about, or uprooted by the war as I. My first concern after the baby's birth would have to be finding a place to live. In the rubble heap that was Nuremberg, that alone would be quite an undertaking. Having my family rejoin me was the next priority, an equally difficult task. If I thought too far ahead my problems threatened to overwhelm me, but I couldn't afford to panic. I resolved to move one step at a time, the first being obviously to have my baby. In the days remaining before my confinement, though, I made some inquiries concerning a place to live, finding the answer always the same —there was simply nothing available. Much of Nuremberg had been destroyed. People were living in cellars and the precarious remnants of ruined houses. Most of the housing that had been spared by the bombs had been requisitioned by the occupation troops. My landlady advised me to try Fuerth, a small neighboring town which had suffered little damage; but I was told that Fuerth, too, was bursting at the seams. My prospects looked grim, as grim as the town in which fate had set me down to give birth to my child.

August baked the skeleton of Nuremberg, bleaching the shells of buildings, raising clouds of fine white dust that glittered in the sunlight. In the still, bright, consuming heat even the weeds that grew in the cracks of the ruins withered and died. The streets were mostly empty, cleared of life like bone of flesh. The narrow cobbled streets had been made narrower by piles of rubble; some were impassable. Here and there walls had remained standing, some with cracked, painted scenes— saints and burghers and masters at their trades and pious sayings in Latin. One night had been enough to destroy what had withstood the seasons of nine centuries. Would there ever again be beautiful old cities, slow-grown and majestic like ancient oaks, or only stronger and better bunkers to shelter the remnants of a doomed race?

On a high sandstone rock the majestic ruin of the imperial castle brooded over its broken city. Once called home to the Hohenstaufens, descendants of the great Barbarossa, later to the Hohenzollerns, dynasty of William II, its ancient walls had also harbored Germany's last and most fateful lord, risen without dynasty and vanished without descendants; a specter leaving ashes. He had come in imperial splendor to the annual party rallies, and the ancient city had resounded with the massive tread of marching boots, the driving chants—*Ein Volk, Ein Reich, Ein Fuehrer!*—invocation of the new trinity to the unfurling of thousands of banners in the marble stadium. *Sieg Heil! Sieg Heil!* Where were they now who had chanted then? In unmarked graves or distant prisons? I found the skeleton of Dürer's house. Not far away in these wasted streets Hans Sachs had pounded his last and composed his songs. Memories of Nuremberg—the piety of Dürer's art and the pornography of Streicher's *Stuermer,* the quiet wisdom of Hans Sachs and the ranting orations of Adolf Hitler.

They were depressing excursions, those walks through the old city, but staying in my attic was no more pleasant. Besides, after three days my K-rations ran out and I had to go in search of food. Even with ration coupons this was a far from simple matter. Supplies were so limited, stores so few that people were unwilling to sell to strangers. What helped me at times was my condition. Once a kind baker woman filled my bag with warm rolls, far more than I was entitled to for my coupons. Then she pressed my hand and wished me luck.

"I've got two boys in the east," she said, wiping her eyes. "May God have mercy on them—and us."

May God have mercy indeed. I fought against the helplessness those words engendered in me. Would God have me bear a child into so much misery? On all sides death was crowding in on me. The living seemed only half alive, hushed and somber—shadows of dirty, gaunt children darting about the ruins; slow-moving, sad-eyed women going about mysterious chores in nonexisting homes; a city of ghosts.

I had discovered a little pocket-sized park where, under a maimed tree, a weathered bench had remained intact. Facing the bench and overgrown with weeds was a grave mound marked with a battered German army helmet. I am not sure why that grave drew me to visit it so that I came back almost every day. It was as if I needed to measure the power of the life within me against the dimensions of that unknown sol-

9

dier's grave, poor fool's grave marked with a fool's cap, summary of lunacy for which millions had died and were still dying. Cry the poor fool the tears that are left, that are always left in abundance. Were the baker woman's two sons in such nameless graves somewhere on the littered battlefields of the east? May God have mercy indeed.

An American soldier came by one afternoon while I sat on that bench. He was whistling and peeling an orange, throwing the peels into the weeds. I don't think he saw the grave, but he looked at me and smiled, holding out to me his half-peeled orange.

"For your baby," he said.

I listened to his whistling as he continued on his way, until I could no longer hear it. I savored the orange, and when the baby kicked with impatient force, I felt a sudden joy that was like liberation. Nothing had changed and yet all looked different, as if life and death had entered into a new balance. I would never forget that soldier's face.

The Sunday before I went to the hospital I had again gone to the little park. As I sat on my bench I heard music from a distance, singing voices, an organ, shreds of melody. I followed the sound, recognizing, even before I had found the source, the strains of Haydn's *Creation*. The music issued mightily from an old baroque church with a smashed cupola, filled to overflowing with people. Many others who could not get in sat in the surrounding ruins to listen and weep. There was great comfort in such tears. I felt bound to the other people by a common grief and to the music by its joy. Both were true, and one did not negate the other. The baby kicked; the chorus praised; I listened on my pile of rubble, drawing from each note its healing power.

Two days later, faithful to his promise, Captain Kerr rushed me to the hospital, where I gave birth to a little girl whom I named Ingeborg. By my bedside was a small bouquet of summer flowers gathered by the nuns to greet the new life. I held my baby and tried to be hopeful about the future.

10

2

CAPTAIN KERR CAME to visit me the day after the birth. He was a large man with a pleasant face and a bearing characteristic of the victorious Americans, casual and self-assured. I had not expected to see him again and wondered why he had come. Inquiring pleasantly about the baby and how I felt, he sat down on the chair beside my bed and put up his feet on a little table. "You're Hungarian, aren't you?"

"Yes, by marriage. But I was born in Germany."

"But you've lived in Hungary for quite a while?"

"About ten years."

"That just about takes care of the whole Hitler time, doesn't it?"

I nodded, wondering what he was getting at.

"You speak English pretty well."

"Thank you. I spent a year in England after I left school."

"German, Hungarian, and English."

"I also speak French."

"Marvelous. That makes it even better."

"It makes what better?" I asked, beginning to get excited.

A sister came into the room. The captain gave her a friendly nod, apparently not noticing her severely disapproving glance at his polished boots on the table. He did not, in any case, withdraw them. "Look, you're kind of at loose ends, aren't you?" he asked with an expression of earnest intentness.

"I beg your pardon?"

"I mean, what will you do when you leave the hospital?"

"I don't know."

"Well, I think I might be able to help you. As you probably know, there's going to be a trial in this town, a war crimes trial. A lot of people will be needed who know languages and who have a clean past."

My tension made it difficult for me to speak; the rapid beating of my heart seemed to fill the room. "And you think there might be something for me?"

He pulled his boots off the table and leaned forward, elbows on his knees. "I think there is a possibility. I'm not sure what is involved. Let me check it out further. I'll probably be back tomorrow." He had noticed my excitement and gently touched my hand. "Things will work out," he said. "Don't worry too much." He reached into his pocket and pulled out a package of Camels. "Here. You really shouldn't have these, but I know how you feel."

I was greatly moved by his concern. How generous they all were—Captain Kerr, Captain Yee, the officers in Pilsen, the young soldier who had given me his orange—generous and self-assured. Their generosity seemed to spring from this self-assurance. Although they had fought this war and were the victors, its bloody passions seemed to have left them untouched.

I awaited the next day with intense impatience, eased only slightly by Captain Kerr's Camels. He came shortly before noon accompanied by another officer, a colonel who was his superior and who asked me essentially the same questions the captain had asked the day before. Then he told me that I might be the right person for a job connected with the International Military Tribunal that would soon convene in Nuremberg. Before he could tell me more about it, however, I had to be interviewed by the CIC. As to his inquiry whether I felt strong enough to have the interview tomorrow, I nodded emphatically, although I was not at all sure that I could even get down the hospital stairs. The colonel told me to be ready the following day at about the same time and left me alone with my anticipation. A hundred questions went through my mind. I had heard that a trial was to be held at Nuremberg, but how could I be connected with it? What kind of a job would it be? Would my language facility be sufficient? Where would I find a place to live? How would I bring my children to Nuremberg?

The unpredictability of fate can be used as a strong argument for the determinist view of life. Certainly my life that summer was governed by coincidences—chance meetings and events of the kind that would earn a novelist the reputation for manipulating his plots. As I worried myself through a sleepless night, I hardly suspected that one of my greatest worries would be gone by morning. It was barely six o'clock when the door opened very slowly and softly and my three children tiptoed into the room, followed by a broadly smiling Cuci. There was enough laughing and crying to convince me that I wasn't dreaming. But I was afraid to believe that it was true, that they were really there in front of me, and when I held them I felt almost guilty with my joy. Was so much happiness possible in such an unhappy time? Or was it only possible in such a time?

It was a while before I was able to piece together out of the excited, often simultaneous accounts the story of their journey. They had come in the back of an American army truck camouflaged with blankets under a cargo of supplies. Farkas, who was eight and had an avid interest in anything that had a motor, had made friends with an American soldier who once a week drove a supply truck across the Czech border to

13

Nuremberg. The soldier also happened to be—another one of those chance events—a Hungarian-American, which was at least one of the reasons that Farkas and he got on so well together. They were able to communicate. Hearing about the dilemma of our separation and the threat of deportation that hung over Cuci and the children, he offered to smuggle them across the border in his truck. Since the Czech border guards rarely checked American military vehicles, the risk of discovery was minimal. The greater risk was in the possibility of my having left the hospital by the time they got to Nuremberg. But Cuci hoped that even if I had left, someone at the hospital would be able to tell her where I had gone. What really made her decision final, though, was the certainty that they would have, at least temporarily, a place to stay. An elderly couple who for a while had also sought refuge with Prince Trautmansdorff had returned a few days before, in compliance with the deportation order, to their apparently only slightly damaged home in Nuremberg. To repay the debt of hospitality they owed the prince, they agreed to take in Cuci and the children when and if they should reach Nuremberg. We were together again; but the thought that this might be the extent of our family now subdued my joy. The children and Cuci fussed over the baby; I wondered whether her father would ever hold her in his arms.

The nuns fed the tired, hungry children, and then they trooped off with Cuci to their temporary quarters. Now, even more than before, the prospective job interview with the CIC looked like a life preserver thrown from a good, strong ship. I wanted to grasp it, hold on to it, and reach safety. After the children had left I got up and dressed very carefully in my one presentable summer dress. It was four days after my baby's birth; I still felt weak and was afraid of dizziness. My greatest fear was that I might pass out on my way to, or during, the interview in a kind of post-delivery repeat-performance of my first American interview in Pilsen.

The jeep was to pick me up about eleven. When it did not

arrive by ten minutes after, I was sure that they had forgotten about me. In my anxiety I walked in the direction from which I knew it would come, my legs feeling weak from descending two flights of siairs, but I was too upset to worry about the extent of my strength. I barely noticed that it was raining. Some two blocks from the hospital I saw a jeep approaching and waved, but to my great embarrassment it was the wrong one. I was about to turn back when Captain Kerr pulled up alongside me. I had difficulty retaining my composure, feeling the way I had back in Pilsen when I had faced the straight-faced major over the tips of his boots, helpless, and ashamed of my helplessness. Captain Kerr helped me into the jeep, introduced me to another captain sitting beside the driver, and draped a blanket around my shoulders. "I'm sorry we're late," he said, "but some fellow picked this morning to break his arm." Captain Kerr did not come to the interview with me. He dropped me at the CIC office, wished me good luck and once more gave me his Camels. "Take it easy," he said before he left, patting my hand the way he had done in the hospital. "I'm sure you'll get the job." I am glad I thanked him, because that was the last time I saw him; a short time later he returned home to America.

The interview was short and informal. A major asked me a number of questions about myself and my family. I told him about my husband's activities as a journalist and our flight from Budapest. He was especially interested in my husband's contacts with certain other people who had opposed the Nazis, a number of whom had at one time or another sought refuge in our house in Budapest. One of these, the Polish Count Badeni, had just left us when he was arrested by the Gestapo only a very short distance from our house. He was an old man. They tortured him, but he did not reveal who had sheltered him. By a miracle he survived and was able to flee to Ireland.

The major took notes on everything I told him, except when I answered his query as to why I had left my husband and come alone to Germany. Then he suddenly raised his hand like a traffic policeman and interrupted me with a pained expression.

"We won't have to go into that, Countess." In a confidential tone he added, "We'll have to leave that one off the record. We'll just say that you fled a combat zone to find a safer area to await the birth of your baby." His meaning was not immediately clear to me. Thousands of people in East Europe had fled the Russian advance, just as they had once tried to flee the German. Why would my answer have to be "off the record"?

"As you know, there is going to be a trial here before an *international tribunal,*" the major said then, and his emphasis served as adequate explanation. "The four allied powers who are now occupying Germany will participate . . ." He paused as if he expected a comment.

"I understand," I said, and he nodded, satisfied.

"I believe you'll be perfect for the job."

I grew tense with anticipation. No one had tested my language ability. My French spelling was abominable, my English not much better. When I accepted the major's proffered cigarette, my hand was trembling.

"It will give you a chance to get back on your feet," he said kindly.

"What is involved?" I asked hesitantly.

"Nothing very difficult. The people who will be tried in Nuremberg are the major war criminals who are now in custody. Some members of their families—primarily wives—are also under detention, but there are at this time no plans to bring them to trial. However, during their husbands' trials these wives are to be billeted in very light detention in Nuremberg. A private house has been requisitioned for this purpose. Your job would be to supervise this house, to take care in general of the day-to-day details, and keep the inmates as peaceful as possible." I looked at the major somewhat overwhelmed, wondering what language ability had to do with such a job. If I was relieved that my French spelling would not be put to the test, the supervision of these ladies at this point in their lives seemed equally formidable to me.

16

"Well," asked the major, "do you think you can do it?"

"Yes," I said quickly and as firmly as I could. "Will I get detailed instructions?"

"Yes. You'll get exact instructions at the house. How soon can you take over?"

"Anytime. Are the women there already?"

"No. They'll be arriving sometime in the near future. But you should be there to receive them."

"Do you want me to go today?"

"Yes, if it's possible. I can give you a jeep to pick up your things. Will you be taking your baby with you?"

"I think I can leave her in the hospital for a few days until I get settled."

"What about your other children—are you going to leave them in Czechoslovakia?"

I had not told him about Cuci's and the children's arrival that morning. I had been afraid that if I asked permission to bring my entire family, I would spoil my chances of getting the job. Later, perhaps, after I had had a chance to prove myself. . . . Now, however, I seemed to have no choice but to tell him. "They arrived unexpectedly this morning," I said hesitantly. Seeing his surprised face, I added quickly, "But they have a place to say, for the time being, at least."

He smiled. "I'm glad for you, Countess. I know what it's like to be separated from your kids. I've got three myself." He turned a framed picture on his desk so that I could see it, a photo of a pretty, dark-haired woman, two boys in baseball suits, and a little girl in shorts. My compliments pleased him.

"I can't promise anything," he said, turning the picture back into its former position. "But I know you'd like to have your children with you. I don't have the authority to give you permission, but I can make a recommendation and put it through the proper channels."

Another face to remember for its kindness, a whole gallery of benefactors. I was grateful—and yet, I was also conscious again of that vague sense of shame for having become so dependent on, and indebted to, the generosity of these men who

1 7

loomed so powerful in this dead landscape, and for having been favored and saved by a series of lucky coincidences. Perhaps the idea of control over one's life is always an illusion, but never have I felt more at the mercy of forces outside myself than during that period immediately following the war.

The major called a jeep for me. On the way back to the hospital I requested the driver to detour to the address Cuci had given me. I gave the glad news to her and the children; then I continued to the hospital, where I picked up my things, kissed my baby, thanked the nuns, and drove off to my new home and job at Nuremberg—Erlenstegen, Novalis Strasse 24.

3

THE HOUSE WAS the last on a dead-end street, set in a garden aglow with summer flowers. It was two stories high with a large red gabled roof, giving it a quaint, somewhat sleepy appearance. Beyond the garden the suburb ended in vast stretches of heath bordered by forests. The colors held me spellbound: shades of heather, pink to deep purple, changing with light and motion under the brilliant summer sky, leaves shimmering green and silver. Cézanne had tried to capture such motion of color and light, contained vitality of growth and change beneath the serenity of summer landscapes. My hands were itching for a brush; what painter could have resisted this view before me? Coming from the dead town, the landscape seemed to be a resurrection.

The driver had walked ahead with my bag into the house from which he now emerged, followed by a young lieutenant who surprised me by addressing me in perfect German.

"Guten Tag, Graefin, I see you're admiring the scenery."

"It's refreshing after Nuremberg."

The young lieutenant introduced himself as Lieutenant Mueller, a German-American attached to the military tribunal's detention section. He and a tall, serious major who was waiting inside proceeded to give me the instructions I was to follow in the treatment of my charges. As I listened with growing apprehension, the lovely vista of heath and sky which had still been lingering before my eyes was soon replaced by the troublesome vision of trying to get Frau Goering, grand dame of Karinhall, to wash dishes in our communal kitchen. The major expounded sternly and at some length about the chastening qualities of hard work. The women were to tend not only to their own needs, such as cooking, making beds, and washing their own laundry, but were to be assigned any other necessary tasks around the house, such as scrubbing floors, washing windows, or pulling weeds in the garden.

Lieutenant Mueller noted my uneasiness with slight amusement. "All you're allowed to do is supervise."

"What if they refuse?" I asked rather timidly.

He blinked at me cheerfully over the rims of his glasses. "You pull rank. You'll be the only countess among them."

"Any refusal to do assigned work will be punished by room arrest and withholding of rations," said the major. "I'm sure that will prove effective, but I doubt that you'll have to resort to it."

"Yes, Major," I said without conviction.

"We anticipate no problems and consider you eminently qualified for the task," the major said briskly.

"Thank you," I said, wondering what made me so eminently qualified to deal with hunger strikes and outbreaks of hysteria, for I did not share the major's conviction about the docility of my expected guests.

"You will be supplied with everything you need. In any emergency you will turn to Lieutenant Mueller or call this number." He handed me a slip of paper and, turning to leave, wished me "good luck."

Lieutenant Mueller remained to introduce me to Frau Kruelle, the plump, dark-haired woman who was the owner of the house. Her friendliness toward me was a little too profuse. Like an oversolicitous salesman she assured me repeatedly of the comfort and the neatness of her house, opening drawers and cupboards, telling me that she had just finished washing all the windows and scrubbing all the floors. I felt sorry for her and a little ashamed. The shame was the same I had felt for myself when I had faced the straight-faced major in Pilsen and walked in the rain this morning to meet the jeep. We were all dependent on the generosity of the victors. Her gratitude was for the permission to go on living in the cellar of her house, even though it had been requisitioned. To be granted that when so many were homeless was generous indeed.

Lieutenant Mueller accompanied us on a tour of the house, which was more spacious than I had expected from its outside appearance. Downstairs, in addition to the kitchen and a fair-sized bedroom, were a large living and dining room; the upstairs contained a bath and four bedrooms with a view of the heath. One wall of the living room was lined with bookcases. A large desk, a piano, a large round table, a number of comfortable-looking chairs, and a somewhat frayed, patterned carpet completed the furnishings. The usual mementoes of a home were still in place—some travel souvenirs, a sports trophy on the piano, family photographs on the desk. From one side of the room two large glass doors led to a patio and the garden.

Lieutenant Mueller brought my bag upstairs and asked me to take one of the smaller bedrooms for myself. I chose one with a small balcony and a magnificent view of the heath. Knowing that the owner of the house would live in the cellar while I occupied this pleasant room did make me feel uncomfortable and vaguely guilty; but if Frau Kruelle harbored any resentment, she didn't show it.

"It's all yours," Lieutenant Mueller said, setting my suitcase on a chair. "Enjoy the view and get a good rest. I don't think your guests will arrive this week."

His prediction proved true. The week passed without the

arrival of anyone. I sat on my balcony watching the changing colors of the heath and lay awake nights listening to the crickets. Gorging myself on the abundant rations, I had to remind myself repeatedly that I had not suddenly been transported into a different world, but that the ruins of Nuremberg were only a short distance away, that my husband's fate was still unknown to me, and that with thousands of others we were in reality dispossessed and homeless.

One of the first things I did after getting settled was to call the Red Cross to initiate new inquiries about my husband. I had done the same in Pilsen but had heard nothing before I left. The lists of the missing were long and growing longer as war-battered families tried to reunite in the face of such obstacles as zonal borders and mass expulsions. One must have patience, I was told. It would take time. If he was still alive and making the same inquiries somewhere in Hungary, was he being told the same?

My own lot meanwhile was certainly bearable enough and almost seemed too good to last. Although the provisions sent down from the mess hall were to be for one person only, there was—by German standards at least—enough to feed a family. Sharing my food with Frau Kruelle eased my guilt feelings about her living in the cellar while I enjoyed the comfort of a sunny room, although she assured me that she was quite comfortable where she was and that the cellar had been made livable when it was set up as an air raid shelter. I saved some delicacies, such as crackers and jam, for my children, but was unable to get to see either the older ones or the baby (whom I missed dreadfully), because I was afraid to leave the house lest my guests arrive unexpectedly or my employers come looking for me and find me absent from my post. Least of all did I want to jeopardize my job. I waited and hoped, wondering how I would cope with my new duties, and how long it would take to put through the proper channels the application to have my children live with me.

As it turned out, my concerns about the job ahead of me

were unnecessary, and I would not, after all, have to face the prospect of requesting Frau Goering to take her turn at the dishpan. At the beginning of the following week Lieutenant Mueller came again, accompanied this time by another major, who informed me that the original plans had been changed and that instead of the wives of the war criminals, I was to expect so-called "free" witnesses who were coming to testify at the trial. The word "free" turned out to be somewhat of a euphemism. Most Germans who had held positions of any significance in the government were held under various degrees of detention; although we were to have some "free" witnesses, the majority of them were restricted in their movements. A number of those who came to testify would eventually become defendants themselves.

I did not, of course, know this when the major gave me my revised instructions. Primarily I felt a sense of relief; my new assignment seemed at least a lot easier than the original one had promised to be. Instead of an overseer I would be a hostess to my guests, a position for which I felt a lot more "eminently qualified." Under my new set of instructions I was to be responsible for the general management of the households—there were to be two houses now under my supervision, the house next door having also been requisitioned. Frau Kruelle and the owner of the neighboring house were given the task of general cleaning; the laundry would be picked up; the food would be brought three times daily from an American mess hall, with a part-time cook taking care of any necessary preparation. All the meals were to be served in Frau Kruelle's house, with the one next door providing only sleeping quarters. It was to be my task to select people compatible enough to share rooms. This, the major warned, would require a great deal of tact and diplomacy, since the witnesses would be of widely divergent backgrounds. In general, he advised me, it should be my primary objective "to keep things running smoothly." Adding an ominous note, he told me that the arrangement of billeting the witnesses in this manner was being tried on an experimental basis which, if it didn't work out, would have to be discontinued.

The major's casually delivered warning worried me, but not so much as had the prospects of the first assignment; compared to that, the possible problems he now mentioned seemed negligible. In the course of the next year, though, I was to think more than once of his words. "Keep it running smoothly" became my motto; translated into specifics, that meant "handle it yourself." Call for razor blades, soap, or extra towels, but never for help to handle the inevitable conflicts and crises arising among people under great tension.

In the next few days, army trucks delivered cots and bedding which were to be used in the house next door. Since the entire house was to be used only for sleeping quarters, quite a number of people could be accommodated. Only special guests would be living in the main house. What sort of quality would make a guest "special" was not immediately clear to me; however, I decided to trust my intuition rather than ask too many questions. After the initial bustle of activity, with both houses prepared, beds made up, and towels on their racks, I settled down to wait for my first guests.

4

A NUMBER OF WEEKS passed. Although I knew that the trial was not scheduled to begin until late fall, I could not help feeling uneasy at times for being thus fed and housed by my employers without an opportunity to prove my usefulness. What I feared most was that some chance event might change existing arrangements before they had even been put into effect. In the meantime, however, I received the anxiously awaited permission to have the children and Cuci move into the house with me, an event both joyful and reassuring in the light of my earlier doubts regarding my job.

Not until the early days of October did my first guest finally arrive—an old man whose erect stature and imposing military bearing were belied by the exhaustion that showed in his face. Retired general, teacher, prolific author, advisor to diplomats and statesmen, Professor Karl Haushofer was seventy-six years old. As the foremost exponent of geopolitics—a volatile hybrid of political geography, Social Darwinism, and ethnocentrism—he had provided the respectable academic basis for Hitler's obsession with *Lebensraum;* but unlike some other theoreticians whose ideas had profound influence on historical events—Rousseau and Marx, for example—fate had allowed Haushofer to live to see his ideas explode into deadly action. He had been the close friend and teacher of Rudolf Hess, who had revered Haushofer at least as much as he had Hitler, and it was through Hess, who worked closely with Hitler on *Mein Kampf,* that a good deal of Haushofer's involved professorial prose was translated into the revolutionary rhetoric of the *Fuehrer,* becoming the ideological force behind Hitler's expansionist drive. There were echoes of Haushofer when the Hitler Youth sang

> For today we own Germany,
> But tomorrow the whole world . . .

as there were echoes of him in the shots and shouts of the SD and SS driving Polish farmers from western Poland to make room for German settlers.

But when I met Professor Haushofer that warm fall evening, my knowledge of his theories was vague at best. I saw only a very tired old man with a disoriented look, like someone who had lost his way. Since both houses were empty, I showed him to one of the pleasant small rooms on the upper floor of the main house, then left him alone to get settled. Half an hour later, when I went upstairs to ask him to dinner, I found him standing in front of the window still wearing his coat, looking out at the heath darkening under a sky streaked with the last remnants of sun. I wondered why he was wearing a coat on so . warm a day, but when he turned, responding to my soft knocking on the open door, I thought I saw him shiver. "How beautiful the heath is," he said.

"It's even more beautiful in the morning sun."

He nodded sadly. "There's something . . . almost brutal in so much beauty now. Nature pays no heed to our sorrows."

26

"In a way I'm glad. Perhaps it's better so."

"Perhaps." He seemed to have tears in his eyes.

"You must have had a rough trip. You look quite worn out."

He turned a sad smile to me. "It wasn't rough. But I am still worn out. It doesn't take much these days to wear me out."

The good ample dinner appeared to lift his spirits, as did the occasional unauthorized appearances in the dining room of one or another of my children. He talked about his own grandchildren, a subject which, like the blooming heath, brought him again close to tears. All in all, it was obvious that he was under great emotional stress, heightened most likely by his age. To help him relax I asked him about his country place in southern Bavaria from where he had come, mentioning some excursions of my own into that lovely area during my student days in Munich. Since he had a lively interest in art—his father had been an artist—we were soon involved in an animated conversation about the Munich art world of the late twenties. In addition to his taste in art (which was decidedly conservative), he talked with great tenderness and fondness of his wife of nearly fifty years. Since she was half Jewish, they had experienced great pressure during the later years of the war, after they had lost the protection of Hess with the latter's flight to Scotland on his curious, unilateral "peace mission." It was this pressure, the fear that his wife might be put into a concentration camp, which Haushofer later cited to his interrogators as the reason for his continuing cooperation with the Nazi regime even after he had lost faith in it.

There was little one could talk about with Haushofer that did not return to the center of his depression. Although a great number of the people I met during my time in Nuremberg exuded the same oppressive sense of failure and defeat, only Haushofer seemed to be genuinely affected by a deep sense of personal guilt. He himself had spent some time in Dachau; members of his family had been imprisoned, but it was in the death of his son Albrecht, murdered by the Gestapo in April of '45, that the father's guilt seemed to have found its symbolic center. Albrecht, like his father an early supporter of Hitler, had worked within the framework of his father's ideas, teaching geopolitics at the University of Berlin and training German diplomats in the subject. Like many other Germans who came to their senses too late, Albrecht Haushofer saw Hitler's attack on Russia as a catastrophe. He became a supportive member of the German underground and tried on several occasions to initiate private peace feelers with Britain. It was this activity which eventually cost him his life.

It was obviously a great effort for the old man to talk about his son, yet he appeared to have a need to. Looking at me across the table, he seemed no longer ashamed of his tears, or perhaps he was not even aware of them. "With the Russians already in Berlin, they murdered him in the street; the bloody monsters shot him down in the street."

"Perhaps now those bloody monsters will be found and punished for their crimes."

He shook his head sadly. "The war crimes trials? They'll be no more than the retribution of the victors."

"No more than that?"

"Do you think the innocents won't suffer the penalties of defeat?"

"It seems to me that they always suffer the most, whether they're Jews, Poles, or Germans. Hitler and Himmler can die only once, but the most atrocious suffering always seems to come to those who never committed an atrocity."

He covered his face with his hands and shuddered. "I see them on the roads, ragged, hungry, and homeless, and I say to myself, my God, what have we done? How did it happen?"

"I suppose that's what they'll try to find out at the trial."

"They will find out *what* happened, but not why or how. History has a murderous chemistry all its own."

"But isn't it people who make history?"

"We may make it, but we don't control it."

He retired to his room shortly after dinner, borrowing an

2 8

old copy of the *Stars and Stripes*. Apparently he spent a restless night. I heard him move about until well after midnight and found him already up when I came downstairs at seven.

"You did not sleep well?"

"I haven't slept well in years." He looked as exhausted as he had the evening before.

"At this rate you will wear yourself out before much longer. Perhaps you should have a sedative before you go to bed."

"Do you have a sedative for a sick soul?"

"I wish I had a few million to dispense for that condition."

He smiled sadly. "There's a difference. The sickness isn't the same for everyone; only some of us will have to live with the guilt of it all."

"I wish I could understand your idea of guilt. You said last night that history is a force beyond our control. Then how can there be individual guilt?"

"Loss of control does not absolve from guilt. Look at it as the responsibility for failure, for not having made better choices."

I hesitated to ask the next question but couldn't resist it. "If Germany had won, would you still feel the same sense of guilt? I mean, for all the terrible things that happened?"

I thought I saw a flash of anger in his eyes. His voice had an edge of sharpness. "Do you believe there were only German atrocities?"

"No. But does that justify anything?"

"That's not the point. The point is that the historical judgment has already come in terms of defeat. Only German atrocities will be tried as war crimes."

"Do you believe, then, that there is no moral guilt involved, only the guilt for failure?"

"Before the court of the victors, yes. But there are two different levels of guilt, the personal and the historical. The first is not within the jurisdiction of the victors; the second has already been judged." For a moment of grim reflection he stared at his shabby but highly polished shoes. Then his voice

29

rose with sudden emphasis. "Look, there must be a moral justification behind a national purpose. Certainly Germany had that after 1918. She had a right to live without being bled dry as the price of defeat. That was the reason Germans rallied to Hitler. He took this honorable purpose and perverted it. That's why Germany could not win this war—not with Dachau and Auschwitz. Brutality is not just primitive and evil; it is fundamentally wrong as an instrument of power. Culture and superiority of mind—those are real and valid instruments of power, but of course they were beyond the understanding of a corrupt and primitive mind like Hitler's. A great culture is a harmonious force, not a destructive one." He was looking at me intently, searching for agreement. When I said nothing, he continued in a sad, quieter voice. "You see, there probably is a moral basis to history, so that success or failure acquires the moral qualities of right or wrong. But all this has little to do with comprehensible standards of justice. As you have said, the innocent always suffer the most; even in just wars, the innocent suffer and die."

The phrase "just war" rang in my ears, an ancient obscenity that made me feel an old anger with renewed intensity. How innocently it was said, and how often, justifying the profession of war and upholding the ancient dogmas that put the great virtues of courage and loyalty at the service of death. My father had been a Prussian officer for whom the first great war was the supreme experience of his life; still, he loved life and lived it vigorously. He was sensitive to beauty and tender to those he loved. But he could not understand my feelings when at the age of seventeen I read Remarque's *All Quiet on the Western Front,* a book which profoundly moved me and which he unqualifiedly condemned, as it was condemned by so many others like him, decent, life-loving, compassionate people whose distorted ideas of virtue would not permit them to see that the dogma of war was the dogma of death. I can still hear my father's angry voice condemning "the pacifist weaklings" and the "degenerate, defeatist thought of a corrupt minority" which had caused Germany to lose the war.

I was grateful to Frau Kruelle for saving me from any further comment by announcing that breakfast was ready, adding with her customary endearing smile that it was a lovely day.

"So it is," Haushofer agreed, returning her smile, "and we haven't even had a chance to notice. I think this place must be an oasis," he added, tasting his juice. "I'm attended by two kind ladies, dazzled by the morning sun, and fed an excellent breakfast. Now if one could only forget what has been and what is yet to come. One should be able to experience happy moments in isolation from past and future."

Frau Kruelle looked sad as she collected our empty juice glasses. I wondered whether she believed that there was such a thing as a just war. I knew that her husband was missing somewhere in Russia. Trying to think of something consoling to say to the professor, I felt rather awkward. How did one console a man who after all that had happened could still talk of "just wars" and for whom the suffering of innocents was therefore lost in the abstraction of history's grand design?

He was examining his little cardboard box of American cornflakes. "What is it?" he asked.

"It's a cereal made of corn. It's eaten with milk and sugar."

He opened his box with interest and poured the contents into his bowl. "That's something we could never grow well in Germany," he said regretfully, adding after a moment, "It's rather good." After a short silence he looked at me suddenly. "You know, there is something familiar about your name. I've been trying to remember in what context, but I can't place it."

"My husband is a journalist. . . ."

He nodded, but it didn't seem to strike a chord. "His uncle was foreign minister of Austria-Hungary during the eighties."

"Of course!" he cried out with almost joyful recognition, "the Triple Alliance, the Serbian negotiations. He had strong German sympathies."

"I'm sorry, but I don't know very much about his career. Diplomatic history tends to confuse me."

"You're not alone. It confuses even the diplomats."

We talked for a while about Austria and Hungary. When

31

I told him about the location of my husband's ancestral seat in the heart of Transylvania, his pale old eyes grew bright with enthusiasm.

"*Siebenbuergen!* Lovely *Siebenbuergen!*" He reminisced nostalgically about the prosperous villages and handsome towns founded more than seven centuries ago by German settlers, calling them "peaceful islands of German *Volkstum*" which had brought to the area "a degree of civilization never equaled by the other population groups." "There is real power," he exclaimed. "What weapons can equal it?"

Followed by her cat, Frau Kruelle came to collect the breakfast dishes. As she turned to shoo the cat out of the dining room, Haushofer protested, assuring her that he was especially fond of cats and requesting her to permit the animal to remain. The cat reciprocated the professor's feelings by rubbing her side against his legs.

"One does not know what unhappy soul might occupy this body," he said as he picked up the cat, which settled purring in his lap. Neither Frau Kruelle nor I quite knew what to make of that remark.

"She doesn't usually take like that to strangers," Frau Kruelle said with a disapproving glance at the cat.

"She recognized my feelings. There may be a communion of souls."

With a look of astonishment, Frau Kruelle departed with her tray.

I remarked, "In that case I wish I could communicate to her that there will be a mighty unhappy soul in my body if she leaves any more dead birds in the garden."

He looked at me thoughtfully. "Strange that you should say that. When I was in India I once saw a woman with a severely burned arm walking quietly out of her house on her way to get some first aid. When I expressed my concern, as well as my amazement at her calm behavior, she told me that she was being punished for her misdeeds in a former life when she had been a cat and had killed birds, not out of hunger but out of blood lust."

32

"Then you believe in reincarnation?"

"I'm drawn to it strongly, more and more, the older I get. How else can one atone for all the errors one has made?"

"The Christians have a theory about it."

He made a gesture of dismissal. "Hell is too primitive a concept. It's too static, without change or growth. But if change and growth are a part of physical life, why should they not be a part of the spiritual too? If there is a unity to life that connects the most primitive with the most complex, if there is an evolution from the lowest to the highest forms, then it seems to me logical that the soul, too, should undergo a kind of evolution."

"That is the belief of the Hindus, isn't it?"

"Substantially, yes. But Socrates said much the same when he described the pure or virtuous soul as light and able to ascend, and the soul that has not freed itself from earthly bonds remaining earthbound and forced to seek another body to inhabit."

"It's a strange thought to be reborn again and again. . . ."

"I would think it less strange and certainly more consoling than the idea of eternal damnation."

In his lap the cat blinked sleepily, purring loudly. I recalled Frau Kruelle's remark about the cat not taking easily to strangers, remembering also that I had hardly ever noticed it in the house before. In view of what Haushofer had said, watching it purr in his lap gave me a slightly eerie feeling. Getting up, I excused myself and went through the adjoining living room to open the two glass doors that led into the garden glowing with color, glorious with Indian summer. I called to Haushofer to come and join me. He nodded and smiled, setting the cat gently on the floor. As he walked across the room, the cat, its tail held high and happy, followed close behind.

5

PROFESSOR HAUSHOFER was not only my first guest; he brought me also the first crisis of my new career. I had left him sitting in the sun in a comfortable chair with the cat in his lap and gone to my room, where I spent the morning on my little balcony working on some sketches, having received the necessary art supplies through the generosity of Lieutenant Mueller, who occasionally came by to check on our needs or just to say hello.

It was shortly before noon when the quiet of the house was suddenly disrupted by an outcry from Frau Kruelle, followed by urgent calls for me. I raced down the stairs and out to the garden, where I found her standing beside the old man, who sat slumped over the side of his chair, his breathing rapid and shallow. Beside him sat the cat, her amber eyes contemplating him. As I ran to the phone, it occurred to me that I had no idea how long he had been that way, and I felt guilty for having been absent when it happened. He might have died if Frau

Kruelle had not by chance found him. He might still die—an inauspicious beginning for my stewardship.

Within minutes of my call an American doctor arrived, administered emergency treatment, and, together with his assistant, carried the patient on a stretcher to his room. The old man had suffered a heart attack. He was to be kept quiet, fed a light diet, and given some medication which the doctor left with me.

Haushofer was conscious when the doctor departed. "You shouldn't have called him," he whispered. "I don't need a doctor. I've been wanting to die for a long time."

I protested, but without conviction, wondering why, at that moment, it was unacceptable to agree with him or permit him to die by withholding medical treatment. One is expected to accept the willful murder of thousands upon thousands of young and healthy human beings in the name of national interest or history, but one may not accept the perfectly reasonable wish for death of a despairing, sick old man.

"I wish it had been big enough to finish me. Why does it take so long to die?"

I stayed with him for the rest of the day. He slept most of the time, his breathing gradually becoming more quiet and even. In the evening the doctor returned for another visit and pronounced the patient greatly improved.

"I promise you to do my best to last through the interrogation, doctor," Haushofer said.

"Don't you worry about that now," the doctor said. "You just rest and get some strength back."

"He'll probably be interrogated tomorrow," the doctor told me downstairs. "They're most anxious to get a deposition from him before he dies. They tell me he's pretty important. If he were not so sick he'd be put on trial himself. But it's only a matter of a little time with him."

"I think he'd be glad to hear you say that."

The doctor looked at me thoughtfully. "Strange world, isn't it?"

Haushofer's interrogation did take place the following day.

3 5

He not only insisted that he was well enough; he seemed anxious to go through with it.

"Perhaps there is a good reason why it didn't kill me. I've been interrogated by the Americans before, but never by anyone who knew my work. This man at least will know what I'm talking about. I want someone to understand. . . ." His voice was weak and breathless; I did not believe that he would last through the interrogation, which in deference to his physical condition was to be held in our living room. Frau Kruelle and I supported him down the stairs, the descent of which was an ambitious enough undertaking for a man just a day over a heart attack; but Haushofer survived it. Although he protested our help, he leaned on us heavily, trying at the same time to maintain his erect bearing as he faced his interrogators waiting at the foot of the stairs.

The man to whom Haushofer was so anxious to talk was in his sixties, white-haired, with a kind face. A Jesuit priest and political scientist from Georgetown University, presently consultant to the American legal staff of the International Military Tribunal in Nuremberg, Professor Walsh was also an expert on geopolitics and had written extensive criticism of Haushofer's theories. I was not in the room during the interrogation, which was conducted in the presence of a court stenographer and an interpreter, although Haushofer and Walsh spoke each other's native language competently.

But the session did not last very long. When I responded to Professor Walsh's sudden and somewhat urgent call for me, I was sure that Haushofer had suffered another attack. This was not quite the case. Apparently, though, he had again become overwrought; his face was flushed, his eyes moist. Fearing that the excitement would indeed trigger another attack, Professor Walsh had broken off the interrogation and dismissed the stenographer and interpreter. He requested me to bring some coffee, and when I strongly objected to coffee for the old man, Haushofer insisted.

"My dear Countess, what are you trying to save me from,

or for? You must stop worrying about me and let the old heart finish breaking."

But if the old heart had reached the breaking point, death was not yet ready to relieve it of its burden. He survived the coffee, as he had survived the stairs, as he would go on surviving the shocks yet in store for him, to see out this fatal year in the life of his country, which he had loved and helped to ruin. The more he physically defied death, the more it seemed to avoid him.

The two men invited me to share their coffee. Haushofer was calmer now; the flush had faded from his face, but there was bitterness in it as he contemplated the table littered with his books and journals.

"A part of my life's work, Countess. It would make a nice fire, but it's needed for evidence."

"Hitler has burned enough books to last me," I said.

"But ideas are fireproof," Walsh countered.

"But not distortion-proof," Haushofer said sadly.

"No. Perhaps ideas have something in common with the element of fire," Walsh said. "To be useful and beneficial they have to be contained. When fire gets out of hand, it destroys; when it's controlled, it gives warmth and energy."

"And how does one control or contain ideas?"

"By preventing their becoming political tools."

The old man buried his face in his hands. "Perhaps I did not have that kind of objectivity. You must remember I was a soldier before I was a geographer, a soldier who returned to a defeated country in 1918 and watched it being mutilated at Versailles. I wanted to restore my country to greatness, because I loved it more than anything else. Everything I ever did, wrote, or thought sprang from that motive."

Professor Walsh fixed his calm eyes on the old man's face. How sure the American seemed, how free. I thought of what Haushofer had said about the court of the victors. But this man's freedom and sureness did not rest upon that kind of power; one could see that in his eyes. The source was within himself. I wondered what it would have been like with the tables turned. I had seen the SS strut in Budapest and Prague, naked power devoid of any saving human grace. If Haushofer was not like that, had not the seed of their brutal, mindless arrogance grown from the soil of his fanatic patriotism?

The cat, having sneaked in when Frau Kruelle brought the tray, lay in Haushofer's lap, purring loudly. His hands, tirelessly stroking the shiny fur, were trembling. "Tell me," he cried, his eyes growing red again and tearful, "how could we err so? You are a priest and do things for the love of God. I was a soldier and did what I did for the love of my country."

"Love of country too easily turns into love of power," Walsh said as if he had read my thoughts.

"Absolute power rarely remains unabused. It should be left to God."

Haushofer stared intently at the cat's patterned back, tracing its lines with his long fingers. He must have been a powerful man once, I thought, strong and sure of himself. There was kindness, too, in the old face. He loved the colors of the heath and the songs of the birds. I thought again of my father.

"Perhaps our error lay in thinking that we could retain control," Haushofer said. "To me the idea was always close to the act. Does not history express itself through actions? I thought of my analyses as intelligent controls which could be applied to the raw energy of inevitable conflict. What is thought without action?" He paused, still studying the pattern of the cat's fur. "There is a passage in *Faust.* It comes after the Easter Sunday walk when Faust returns to his study and tries to decide which might have been the original element in creation. He thinks first of the word, then of mind, then of power, and finally of action—*'Im Anfang war die Tat!'*—rising, as it were, out of primordial darkness, prior to word and mind, the expression of a blind and compelling courage."

"I won't argue Goethe's version of theology," Walsh said with a smile. "But we were talking about error. Let's not forget what happened to Faust."

3 8

"He was redeemed."

"By God's grace."

Haushofer suddenly raised both arms toward Walsh in a pleading gesture. "And Germany?"

"God has a lot of grace."

"Give us a guiding light. . . ." Haushofer cried, his eyes brimming with tears. "What is to become of this land?"

Walsh looked at him thoughtfully for a moment but made no reply. "We have to continue the interrogation tomorrow. I'll be back at the same time. Please try to be calm."

I accompanied Professor Walsh to the door. He urgently asked me to try to calm the old man. "I've tried that since he came. It's a losing battle."

"I know. But we do want him to last awhile."

"His interrogation must be very important."

"If we shall ever come even close to an understanding of the last twelve years."

I thought again of my father celebrating the memories of war; of my husband, steeped in reverence to the crown, waiting for the restoration of his lord to the vanished Habsburg throne. It was not just the last twelve years that defied understanding. They would find out *what* happened, but not why or how, Haushofer had predicted. He was probably right. Where was the beginning? If he was the corrupter, he was also the corrupted, a part of the pattern that bent and channeled thought into mindless loyalties, keeping men enthralled by forms that had become devoid of substance, holding them steadfast in fealty to corrupted ideals.

"I think he himself has more questions than answers. I suppose we all have."

Professor Walsh looked at me serenely. "There is nothing wrong with questions. They teach humility."

After he left I went back to the old man, who was still sitting in the now almost dark room, stroking the loudly purring cat.

6

Haushofer's interrogation was resumed the following afternoon. He had spent the morning preparing himself, busily making notes on a dog-eared pad, and he appeared to be more composed. But my preoccupation with my one and only guest was about to come to an end.

Late in the afternoon a rather violent assault on the doorbell brought me racing to the door. The sound was so frantic, I thought one of my children had been in an accident. Actually, an American ambulance with a very impatient-looking driver was parked in front of the house, while facing me in the doorway were two unkempt civilians and an American lieutenant.

"These men are to be billeted here until further notice," the latter said, waving a military order under my nose and indicating his charges with some disdain.

"But this is not an infirmary," I said.

He grinned. "That's all right. They'll survive—unfortunately." He took out his wallet, gave each of them several German bills, and ran back to the ambulance, which took off like a rocket.

My God, I thought, what am I going to do with two hospital cases? The men's faces expressed a mixture of astonishment and relief. They stared at me as if I were an apparition.

"Where are we?" asked the older of the two.

"In Nuremberg."

"In Nuremberg?"

"Yes. Are you very ill?"

"Only at heart," the younger quipped with a melancholy smile.

"But why did you come in an ambulance?"

"Only God and the Americans know."

Just then Cuci returned, pushing the baby in the carriage, with the other three children trooping behind her. The older man watched disbelievingly as they disappeared into the house. *"Na, das ist ja allerhand . . .* the idiot dropped us in the wrong place. This is certainly not an internment camp."

"It isn't. You're supposed to be here voluntarily."

They both laughed. "I understand. It's what we used to call *freiwillig gezwungen,"* said the older one.

"Voluntary compulsion is certainly within the realm of the German experience," said the other. He was much younger, tall, and would have been of a pleasing appearance had it not been for the several days' growth of beard, the deep shadows around his eyes, and the deteriorated state of his clothing.

"Well, if this is not a prison, what is it? Why are we here?" the older one asked. He appeared to be well into his sixties, with unusually short legs and a head which seemed disproportionately large, an effect intensified by a thick mane of rather long gray hair.

"This is supposed to be an official American billet for voluntary witnesses to the war crimes trial."

They exchanged a significant glance. "So that's the answer," said the younger one. "I don't recall volunteering, but this place is certainly a big improvement over my last residence."

"Come to think of it," said the other, "if we were still in military custody, why would he have given us our money back? But forgive us, *gnae' Frau,* we haven't even introduced ourselves . . ." He bowed with somewhat exaggerated formality, as if he wished to emphasize the disparity between his manners and his appearance. The effect, however, was more theatrical than dignified. "Professor Heinrich Hoffmann. I'm most delighted to make your acquaintance."

The younger man introduced himself as Dr. Wilhelm Scheidt. They had come from different internment camps and had made the trip in the ambulance under guard. In addition to having had no idea of where they were going, they had not been able to see out of the covered windows of the ambulance either. Hoffmann confessed to me later that he had been in a cold sweat for fear they were being taken to the Russian zone for interrogation.

Like tens of thousands of other Germans who had had close affiliation with party or state, Hoffmann and Scheidt had been imprisoned since the end of the war. Hoffmann had been Hitler's and the party's official photographer, as well as one of Hitler's closest friends. It was Hoffmann who had introduced Hitler to Eva Braun, the woman who became Hitler's wife only hours before her death. He had other "family" connections in high party circles, his daughter was married to Baldur von Schirach, the *Reich* youth leader, but Hoffmann himself, although an avid and early supporter of Hitler, and a party member since the twenties, had never held any political office. His title of "Professor" was an honorary one and, as he liked to emphasize, the only title he ever received through his affiliation with Nazism. However, his unofficial position as "official photographer," which clearly had fallen to him through Hitler's patronage, had made Hoffmann a multimillionaire. He undoubtedly owed his success to three characteristics which became quickly apparent even after a short acquaintance: a flamboyant personality, resourcefulness, and an untroubled opportunism. Not only did his country's present shame and suffering appear to have left him untouched; he seemed unaware of them. As far as his own fortunes were concerned—and they were apparently all that concerned him—he was an unshakable optimist. What's more, this optimism seemed justified. During the following year I had ample opportunity to take notice of his brilliant capacity to make life profitable for himself.

By contrast, Scheidt was unassuming, quiet, and depressed. A former career officer, he had been the historian for the OKW, the High Command of the Wehrmacht, and had had some involvement in the long-standing and ill-fated resistance of the army which culminated in the unsuccessful assassination attempt on Hitler on July 20, 1944.

At dinner that evening my two new guests were clean-shaven and looked considerably more civilized than they had at their arrival. The problems of laundry and the lack of certain basic necessities were for a time the topic of conversation. When I told them that they could send their laundry out along with the household linens, they were greatly relieved.

"Strange, how the focus of importance shifts," said Scheidt. "What was once taken for granted becomes the preoccupation of one's existence."

"What is even stranger is the fact that one can spend one's life thinking one is concerned with basic problems and then wake up one day to realize one has never understood what they were," Haushofer said. He appeared to have weathered his second interrogation well; his expression was one of composure and resignation.

Scheidt nodded. "I know what you mean, Herr Professor. Reality becomes an abstraction, words about events instead of the events themselves. Then one day reality makes you remember it by falling on top of you."

Hoffmann and Scheidt exchanged experiences about various prisons and internment camps they'd been held in since the collapse, with Hoffmann doing most of the complaining about inadequate rations and occasional mistreatment. Asserting repeatedly that he had been only a photographer, he said that he couldn't understand why anyone would want to arrest him.

"The Americans have told me that the Russians have me on their most wanted list—my God, when I think that I drank friendship with Stalin!"

"The Russians are after everybody's skin," said Scheidt. "I suppose it's their answer to our *Commissar Order.*"

"I understand that order was not carried out by most commanders," Haushofer said.

"That didn't stop the SD from carrying it out," Scheidt countered bitterly.

Inquiring about the nature of the *Commissar Order*, I was told that it concerned Hitler's directive to the German military commanders to summarily execute all representatives of the Communist party in German-occupied territories of Russia.

"With poetic justice the Russians are now doing the same to our party people."

"From what I hear, Russian terror is not restricted to party members," I said.

"Neither was German," said Scheidt.

"An eye for an eye?"

"Yes," said Scheidt. "An eye for an eye."

"But isn't it always the wrong people who are made to pay?"

"That's certainly true," said Hoffmann. "Look at me. I never meddled in politics. I never hurt anyone in my life. I would like to know what they think they're punishing me for."

Haushofer and Scheidt exchanged a glance, sharing each other's contempt for their dinner companion. Frau Kruelle came in to collect the dishes, followed inevitably by the cat (which promptly jumped into Haushofer's lap), and by my youngest son Antal, age four, who had a passion for watches and demanded to see Hoffmann's. By the time Cuci came running after Antal, the boy was spellbound watching Hoffmann

4 4

do magic tricks with his watch. Obviously pleased with the success of his performance, Hoffmann extended it for the benefit of Cuci and Frau Kruelle. Haushofer and Scheidt took their coffee in silence; Hoffmann's antics seemed to deepen their depression.

Later in the evening, before he retired, Haushofer pulled me aside.

"I will be leaving tomorrow. Professor Walsh is taking me back home."

"I'm glad for you that the interrogations are over."

He smiled sadly. "Not yet, not quite. I'm honor-bound to do the last interrogation myself. Then I will be free."

"But you'll be free when you get home, won't you?"

"I mean free to depart this sad earth."

"You mustn't . . ." I stopped myself from finishing the routine sentiment that had come reflexlike to my mind. The old man was serious. He was trying to be honest with himself. He hardly deserved the hollow comfort of platitudes.

"It must be strange to hear someone my age talk of suicide."

"More painful than strange."

He was stroking the cat. "Tell me," he asked, "what is your prognosis for my soul? Will it rise or sink?"

"Christians believe that repentance brings God's forgiveness."

He nodded. "What is done cannot be undone."

I had never realized how much pain there was in those words. They seemed to contain the judgment and the sentence as well.

45

7

PROFESSOR HAUSHOFER had been somewhat premature in his leave-taking. He was not picked up the following day but was instead notified that his presence in Nuremberg would be required for a few more days. After spending a day in restless uncertainty, he was told the reason: Rudolf Hess, his friend and former student, had just been brought to Nuremberg from England, where he had been imprisoned since his famous flight to Scotland in 1941. With the other top Nazis in custody, he was to stand trial before the allied military tribunal. Hess, however, showed signs of mental illness and appeared to have amnesia. To test his memory he was to be confronted by people who had been close to him. Haushofer was one of these.

Anticipation of the meeting caused the old man so much anxiety that he suffered what appeared to be another small heart seizure. But he did not lose consciousness and begged me not to call the doctor. This was in direct conflict with my instructions, which were to watch him closely and report any recurrence of his illness. But there are instructions of the heart which supersede all others. I would not interfere with the old man's wish to die; God would decide whether he was to live to face his former student or be spared it by death. A certain irony in my decision, however, did strike me. I was disobeying orders in favor of one of my countrymen who was accused of bearing a large share in what may have been the most massive, most infamous, and most thoroughly organized crime in history, a crime which could have reached its fantastic proportions only because men like Haushofer preached and followed a doctrine under which the individual conscience must be sublimated to the collective needs and goals of the state, and which invested with the highest virtue the act of blind obedience.

Scheidt and I supported Haushofer to his room and remained for a while at his bedside.

"I can sympathize with him," Scheidt said, watching the old man doze. "At least he's old. What is left for us?"

In the silence that followed I could feel his tension. "It's all over for us," he said, very softly but with a kind of urgency, as if he wanted to convince me. "You know what one interrogating officer told me? He said that there's a plan being discussed among the Allies to turn Germany into an agrarian country, to strip it of all heavy industry and never again permit it to have an army. It's being done already. Whole factories are being shipped off to Russia."

The old man moaned softly and began to snore.

"I understand his son was executed right at the end," Scheidt said.

"Yes. The Russians were already in Berlin."

"All that counts for nothing now, all that slaughter and sacrifice. The only thing that counts now are the Nazi crimes, and they want that filth to spill on all of us. The fact that there was a real and long-standing resistance to Hitler doesn't seem to matter."

"Perhaps because it wasn't successful."

"Of course. Nothing succeeds like success. When our glorious *Fuehrer* was at the height of his triumphs, they all came to pay him court—do you remember? The Windsors, Lloyd George, the Lindberghs. . . . And they all did business with him —England, France, America, Switzerland. When the German resistance was already trying to get rid of Hitler, Chamberlain was still busy negotiating with him. When we asked for Allied support later, it was denied. But we, *we* are being condemned for having given him our early support when he seemed to be performing miracles for Germany." He paused somewhat breathlessly, turning his bitter eyes on the old man's face. "Do you know how many people lost their lives after July twentieth? Thousands—hanged, tortured by the black swine; the best Germany had to give—Oster, Canaris, Beck, Moltke, Kleist, Stauffenberg, Schulenburg, Bonhoeffer, Goerdeler . . ."

"And Albrecht," the old man said in a half whisper. "It was all too late. . . ." His eyes were still closed. Scheidt said nothing. The old man asked for a glass of water. As I handed it to him I asked him how he felt now. He smiled sadly. "Well enough to see Hess, I'm afraid."

"I'm sorry the prospect upsets you so."

"I would have liked to remember him as he was before. . . ."

He reminisced about Hess in a voice that was almost inaudible, a monologue of fragments aimed as much at himself as at us: Hess fleeing from the Bavarian police after the Beer Hall putsch in 1923 and finding temporary refuge in Haushofer's country house; Hess being taught English by Frau Haushofer, or assisting the professor in a research project. For one who knew of Hess primarily as a vicious anti-Semite, a deluded fanatic and practically co-author of *Mein Kampf,* Haushofer's reminiscences were curious to hear. But the old man appeared to have a real affection for the Hess he remembered as an intense-eyed student, still wearing the ragged uniform in which he had returned from the war, and whom he described as a young man consumed by bitterness over his country's defeat and as a revolutionary of boundless commitment and courage. His feelings for his former student had a strong paternal quality, but they were also tempered by a kind of condescension: he thought of Hess as a man whose integrity and capacity for devotion considerably exceeded his intelligence.

"But he was always in the thick of action. He was twice wounded during the war and once during a street battle with the Communists. Later he had his head smashed in with a brick that was intended for Hitler. He probably saved Hitler's life by intercepting that brick."

"It's a curious thought that the course of history might have been altered by a flying brick," I said.

Haushofer smiled at me briefly. "You see, dear lady, even the course of a brick is more often than not beyond the control of the one who throws it."

"If an idiot like Hess sticks his skull in the way," Scheidt muttered.

Haushofer glared at him. "Now we all know better, don't we, when it's too late."

Scheidt took the old man's rebuke in silence.

"Let's leave him so he'll rest," I suggested, to avoid any further argument.

"I wouldn't mind trading places with Hess," Scheidt said, following me into the living room. "I wish I could lose my memory of the past."

"The good with the bad?"

"The good . . ." he repeated softly. His look mingled sorrow with devotion and made me feel uneasy.

"I would need the good to sustain me."

"If it can. If there is enough of it."

"One has to try to retain a sense of proportion. There is always something . . ."

"What proportion?" he interrupted almost sharply. "If we all had a true sense of proportion, we'd kill ourselves." Despite the sharpness of his tone, his eyes had a pleading look. They were fixed on my face with an intensity that was too personal and too demanding, as if I had the power to free him from his regrets and end his misery. "I'm sorry," he said after a moment. "It's just that sometimes I get the feeling that I'm dead already, as if the spirit had died. I no longer understand the past or the present. I'm like a stranger to my own life. . . ." He paused, then added abruptly, "My wife is leaving me."

The announcement startled me and added to my discomfort. It was made as if it held particular significance for me. "I am sorry," I said more stiffly than I had intended.

He got up. "No, I am sorry. I'm burdening you with my problems. You've got problems of your own."

"I don't know anyone who hasn't in these times."

I went back to check on Haushofer, who appeared to be sleeping soundly and continued to do so right through dinner. Later in the evening I brought him some milk and bread and kept him company until after midnight, when he fell asleep again. He seemed resigned about seeing Hess. When I asked him whether he had had prior knowledge of Hess's flight to Scotland, he did not answer. "It was a mission of peace—too late," was all he would say. Later it became known that on his arrival in Scotland, Hess had carried two visiting cards, one from Albrecht, the other from Karl Haushofer, and that both father and son had been involved in the planning of the unsuccessful mission.

Haushofer's confrontation with Hess took place the following afternoon. Hess did not recognize his former friend and teacher, and when the old man returned from the courthouse the ordeal of the experience was clearly visible in his face. He no longer walked erect. He seemed drained of strength and emotion. Although he wished to eat alone, I persuaded him to come to dinner, hoping that the company of people would help him to get over the shock of the meeting.

Hoffmann, who had been out all day and apparently did not know of the Hess-Haushofer meeting, dominated the conversation. He was greatly excited at having discovered the reason for his sojourn in Nuremberg. "The Americans found my archives in Munich and brought me here to sort them for the trial. They are evidently considered important evidence. What a job that will be! There are tens of thousands of photographs—and those are only my Munich files. I guess the Russians got my Berlin files, if they weren't burned out. It'll take months to get any order into those files. The index has been lost, you know . . ." He was thoroughly delighted with the prospects of his new job, which had liberated him from the discomforts of the internment camps and promised good food and warm shelter for the coming winter. The fact that he, the erstwhile friend and boon companion of Hitler, was now working for the prosecution of the Allied Military Tribunal which had branded his late friend and the latter's associates as war criminals, did not seem to bother him in the least, nor apparently did the fact that his son-in-law, Baldur von Schirach, was to be one of the indicted.

"There's a lot of history in those photographs, a lot of history . . ."

"All of our folly and our shame," Scheidt said softly, looking at me.

"I have a picture of Hess, a very old picture my wife took in Munich," Haushofer said. "I forgot that I had it in my wallet. I hadn't looked at it in years, but today I looked at it. I wanted to make sure that the man I remembered was real, not the one I saw today."

Hoffmann looked astonished. "Hess is in Nuremberg? Already?"

The old man's hand trembled as he reached into his breast pocket for the wallet and pulled from it a faded photograph. The picture showed a slim young man standing in a garden, wearing a shabby uniform, facing the camera unsmiling, eyes blending darkly into the heavy brows. "We wanted to give him a decent suit, but he wouldn't take it. That old uniform was his badge of honor, he said. I don't think he wore a suit until after he was married."

5 1

Scheidt's face expressed bitterness and contempt as he studied the photograph. "Perhaps the man you saw today was more real than the one in this picture."

"It was a burned-out hull of a man. . . . He looked . . . consumed. He did not recognize me or anybody else."

"He always was a little strange, but I greatly preferred him to Bormann," Hoffmann volunteered. "I guess I've known Hess almost as long as you have, Professor—since way back in Munich when he got his head cracked with a rock at a rally. Maybe that's what made him a little wacky."

"On the way back through the ruins of the old city, I kept seeing his face," Haushofer said as if he hadn't heard Hoffmann. "I thought of something I had read in the *Vedas,* that the state of our inner being reflects the world without."

"The proportions of our reality," Scheidt said, glancing at me. "I agree."

"I don't. I share the same world, but I refuse to equate my inner being with either Hess's or the ruins of Germany."

Haushofer looked at me sadly. "You share the same world, but not in the same way. Our reality reflects our choices."

In his old face was a stillness projecting finality, rehearsing death. He left the following day with Professor Walsh, returning to his home in southern Bavaria. There, as he had promised Walsh, he finished his last work, an analysis of the impact of his ideas on the development and course of National Socialism. He was to be called as a witness during the trial, but this last duty he shunned. When a stroke failed to kill him, he finally helped himself to the death so long denied him. It was the following March that I read the notice in the newspaper that Professor Haushofer and his wife had committed double suicide through poison. Their bodies were found by their last surviving son, Heinz.

While he was confined in Berlin by the Gestapo in their notorious Moabit prison, Albrecht Haushofer wrote a number of poems which were later published under the title of *Moabiter Sonette.* On April 23, 1945, when the Russians had already entered Berlin, Albrecht Haushofer and a number of other prisoners were told by their captors that they were free. They were escorted to the street. There, in the dying moments of the nihilistic frenzy that was Nazism, they were shot in the neck. A small number escaped. Among them was Heinz Haushofer, who had been held in the same prison in *Sippenhaft*—the system under which relatives of enemies of the state were also arrested and not infrequently put to death. It was Heinz Haushofer who found his brother's body after the executioners had fled from the advancing Russians. In his brother's dead hand was clasped the notebook containing the poems.

I don't know if the old man knew about his son's poems; if he did he never mentioned them to me. But there is one bearing the title "The Father." It retells the ancient legend according to which once in a millennium a mortal is given the power of the gods to release or keep confined the spirits of evil that live imprisoned in the darkness of the ocean's depth. These are the last two stanzas of the poem:

> The lot fell to my father;
> It once lay in the power of his will
> To cast the demon back into his prison home.

> My father broke the seal;
> He did not see the evil's vapor rise
> Into the world. He let the demon fly . . .

8

On October 20, the indictment against the major war criminals and criminal organizations was presented to the International Military Tribunal. The trial itself was to begin a month later. As the opening date approached, the witness houses became increasingly busy, but the new guests stayed for the most part no longer than one night, or until private accommodations for them could be found—a formidable task in a city as nearly destroyed as Nuremberg. The reason they were not permitted to stay in the witness houses was, quite simply, that they were not witnesses but defense attorneys summoned by the IMT to take over the thankless and difficult job of defending the accused against charges that appeared—even before the trial had begun—overwhelming and irrefutable. Assembled from all over Germany, and in one or two cases from Austria, they represented in many instances the top legal talent of the country. Among them were Dr. Rudolf Dix, former president of the German Bar Association, and Professor Herbert Kraus, an expert on international law, both charged with the defense of Schacht. Another pair with a long list of impressive judicial and academic credentials were Professors Exner and Jahrreis, the attorneys for General Jodl.

The mood of these men reflected the grimness and distasteful nature of the task before them. They were faced with incredible difficulties: dependent completely on the victors for the most elementary necessities of life, as well as the facilities and materials for the fulfillment of their duties; limited, as were all Germans, in their freedom of movement; without free access to witnesses and documents; and operating within a legal system that differed substantially from their own, they were expected in many cases to defend their clients against charges of crimes so monstrous as to make a mockery of the very idea of human justice. They were caught between the staggering proportions of the crimes and the very real flaws of the tribunal and the statutes within which they were to work. None of the attorneys appeared to question the need for a trial, only the composition of the tribunal and certain of the statutes, especially the one that dealt with the crime of conspiracy, a concept alien to continental law which, through the indictment of mass organizations as criminal, implied the collective guilt of large sections of the German people. It was the effort to separate as much as possible the people from the crimes that had been committed in their name, to rescue and preserve a memory of decency for Germany, that was to become the almost hopeless mission of the German defense at Nuremberg.

But as I listened to my guests discussing the validity of statutes and the applicability of laws, I remembered other voices, other sounds. They forced themselves into the learned debate, obliterating it.

The year before, during the time of our refuge in west Hungary with the Bishop of Gyoer, trains carrying Jews, apparently to camps in Austria or Czechoslovakia, had come past the village at the same time every day for nearly a week, and the sound of their awful passing had shut out all others. Through the small windows of the cattle cars, we had caught occasional glimpses of their tightly packed human cargo marked like vermin for destruction. I remembered the cries and the already strangely distorted faces. Each day at the passing of the hell-bound trains, the bishop, who was our host, had knelt with his priests by the side of the tracks, prayed, wept, and raised his cross in supplication. In one of the village cottages an elderly Jewish couple from Austria had been given refuge. Frequently, at night, my husband or I had taken them provisions. One night, during the week the trains came past the village, we were awakened by shouts and cries and the sound of cracking whips, sharp as gun shots. We had cowered by our dark windows as contingents of Hungarian SS drove hundreds of Jews through the village streets. The following morning the Jewish couple were gone; so were all the other inhabitants of the cottage. I don't know whether any of them survived.

I had caught only a glimpse of the spectrum of terror with which the tribunal would have to deal, but even from that glimpse its failure seemed predetermined, as inevitable as the failure of the bishop's prayers to stop the trains. I was beginning to understand what Haushofer had meant when he said that the tribunal would find out *what* happened, but not why or how. Perhaps what was on trial in Nuremberg was something at the core of human nature itself, an elemental ferocity that has made of human history the slaughter bench Hegel saw. An ancient, simpler code than the tribunal's was needed to settle scores, and even as the court prepared to convene, cumbersomely and ceremoniously, that ancient code was being upheld without delay or ceremony. It was the turn for German prisoners to die in Russian prison camps, as Russians had died in German camps; it was the turn for Germans to be deported for forced labor and expelled en masse from their homes. Refugees by the thousands poured daily into Bavaria, mostly from Bohemia. There were similar expulsions from Upper Silesia, East Prussia, and Transylvania.

Wood carving of Burg Ranis in Thuringia, ca. A.D. 900, the birthplace of Countess Kalnoky.

Burg Ranis.

Family dinner with guests.

Below: *Dining room at Burg Ranis.*

Countess Kalnoky and her son, Antal.

Opposite: *Engagement portrait of Dietrich von Breitenbuch and his wife, the parents of Countess Kalnoky.*

Left: *Cuci with Antal and Ingeborg (Bobby).*

Opposite: *Countess Kalnoky and her husband, Hugo, on their wedding day.*

Countess Kalnoky wearing the Kalnoky family jewels and a gown from the Middle Ages.

Above: *The Count's daughter, Eleanor. (Photograph by Heinrich Hoffmann.)*

Left: *Countess Kalnoky listening to one of her guests at the guest house. (Photograph by Heinrich Hoffmann.)*

Until the beginning of the trial the attorneys kept on coming and going. On several occasions Professor Exner brought Frau Jodl, the wife of the general he was to defend before the allied tribunal. Although harassed and drawn, she was still a handsome woman who appeared to be sustained only by her purpose: to save her husband's life. To this end she had joined Professor Exner's staff. She was Jodl's second wife, and that only for a few months, having married him shortly before the war's end. What she had shared of her husband's life were its darkening hours, with the darkest yet to come. I felt for her, wondering that this pity had not been eclipsed by the horrors I had seen. The world was full of victims.

Frau Jodl's presence brought an urgency and involvement on the part of the attorneys involved in her husband's defense. Exner and Jahrreis were among the few defense counsels at Nuremberg who appeared to be genuinely concerned about their clients. Not all took their mission so seriously. Some, in the spirit of Hoffmann, looked upon the trial as a meal ticket that would get them through the winter. I even heard one attorney quip that he hoped his client would not desert him by committing suicide, as had Dr. Ley, the alcoholic head of the *Arbeitsfront,* who had hanged himself in his Nuremberg jail cell shortly after the indictment had been handed down. The individual attitudes of the attorneys depended then largely on the type of client each was slated to defend. Dr. Dix, a man of impressive appearance and a cosmopolitan manner, as well as an attorney of long-standing fame, did not seem to share much in the common concerns of his colleagues. Unlike a number of other attorneys (the counsels assigned to Streicher and Kaltenbrunner, for example), who for all practical purposes had to view their clients as indefensible, Dix looked upon his client, Dr. Schacht, as a man who had been wrongly indicted under the war crimes charge. Similar views about their clients were shared by the counsels for the indicted military men, who, in addition to General Jodl, were Fieldmarshal Keitel, Hitler's Chief of Staff, and Admirals Doenitz and Raeder. Dr. Kranzbuehler, the attorney for Doenitz, was himself an officer of the

German navy and the only one among the attorneys who wore a uniform, although it was stripped of its rank markings, as was the rule for all former members of the German military.

I was kept quite busy during those days by the constant turnover and changing number of guests. There were small problems. In the neighboring house the cuckoo clock disappeared, evidently the victim of an insomniac's wrath. We had locked up the noisy bird at night, but its insistent knocking apparently sealed its fate. We found that we were short on chairs. More were supplied in short order, arriving in an army pickup truck—painted wood, wicker, and faded damask, a mixture of styles as motley as the people who were to occupy them in the months ahead. As the chairs moved in, the family photographs on the desk were quietly moved out, gathered into her cellar by Frau Kruelle. Our operation was becoming professional, but certain "unprofessional" touches remained, provided mostly by my children. The baby, who was now two and a half months old, was developing a fairly robust voice which would now and then startle a group of counsels immersed in learned debate, while Antal, whenever he could get away from Cuci, continued to waylay unsuspecting arrivals, asking to see their watches. The cat was behaving with more decorum; since Haushofer's departure I had not seen her again in the house.

All in all I was content, and grateful for the job that provided me with security for my family. The baby was thriving; the children were healthy. But if we had found a haven for the winter, my husband's fate still remained uncertain. The Red Cross still had no information; with countless others I worried and waited. Being busy helped, since it limited my time for brooding. Unfortunately, many of my guests had little else to do with theirs and so were worn down by time and the uncertainty of waiting.

Scheidt was one of those. He had been kept waiting for weeks and in the process had grown increasingly depressed. He appeared to have had close connections with the German resistance, but he feared that he lacked sufficient proof of his involvement and that it would not be considered a great enough counterweight to his earlier support and services for the regime. While he was in Nuremberg he was visited by two men whose names figured prominently in the resistance. They were Ludwig von Hammerstein, whose father, a former Commander-in-Chief of the German army, had been a bitter enemy of Hitler, and Ewald Heinrich von Kleist, who had himself at one time been waiting to assassinate Hitler, the attempt—like so many others on the indestructible dictator's life—being foiled when Hitler abruptly changed his schedule. Kleist's father, one of the earliest members of the opposition, had died on the gallows after the '44 coup. The extent of Scheidt's own involvement was not known to me, but his bitterness over the allied indictment of the OKW and the General Staff as criminal organizations was great. He considered this indictment vindictive and unfair because it placed these groups in the same category with the SS and the SD, despite the long-standing and often active resistance to Hitler among so many of the officers involved.

"If there ever was a conspiracy among any officers of the German army, it was the conspiracy to get rid of Hitler," he said to me on one occasion. "Not that I ever had any illusions about the fairness of the trial, but this is no more than blatant propaganda to discredit the army before its own people. The only crime the German army is on trial for is defeat. This is the price we pay for unconditional surrender."

He seemed to be torn between his shame and sorrow for the events of the past, and his resentment against the victors. But in his general depression it was difficult to separate his own situation from the one at large. His wife's threat to leave him obviously caused him a great deal of pain. She was Hungarian, and he implied that she was leaving him because she would not remain married to a German.

He sought me out whenever he could, and because my company appeared to relax his tension, I spent what time I could spare with him, although I felt considerably uneasy in his presence. There are certain things a woman doesn't need to be told in words. Scheidt was too sick at heart to flirt; what he was asking when he looked at me was more serious. It gave silent expression to a need extending beyond infatuation to the compassion and comfort contained in love. A simple flirtation would have presented no problem, but Scheidt's plea moved me, and I could not help but respond, inwardly at least. I felt quite vulnerable and alone, wondering how I would be able to continue extricating the warmth and compassion due Scheidt as a fellow human being from the tangle of feelings inherent in such a situation.

Once, on a lovely, clear day in early November, I had set up my easel in the living room by the glass door that led into the garden. It was midmorning, and the house was quiet. Cuci was out with the children; Hoffmann was at the courthouse, sorting his archives; several attorneys who had stayed overnight had checked out after breakfast. Only Scheidt, who was restricted to the house, remained, and his restlessness seemed like a palpable force, a third presence in the room. I was already sorry that I had brought down my easel. It was a situation I should have tried to avoid. Yet it did not seem fair to avoid him, especially when no one else was in the house. Although he loathed Hoffmann, Hoffmann did at least distract him from his brooding, while the lawyers gave him a chance to argue about the trial. I knew that Scheidt craved my presence, probably for all the reasons that make a man turn to a woman for comfort when he is hurt in body or soul, but I didn't think that he had tried to disentangle the web of his feelings, the way I had tried to do with mine.

I tried to concentrate on the paper before me. What had lured me were the colors of the chrysanthemums beneath sky and tinted leaves; everywhere the colors of autumn were brilliant, yet muted, life holding its breath in the foreknowledge of death. Always painting had restored me, helped me to possess the beautiful and to control the ugly, giving form and perspective to experience. But Scheidt's presence was too disruptive. There was pressure even in his silence. He alternately sat and paced, stopping now and then before the bookcases to look for the hundredth time at the titles in Frau Kruelle's library. As if he had a need to torment himself, he had started to read Schiller's *Wallenstein,* finding numerous parallels between the Thirty Years War and the present, as well as between Hitler and the enigmatic figure of Wallenstein. But the drama only added to his depression. When I suggested that he try to relax by reading one of the numerous well-thumbed detective stories on the shelves, he rejected the idea with some vehemence. Mostly he complained that he found it too difficult to read in any case, because he could not concentrate.

I had made several attempts to sketch out my picture, none of them successful. When I folded up my easel and started to leave the room, he stopped me.

"You're leaving because of me."

His directness and accuracy startled me, but perhaps it was better to say what had remained unspoken and so clear the air.

"Your tension is contagious."

"I'm sorry I upset you."

"You don't upset me, but you do make me feel uneasy. I know how unhappy you are and I wish I could help you."

"You can and you have."

"I'm glad."

"You know how much I admire you."

"That's what makes me so uneasy."

He began to pace again. "My feelings about our situation are ambivalent . . ."

"I wish you wouldn't call it that."

He stopped in front of me. "You feel not involved?"

"Perhaps not quite in the way you think. Besides, that is really not the point."

"Isn't it? All our lives we've been told that feelings and emotions must be controlled. Before one can fulfill one's love, one has to marry; for everything there was a law . . ."

61

"There still is," I said with as much emphasis as possible.

He looked at me for some moments in silence, but in his eyes was a desperate intensity, making me think of someone drowning, trying with his last strength to reach the safety of shore. "Don't you see," he said at last, "living according to the law has been meaningless for me. I don't know how it has been for you, but perhaps we would all be better off if we would rely more on our feelings, respect our feelings instead of the laws. Should love be legislated, or should it have freedom?"

Law, love, freedom—how did the words translate into living? I thought of my husband, imprisoned in the forms of ancient custom; proud, loyal, rigid. Love turned to rite and worship, so that it lived freely only in his eyes. He was both lord and vassal, demanding and giving unconditional obedience, locked as much as were his peasants within the web of the sovereign pattern into which he was born. What freedom? Will and spirit must be broken to fit the pattern's design. He was educated by the Jesuits at Kalksburg in Austria, harnessed with dogma and saddled with the code that would forever bind him to the past, church and throne and the fallen empire. Love? What he remembered of his boyhood was hate and fear, the slow suffocation of the will. The memory of hate remained, coupled with regret, as for something precious lost so long ago that it was barely remembered, remaining only in outlines of feelings, like shapes in the dark.

And I? Did I know freedom? When I was sixteen I refused to go to communion on Good Friday. There was an awful battle, but I won, and the victory at once exhilarated and frightened me, for it left me alone in the isolation of my will. I longed more for love than such awesome power. Joy and longing had created me a lover who roamed with me through the meadows and forests of my childhood, a lover made of myth and woodland spirit, and love was the eternal promise consummated on beds of wet grass scented with pine. I had loved then with an ecstasy transcending the possible, and yet it had all been real and tender, like the first morning light creating halos for flowers from the mists of night.

"You're not answering me," Scheidt said. "Have I offended you?"

"No. I was thinking. . . ."

"About what?"

"About the reality of the things we've talked about, like love and freedom."

"You don't believe they can be real?"

"I would believe in love more than freedom."

"Do you believe in my love for you?"

"No."

He was silent for a moment. "Why? Are you afraid?"

"No, not afraid. I just believe you're seriously misinterpreting the feelings you think you have for me. We're all at loose ends. It's only natural to look for comfort."

He looked hurt. "I'm not a child."

"Children are not the only people who need comforting."

"You're making fun of me."

"Not at all. I respect your feelings for me and I'm touched by them."

He nodded, his face expressing bitterness and resignation. "I apologize if I've caused you any embarrassment."

I was glad the matter had been brought into the open. For a time he behaved toward me with rather exaggerated formality, but this did not last long. For one thing, his limbo of waiting was at least temporarily interrupted when he was at last taken to the courthouse for interrogation. Afterward he worked on a deposition. As it turned out, Scheidt was to stay at the witness house for almost six months, but the subject of his "love" for me was raised only once more, at a later time, and under curiously ironic circumstances.

9

Near the end of the month I received a call from the court-house, instructing me to hold in readiness a room in the main house. It was the first time that I had received such a directive. Until now all my guests had arrived unannounced, and their placement had been left entirely to my discretion. Naturally, I awaited with some suspense the guest for whom this special reservation had been made.

He arrived the following day accompanied by an officer and two guards, a tall, yet—next to the young M.P.s—almost frail-looking man in his middle forties. I was struck by his face, which was a study in contrasts: exceedingly pale and deeply lined under the kind of straight bluish-black hair one connects most often with Latins; eyes that were unexpectedly blue and whose expression was startlingly frank, mingling vitality and desire. Above the mouth and across one cheek were the dueling scars that testified to his onetime membership in an exclusive student corps.

If I had ever had any doubts about the voluntary nature of the establishment I was managing, they were about to be confirmed; still, I was in no way prepared for what was about to come.

"This man is to be held under room arrest," the accompanying officer told me. "He is not allowed to have contact with any of the other people billeted here. You are responsible for his confinement."

I wasn't sure whether I had heard correctly. "You mean I have . . . to watch him?"

"Just lock the door and keep the key," the officer said nonchalantly.

"They're not going to stay?" I asked, indicating the M.P.s.

"*Gnaedige* Frau, I give you my word of honor that I shall cause you neither inconvenience nor embarrassment," my new guest said with the faintest suggestion of a smile.

The officer looked at him distrustfully, evidently unable to understand German. "Look," he said to me, "this is a darn sight better than jail. It's most likely far better than he deserves. He won't try any nonsense."

The man nodded, his smile deepening into irony. "I promise I won't . . . try any nonsense."

"Okay, let's lock him up, fellows," the officer said to the M.P.s, and turning to me, "Please show us the room."

I walked ahead upstairs. Expecting someone special, I had reserved the largest, most comfortable of the bedrooms. As it turned out, my new guest was indeed someone special, though not quite in the way I had expected. His name was Rudolf Diels; but when the door locked behind him and the officer handed me the key, that name still meant nothing to me. It was Hoffmann who enlightened me about my new guest's identity. Seeing me carrying a tray upstairs at dinnertime, he inquired whether we had now instituted room service.

"Not exactly. They call it room arrest."

Hoffmann raised his eyebrows and looked interested. "And the best room, too. Anyone I know?"

"Perhaps. But he's not allowed to talk to anyone. His name is Diels."

"Rudolf Diels?"

"Yes."

"Humm. I thought he was dead," Hoffmann said. Then he suddenly began to laugh. "Are *you* supposed to keep him locked up?"

"Yes. Only I don't find it particularly amusing."

"You will when you find out who he is—or do you know?"

"No . . ."

"My dear Countess, you have the rare honor to be the jailer of the founder and original head of the Gestapo."

I think I very nearly dropped the tray. In any case, I must have looked as if I were about to faint, for Hoffmann rushed to my aid and carried the tray the rest of the way. "Now, now, calm yourself. He's not Himmler. Diels hasn't been with the Gestapo since '34."

Hoffmann held the tray while I knocked and unlocked the door. My hands were trembling. Then I remembered that my prisoner wasn't supposed to communicate with anyone in the house except, presumably, me, his jailer. I thanked Hoffmann for his help and, explaining my orders, requested him to leave.

He appeared amused. "You take everything very seriously, Countess. I've known Diels for years. If I wanted to, I could talk to him through the wall. After all, I'm his neighbor."

"Just don't do it while I'm around," I said, feeling both foolish and inefficient.

My heart was beating like a tom-tom when I entered the room, balancing the tray in one hand. Diels jumped up helpfully, relieving me of the tray and closing the door.

"Don't worry," he said. "If he talks to me, I promise I won't answer. I much prefer talking to you."

"You heard us?"

"I was listening by the door," he said with mock remorse. "One loses one's good manners as a prisoner."

"Do you know who I was talking to?"

"Of course: Photo-Hoffmann. I recognized his dialect. Be-

66

sides, I knew he'd be here." He looked at me expectantly, as if he were waiting for me to follow a cue.

"I suppose being well informed is a part of your . . . profession . . ."

He smiled ruefully. "I see my reputation has preceded me. How shall I defend myself?"

"You needn't. I'm no judge."

Turning to go, I added mechanically, "I hope you enjoy your dinner."

"Countess, please," he called after me. There was a note of very real concern in his voice. "Your face belies your words. It shows your judgment."

"Why should you care what I think? You don't know me."

"I should very much like to know you, and I would like it if you would get to know me better before you judge me." His smile was disarming, his eyes too frank; mingling plea and pleasure, their gaze on me was like a touch. "After all—I am your prisoner."

He seemed to enjoy his little scene, which appeared at least in part inspired by the absurdly peculiar circumstances of our relationship. There was certainly some mockery in his flirtation, but its effect on me was to free me of my first reaction of panic and restore my balance. The ominous echo of the word Gestapo still rang in my ears, but when I locked the door again behind my prisoner, I felt more silly than afraid. The idea that I was responsible for keeping that man locked in his room seemed as ludicrous to me as it apparently did to him.

The rest of our little company was equally amused. By the time I arrived at dinner a few minutes late, Hoffmann appeared to have informed everyone of the situation.

"The Americans probably know that Diels would never run away from a lady. It would be completely against his principles," Hoffmann said with a grin. "He may run away *with* a lady, but never from one."

"I won't put him to the test," I said, laying the key beside my plate.

"You'd better beware of him, Countess. He's a devious fellow," Hoffmann said with mock seriousness.

"I suppose the founder of the Gestapo would have to be."

Hoffmann shrugged. "He knows a lot of tricks, but they weren't enough to stop Himmler."

This may well have been an accurate appraisal of Diels measured by Gestapo standards; to compare him to Himmler as if he were merely a smaller exemplar of the same monster species turned out on closer examination to be unfair. Diels's plea that I should try to get to know him better before I judged him appeared to have some merit. He was at any rate a lot less sinister than my immediate reaction to the word Gestapo had painted him in my mind.

Diels had indeed founded the Gestapo in 1933 at the behest of Hermann Goering, who had become Minister President of Prussia in Hitler's government. In those early days of the regime, directly after the attainment of power, rival Nazi factions fought each other for shares of that power often with as much viciousness as they fought their political enemies. This kind of jealous factionalism was to plague the Nazi state throughout its brief and violent existence, resulting in a fairly impenetrable jungle of competing agencies and overlapping authority, but it had its acutest phase during that first year.

Among the most covetous of the new lords was Goering, who, along with objets d'art, mansions, and exotic costumes, collected titles and spheres of influence. As Minister President of Prussia he was already head of the Prussian police; his aim, however, was the eventual control of all the police forces in the Reich. In this ambition he had a rival in a relatively obscure Bavarian who at that time was the head of the Bavarian police as well as the commander of the SS; his name was Heinrich Himmler. But it was Goering who through his control of Prussia had by far the larger power base. To consolidate this power, Goering turned to a heretofore insignificant section of the Prussian police which even under the republic (and in violation of its constitution) had been concerned with political intelligence. His plan was to build this agency into a major intelligence force. His choice to execute this plan was a young career official who had already been a part of this intelligence division under the republic, namely Rudolf Diels. Under Diels's direction the agency grew considerably in size and scope, and under a law passed through Goering's initiative it became autonomous, responsible only to him. Goering called his creation *Geheime Staatspolizei,* shortly thereafter to be known as the Gestapo.

If the history of the early pre-Himmler Gestapo is no more savory than that of most other such political intelligence agencies—its prime function appears to have been to suppress remnants of political resistance—it was nevertheless a long way from the instrument of absolute terror it was to become under Himmler and Heydrich. The men Diels brought into the agency were, like him, career officials. Few were Nazis, though with the characteristic conservatism of the civil service they shared the Nazi hatred of both social democracy and communism. The terror in those early days came primarily from the SA, which Goering had declared a police auxiliary force in the fight against remnants of the left. But even Goering appeared to have been unprepared for the ruthless diligence his deputies brought to their task. Before long his new Gestapo had its hands full just containing the revolutionary fervor of its supposed allies. Goering appeared to have unleashed a force he could not control.

The chronicle of SA atrocities during the Nazi revolutionary period foreshadows the horrors of later SS and Gestapo methods, but these had not yet become standard operating procedures. There was still the difference between on one side the career service and on the other the army of revolutionaries riding the cruel crest of their triumph above and beyond all law, heedless now even of the commands of their masters. This difference, however, was to disappear shortly, when the very lawlessness of the doomed brown mercenaries would become codified by their black-uniformed successors and Germany turned into a criminal state. It was in June of 1934 that Hitler finally moved in characteristic fashion against the Brownshirts who had done so much to bring him to power and who had now become a threat to that power. In a bloody purge the entire SA leadership was murdered. The field was open for the even more sinister Himmler and his SS.

By this time Diels was no longer with the Gestapo. During his brief tenure, though, he fought SA outrages with considerable courage, an undertaking in which Goering gave him reluctant, tacit support. Diels was responsible for the closing of a great number of SA "bunkers," those notorious, somewhat impromptu detention facilities where the victims of SA raids were beaten and tortured. On some such occasions Diels's Prussian police, armed with hand grenades and machine guns, faced its revolutionary adversary across drawn battle lines and liberated SA victims at gunpoint. He was less successful in closing down some equally notorious SS facilities but, apparently undaunted, went to court against SA and SS offenders— quite a daring undertaking even in those early days. Finding some judges who matched his daring, he even succeeded in getting convictions. The sum of his efforts earned him the bitter enmity of both the SA and the SS, and in the fall of 1933, in what appeared to have been an SS coup to gain control of the Gestapo, Diels barely escaped from an SS detail hunting him. Fearing for his life, he fled to Czechoslovakia. Himmler, of course, had long been waiting to break into Goering's territory, and this apparently was his first offensive; but Goering survived the first round and brought Diels back, guaranteeing his safety and reinstalling him in his former office. In honor of the truce between the two rivals, Himmler and Goering, Diels was given a black uniform and made a *Standartenfuehrer* in the SS, which in no way prevented Himmler from keeping him on his "deathlist." In a similar temporary truce with the SA, Diels at the suggestion of Goering had become a *Gruppenfuehrer* in the SA. He was then a ranking member in two organizations that counted him among their most hated enemies—a situation not at all unusual in the cauldron of Nazi politics, and which Diels survived only through Goering's protection.

Shortly after his return from his brief exile, Diels managed to persuade Hitler and Goering to agree to a fairly widespread amnesty for political prisoners. About five thousand were released, an event of which Diels was justly proud and which appeared to sustain him inwardly through the mass of postwar accusations leveled against him.

But his power to temper the terror was about to come to an end. The truce between Himmler and Goering proved short-lived. Himmler had long been expanding his power. Outside Goering's territory the *Reichsfuehrer* of the SS controlled a widespread police intelligence network. In his efforts to break into Goering's Prussian stronghold, Himmler eventually found allies among the proponents of centralization in the Reich government. By early 1934 local government in the *Lander* had been reduced to purely administrative functions. Among the powers taken over by the Reichsministry of the Interior was the control of all German police forces. Goering's power over Prussia was broken; Diels resigned in April and was replaced by Himmler as head of the Gestapo.

Transferred to Cologne, where he assumed the office of *Regierungs-President* (head of local administration), Diels continued to enjoy Goering's protection, and some years later even became related to the Reichsmarshal by marrying the widow of his brother. But in 1944 Goering's power was apparently no longer strong enough to save his former protégé from Himmler's unsubsided wrath. Diels spent most of 1944 in a Gestapo prison. His marriage to Goering's former sister-in-law was dissolved by the Reichsmarshal, who sent word to Diels—so the latter told me—that he didn't want to have a "hanged man" in his family. (Considering Goering's later action in Nuremberg —he eluded the gallows by taking poison—he must have been really determined to avoid that stigma.) Diels, however, escaped the gallows through an accident that saved the lives of a number of other Gestapo prisoners: an allied air raid destroyed the prison and the court building and killed Roland Freisler, the notorious prosecutor of the People's Court.

This, roughly, was what I learned about Diels from bits and pieces gleaned from conversations with him and some of my other guests. One guest especially was not only able but exceedingly eager to talk about the erstwhile Gestapo chief. Fraulein Limberger, an attractive woman in her fifties who had been Goering's librarian and later his private secretary, arrived the day after Diels. Her excitement was great when she found out that he was in the house; but her disappointment was even greater when she learned that she would be unable to see him. She compensated for this deprivation by talking about him and sending him her heartfelt good wishes through me, watching me with obvious longing when I balanced my tray up the stairs at mealtimes.

Fraulein Limberger had been present at Diels's wedding to Ilse Goering, which evidently had been engineered by Goering to strengthen his protection of Diels through family ties. That Goering had a fondness for Diels was obvious, but any reasons for this were unknown to the secretary, or at least she seemed to think that no particular reasons were necessary, since Diels's charms were such that it was impossible not to like him. If Diels knew of any particular reasons for Goering's long-lasting fondness and concern, he never mentioned them to me. He did, however, reveal a grudging admiration for his former chief. When he talked about Goering, he endowed him with a certain romantic aura reminiscent of a Homeric hero, describing the enormity of his rages, the generosity of his friendship, his childlike delight in pomp, his exuberant abandonment to pleasure. Diels seemed to see in Goering's elemental vitality and arrogance an enlarged image of himself, and in his hero's heedless breaking beyond the barriers of law and conscience the ominous, forbidden, yet secretly desired fulfillment of the romantic ideal.

If Diels talked with reluctant admiration of his former

chief, he appeared to have been less than enthusiastic about his arranged marriage. According to him it had been a marriage in name only. He talked little about his former wife but a great deal about his numerous love affairs. Fraulein Limberger, though, with obvious emotion, told me about Ilse Goering's great love for Diels and her grief when her brother-in-law forced her to give him up. The secretary seemed greatly moved by the unhappy love story she was recounting to me and glanced sadly more than once in the direction of the stairs that led to Diels's locked door.

Tears in any case seemed to be the theme of Diels's romances. From his own accounts I got an image of beautiful women swooning at his feet and attempting suicide out of unrequited passion. These accounts were not meant to be taken seriously; they were one part in his repertoire of seduction. He had quite definitely an image of himself as being irresistible to women and behaved accordingly. During the first few days of his stay I was subjected to every trick in his routine of flattery and flirtation, an experience which proved both fascinating and amusing and in no way emotionally taxing, as had been the episode with Scheidt. It was obvious that Diels collected love affairs like trophies, to please his ego. Working on my seduction also interrupted the monotony of playing solitaire; it was a change of games.

I was forced, though, to reconsider my appraisal of Diels's romantic attraction when on the third day of his stay a young woman arrived and tearfully begged permission to see him. Delicate, dark-haired, and rather pretty, she had traveled a great distance. God only knew how she had found out where to find him. Now, so close to the object of her desire, she seemed unable to believe that I could not permit her to see him. She sat down on the stairs and cried. Since I didn't have the heart to throw her out or call the courthouse to complain, she was still there in the evening, sitting on the stairs with a hurt, bewildered look, crying intermittently. Her presence caused quite a stir. Fraulein Limberger cried with her, sending occa-

7 3

sional longing glances upstairs. Hoffmann decided that I was entirely too rigid in my obedience of instructions, and for once Scheidt agreed with Hoffmann. "You're being terribly German about this," he said. I was obviously becoming the villain of the piece. Fortunately, two attorneys who had just arrived for dinner sided with me. "If it comes out, the place will be closed down," one of them said, bringing the argument to a close but hardly solving my problem. The girl made no move to leave but simply remained sitting on the stairs, mute and heartbroken. I asked her to join us at dinner, but she didn't respond to my invitation. Finally Fraulein Limberger managed to coax her into the living room and got her to eat something.

When I brought Diels his dinner he looked at me accusingly. Evidently Hoffmann had been unable to resist telling him through the wall that he had a visitor. I was aware that they had been communicating in this manner, but since I couldn't prevent it I had ignored it. I didn't want trouble, but beyond keeping Diels locked up in his room there was really nothing I could do to keep him incommunicado. Besides, the whole situation was just too ridiculous to take seriously and was becoming more so by the minute. Looking at Diels's mournfully accusing face, I suddenly burst out laughing. I certainly pitied the poor girl downstairs, weeping in the sympathetic company of Fraulein Limberger, but the absurdity of the scene got the better of me.

"You are a hard woman, Countess," Diels said.

"Look, I feel very sorry for the young lady . . ."

"Erika . . ."

"It was very foolish of Erika to come."

"Lovers are fools," Diels said, sounding theatrical. He appeared to be only half serious, like an actor playing a part, calculating its effect on his audience.

"I'm sure I've heard that before somewhere."

"Undoubtedly."

I thought he looked rather pleased about the girl's visit. His eyes had an "I told you so" expression.

7 4

"Aren't you concerned about her?" I asked.

"Why? Won't you even put her up for the night?"

"I'm not supposed to, but I guess I have no other choice. If she doesn't leave tomorrow, though, I'll have to call the court-house."

"Let me talk to her through the door."

"That'll make matters worse. She'll probably become hysterical."

He shrugged with mock exasperation. "One can't reason with women." Unable to hide his satisfaction, he added, "I wonder how she found me."

"So do I. She wouldn't tell me. I wish whoever told her where you were hadn't neglected to inform her that she wouldn't be able to see you."

"I still say you're a hard woman."

I left, exasperated, feeling a bit like the villain in a farce when I locked the door and went downstairs to face the silent reproach of Fraulein Limberger.

"All I need is a nasty laugh and a mustache to twirl and my character would be complete," I said to Frau Kruelle, who appeared to be my only ally in the matter, severely disapproving of Erika's intention upon discovering that she was not Frau Diels.

I put Erika in Fraulein Limberger's room, though I didn't trust either of them. I'm not exactly sure just what I expected, but at that point ropes made of bedsheets or ladders wouldn't have surprised me.

If any such exotic events occurred during the night I was not aware of them. On the following day Erika, in any case, looked quite as unhappy as she had the evening before, and Fraulein Limberger remained equally in a state of depression.

It was curious how, against the background of war crimes and war guilt, devastation and suffering, this little drama continued to occupy my guests. Vicariously they seemed to identify with the thwarted lovers, experiencing their emotions as a pleasing diversion. Perhaps it was because the affair was so completely out of place that Erika became a celebrity in our living room. Frau Jodl, for example, caused no such stir; Fraulein Limberger barely gave her a glance. But then, Luise Jodl's problems were not remarkable by the standards of the time.

The affair finally reached its unhappy conclusion when Lieutenant Mueller sympathetically but firmly escorted Erika from the house after Fraulein Limberger had enclosed her in a weepy embrace and exchanged addresses with her. For the rest of her stay, which was not very long, Fraulein Limberger was markedly cool with me, while Diels played the part of the pining lover kept from his beloved by a cruel fate—personified by me. But I did not have to play the part of the "heavy" too much longer. About a week after Erika's unwilling departure, her lover was picked up in a jeep under heavy guard; Fraulein Limberger departed several days later. It was a relief not having to lock that door on Diels anymore. I had no way of knowing, of course, that I had not seen the last of him.

10

ABOUT A WEEK before the beginning of the trial two military vehicles brought five new guests. They were accompanied by a German-speaking captain and another officer, as well as by a guard of three enlisted men. Next to the well-pressed, handsomely uniformed Americans, the five, all but one of whom were dressed in rough American-issued clothing, looked shabby and drab. The consciousness of this seemed to be reflected in their grim faces. One of the five, a tall, gaunt, almost completely bald man, especially caught my attention because of his motley, unkempt appearance. He wore a battered German army jacket stripped of all rank markings, a pair of dirty threadbare trousers, a dark blue beret covering his baldness, and an incongruous scarf of frayed red silk wrapped around his neck.

I thought that after the experience with Diels nothing would surprise me, but when the German-speaking captain, whose name was Wulff, told me that the five newcomers were prisoners of war who were to be restricted to the house and given exercise privileges in the garden, I was dumfounded. If he had handed me a rifle to guard them I would probably have been stunned enough to take it. But this turned out to be unnecessary. After the officers left, one of the enlisted men posted himself before the house; another stayed by the side of the man with the red scarf. It was then that I realized that he had a personal guard.

I was rather perplexed. Nothing in my previous experience had prepared me to run a prisoner-of-war camp. My new guests appeared to share my misgivings; they looked puzzled and suspicious. Explanations and introductions were as usual left to me. My well-guarded group, I discovered, consisted of four ex-generals and one foreign service officer. Two of the generals, *Generalmajor* Ulrich Kessler of the Luftwaffe, and General Ernst Koestring, the former German military attaché in Moscow, were German; the other two, Generals Kalman Hardy and Erwin von Lahousen, were Hungarian and Austrian respectively. Lahousen, the one with the red scarf and the personal guard, was, as I found out later, one of the very few survivors from the core group of anti-Hitler conspirators in the *Abwehr* (the German counterintelligence service) under Admiral Canaris and General Oster, both of whom were hanged after the abortive July 1944 coup. The personal guard appeared to have been assigned to Lahousen to protect him against possible reprisals for his resistance work. The fifth member of the group was Emil von Rintelen, a foreign service officer with little affection for his erstwhile superior, Foreign Minister von Ribbentrop. All but Lahousen had been brought to Nuremberg from imprisonment in the U.S.

I proceeded to assign my new guests to their rooms. The fact that they were prisoners of war and that there was now a guard before the house made me feel uneasy and depressed. How grim their faces were. My father, too, had been an officer in the other war; but his face had never been grim when he spoke about his war. Pain and death were for him part of a romance. I wondered if these grim-faced men were different and if this war had killed that awful joy, burying it beneath the ruins of the devastated land. No romantic legend now, only the reality of destruction—hunger, cold, homelessness, guilt.

I had gone into the living room to turn off the radio, which was blaring away with no one to listen. Most likely it had been left on by Scheidt, who turned it on for every news broadcast and invariably, to Frau Kruelle's great annoyance, forgot to shut it off. Just then a Handel harpsichord concerto was being announced and I sat down to listen for a while. Under the table I spotted Farkas's ball, muddy and covered with little bits of leaves. He had been looking for it. Until now the children had been spending most of their time outdoors, with the entire heath for their playground, but the weather was beginning to turn cool, and I wondered how and where they would be able to play during the coming winter without disturbing the guests. My mind wandered with the strains of the music. The stately yet joyous dimensions seemed too much for the small receiver, so that the sound was sometimes cramped and unclear. Still, the pure structures were discernible, and my imagination supplied the missing resonance.

A loud, sharp knocking at the door interrupted my preoccupation. From its noisy insistence I concluded that I must not have heard earlier, more discreet, attempts to gain entrance. I turned down the radio and went to open the door. I was faced by General Lahousen and his guard. The general bowed stiffly and without smiling, his faultless formality in incongruous contrast with his appearance. He had neither shaved nor changed his clothing, from which I concluded that he did not own a razor or another set of clothes.

"Please forgive this intrusion," he said. "I heard the music, but it was he"—he indicated the guard—"who nearly broke down the door."

"Do come in, please."

"The largo," he exclaimed, rushing to the radio. He was followed by his guard, who sat down near him.

"Turn it up if you wish to hear it better."

He raised the volume to maximum loudness and adjusted the tone, glancing at me questioningly.

I nodded and tried to reassure him with a smile, but he seemed already to have forgotten about me. He stood very still beside the radio, listening to the music. The pallor and gauntness of his face exaggerated its sharply chiseled features. His prominent profile, white and immobile, appeared to belong to a classic statue, not to this soiled, untidy figure. He betrayed no emotion as he listened, though now and then the stillness of his features was broken by a twitching around the lips. I thought it a nervous symptom until quite suddenly he let himself drop into a chair and, burying his face in his hands, began to sob with barely stifled sounds. The guard looked startled and glanced at me questioningly; nor was I sure what to do. My first impulse was to rush to him and offer comfort, but I hesitated, obeying mindless embarrassment. Was there not an unwritten law that prescribed that men must not cry? To be masculine and brave was to be deaf to pain, one's own and that of others.

The young soldier guard had retreated to the far end of the room, where he studied the twilit garden beyond the French doors and glanced now and then over his shoulder at his charge. His discomfort was quite obvious. Would he report to his superiors, I wondered, that he had seen a German general cry, seen him break the code that bound them all—a German general, of all people? I went to Lahousen, sat down beside him, and laid my hand on his arm. He did not react, but I left my hand there, pressing his arm gently for reassurance. The music was still playing, the sound rising above and around us, a bond between strangers. Was the spirit of Handel the same that had raged at Auschwitz and Treblinka? Light into shadow and shadow into light, a fusion of polarities. Dionysus blessed the sparkling wine and the joyful feast, but his rage turned the wine into blood and the celebrants into raging beasts. How did the blood of Christ become the wine of communion? Wine into blood and blood into wine. Fusion. Evil in the name of good,

and good in the name of evil. So many pretexts for murder—
fatherland, revolution, religion, race, class. So many zealots
looking for a cause, so many ends to be achieved at all costs.
What label fit this man sobbing beside me?

Lahousen put his hand, damp from his tears, on mine,
pressing it gently, but he did not look at me or say anything.
The concerto was over and the announcer was talking. Now
the young guard approached hesitantly, looking at Lahousen
with a mixture of curiosity and awe.

"You all right, Mac?"

His head still bowed, Lahousen nodded. Pulling a dirty
handkerchief from his trouser pocket, he blew his nose and
wiped his face.

"If there is anything I can help you with, anything you
need, please let me know."

He looked at me as if he had not seen me before, taking
recognition of my full presence. His eyes were red and his face
looked mottled, but his look was free of embarrassment, which
gave me a feeling of gladness.

"Thank you," he said in a low voice. "I have no soap or
razor blades."

"I'll talk to Captain Wulff about it. For the moment I'm sure
we'll be able to help you out."

He was looking at his guard's brightly polished boots and
creased trousers as he stuffed his dirty handkerchief back into
his pocket. "We've come a long way, haven't we?" he muttered.

It was very near dinnertime. I gave Lahousen some of my
soap, but there was only one immediate source I could think
of for razor blades and that was Hoffmann. While the general
returned to his room in the other house, I went up to see
Hoffmann, who occupied one of the small bedrooms in the
main house. He appeared to have just returned from the court.
His door was open and a young M.P. was with him.

Hoffmann greeted me expansively. "Come in, come in,
Graefin. I was just showing my friend here some of my drawings."

8 1

He introduced me to the M.P., who offered me a stick of gum. I would have preferred a cigarette. Hoffmann, of course, had plenty of both gum and cigarettes, as well as those other American luxuries, chocolate and instant coffee, soap and even whiskey. I had noticed for some time that he was doing a flourishing business, trading his autographed drawings with his American "customers" for those rare commodities which he locked in a trunk (sent by his wife and stored under his bed). His customers often were soldiers who drove him back and forth between the court and the witness house and who affectionately called him "Uncle Heini." But Hoffmann's popularity was spreading wider than that. I had heard that he was doing quite well peddling his wares among allied court personnel in general. In any case, he was making a successful and lucrative career out of his intimate association with Hitler.

Hoffmann was not a bad artist. His sketches caught the robust humor of his native Bavaria—inebriated monks and fleshy-faced burghers waving their beer steins. It was a style of good-natured caricaturing that had been prevalent around the turn of the century. I remembered having seen copies of magazines that had carried similar illustrations. He was now putting the finishing touches on a sketch for his visitor, deepening the shadows and laugh lines around the eyes of his jolly beer drinker, adding a wart on the side of the nose. He chattered as he worked, a cigarette bobbing up and down at the side of his mouth, his Bavarian dialect becoming as picaresque as the character in his drawing. He seemed to be playing the ur-Bavarian for his American visitor, despite the fact that the fellow obviously couldn't understand a word he was saying.

If Hoffmann's artistic style belonged to a period sometimes called the Munich-Bohemian, his life-style most certainly did also. His room was the bane of Frau Kruelle's housewifely existence, perpetually littered with half-finished drawings, overflowing ashtrays and glasses smelling of whiskey, hard and soft pencils, assorted items of clothing, notes, letters, and photos. She had sworn never to enter his room again until he mended his ways, to which he had replied that that suited him just fine, since he never could find anything after she had tidied up. And there the matter rested in a deadlock.

"It's a good thing we don't have military inspections," I said, "or you'd spend the rest of your life in the guard house, Herr Hoffmann."

He grinned. "From what I saw downstairs it would seem to me that we *are* in a guard house. Did they send that handsome fellow to stand in front of the door because Frau Kruelle complained that I didn't keep my room tidy?"

"I think she would probably demand more drastic action if she could."

"Like having me shot at sunrise."

"They'd have done so for less than that at Dachau," said Scheidt, who had come from the bathroom and overheard the last of our conversation.

"We must be glad then that the color of the uniform at our door has changed," I said.

"Better enemy khaki than those black swine."

The young American who had been listening to our exchange with apparent interest, although with an equally apparent lack of understanding, had stopped smiling at the word Dachau and looked suddenly mistrustful. Hoffmann had noticed. All his resentment poured into a single glance at Scheidt before he broke into his jolliest smile, raised his finished sketch, and cried out, "It's finished!"

"Congratulations," Scheidt said sourly and went on downstairs.

The G.I. smiled again. I added my approval, remembering my mission.

"Herr Hoffmann," I said, "I didn't mean to interrupt your . . . business, but I seem to have a small crisis on my hands, and I wondered whether you would be good enough to help me out."

He bowed with mock ceremony. *"Graefin,* I'm always at your service."

I told him about Lahousen and asked him to lend me two razor blades for the general, assuring him of prompt repayment through Captain Wulff. His hesitation was only in his eyes in an instant's expression of wariness before he began to rummage on his littered table.

He presented me with the requested two blades. "My compliments to the general."

There was an element of irony in this exchange that I did not recognize at that time. I was borrowing from Hitler's closest friend for the man who had once carried explosives to the eastern front when Hitler was there for a visit, explosives that were to be used to blow up his plane on the return flight to Berlin. On that occasion, too, Hitler's guardian demon protected him—the bomb did not go off.

At dinner my new guests looked a lot more presentable but no less grim. The only exception was General Hardy, who was so delighted to find an "almost" Hungarian with whom he could talk about his homeland in his native tongue that he got quite carried away with enthusiasm and, appearing to forget the presence of the others, monopolized me completely. I tried to listen to him with due interest, although I felt distinctly uneasy about the prevailing mood of the rest of the company. Being left to the mercy of Hoffmann, the other newcomers were looking even more sour—if that was possible—so I tried to monitor the conversation (which seemed to come primarily from Hoffmann) at the other end of the table, while still listening to Hardy. Anyone who has ever tried to follow two different conversations in two different languages at the same time will bear me out when I say that it is a considerable strain. I must have looked harassed, because I noticed Scheidt looking at me with an amused expression. When Hardy finally paused in his Hungarian rhapsodizing, having probably noticed that his dinner was cooling, I heard Hoffmann remind a bewildered General Koestring that they had met at an embassy party in Moscow when Hoffmann had accompanied von Ribbentrop there in 1939. Continued reminiscences by Hoffmann about that fateful trip, which resulted in the Nazi-Soviet nonaggression pact, drew only embarrassed muttering from Koestring; and when Hoffmann told the assembled company that Hitler had sent him along on the Ribbentrop mission to bring back his own personal impression of Stalin because Hitler had more faith in his judgment than in that of his diplomats, I had the distinct impression that Koestring and von Rintelen were turning yellow, unless it was the fact that I was beginning to feel sick. The tension was growing as thick as Hoffmann's Bavarian accent. I caught Scheidt looking at Koestring and Rintelen with an ironic "I told you so" look, and I wondered if he had briefed them before dinner on the presence and character of Hitler's strange boon companion.

In retrospect the situation has about it a certain hilarity, but the joke was too sick and its consequences too devastating to produce any laughter. They were all men of skill and character who had served a corrupt master, only to be superseded at critical moments by the court jester. For all his diabolical brilliance Hitler had been severely limited—Haushofer had called him "a half-educated bungler"; Hindenburg had referred to him as "that ex-corporal with the dirt still under his nails." They had admired his brilliance and overlooked his limitations with indulgent contempt. *Mein Kampf* was, of course, not fit to read for a literate person; "revolutionary polemics," Scheidt had called it. The excesses would be controlled and channeled like energy in a high voltage cable. They had thought that Hitler could be used, and in the process had themselves been reduced to puppets in his savage comedy. The incredulity on the faces of Koestring and Rintelen as they looked at Hoffmann attested to the fact that they had not yet come to terms with their experience.

I wondered whether Hoffmann was aware of the effect he was having on his dinner companions. I don't know how he could have failed to notice it, but it didn't seem to faze him in the least. He appeared to have his own sources of strength; unlike most of the others, he seemed to have no regrets. His loyalty to his friend Hitler was undiminished, quite untouched by all that had happened, and so was his pride at having been the intimate of so powerful and great a man. Hoffmann unquestionably showed a remarkable integrity of conviction; that this integrity should have been displayed by a man who in all else was the supreme opportunist, for a man who was probably the supreme villain, was like an ironic footnote to an obscene chapter in history. Worse than seeing Hitler as the charismatic representative of evil, casting his spell upon his nation, was seeing him within the tawdry dimensions of Hoffmann.

I was grateful when Frau Kruelle came to collect the dinner plates, interrupting Hoffmann at least temporarily in his Russian reminiscences. To cut short the enforced companionship of the dinner table, I announced that for those who preferred it coffee would be served in the living room. The extra work caused by this arrangement would not endear me to Frau Kruelle, but it was the only sure way I could think of to liberate Hoffmann's forced audience. As we ate our dessert of canned fruit, General Hardy told me his opinion of Hoffmann in Hungarian, and although Hardy had not mentioned Hoffmann's name, he glanced at us with what seemed a glint of suspicion.

"You're speaking Hungarian, aren't you?"

"Yes."

"It sounds a bit like Russian."

"I don't know Russian, but I understand there is a considerable difference."

"There is no similarity whatsoever," Hardy said in gruff German.

"I've always admired people who speak foreign languages the way you do, *Graefin*. I never had much of a talent for it myself."

"But you have so many others, Herr Hoffmann," Scheidt said with an ironic glance at me which embarrassed me because Hoffmann caught it.

I rose, breaking up the dinner, and the company adjourned

in small groups to the living room, I in the enthusiastic Hungarian company of General Hardy. Glancing over my shoulder as we were drinking our coffee, I saw Hoffmann alone in a corner of the room. Not far from him Lahousen sat also alone, staring at the floor, his guard standing bored and gum-chewing behind him. When I looked back some moments later, Hoffmann, his cigarette dangling from the side of his mouth accenting the rhythm of his speech as a conductor's baton sets the rhythm of a band, was talking to the guard and the guard was laughing.

11

ANOTHER NEW ARRIVAL was added to my guest list a few days later. Dr. Hans Luther, a former chancellor of the Weimar Republic, director of the Reichsbank and ambassador to Washington during the early years of Hitler's regime, was a man in his sixties who had been called to testify in the proceedings against Schacht. Dr. Luther's varied political career stretched well across two tumultuous decades—with Stresemann he had signed the Locarno Pact, which was supposed to open a new era of cooperation between Germany and France and which paved the way for Germany's admission to the League of Nations; he had participated in the negotiations for the Dawes plan and worked with Schacht on the reconstruction of the bankrupt German financial structure in the wake of the disastrous inflation of the early twenties. But although politics appeared to have been his life's main occupation, it was by no means his preoccupation. A charming, witty, and versatile conversationalist, Dr. Luther brought some urgently needed diversion into our gloomy company. If he was not unaffected by the fate that had befallen his country, or free of the Nazi legacy of guilt, he did not appear so oppressed by it as the others. He had kept his sense of humor, which often helped to break the prevailing tension.

But on November 20, the day the trial began with a reading of the indictment, even Dr. Luther succumbed to the general sense of despair. At the witness house the mood was black and almost unbearably tense. The expectation of the event had been different from the event itself. The charges in the indictment were known and the trial date long set, but when the expected became reality, with pomp and drama and conqueror's power, all the shame and sorrow of the recent past gathered into that one day to be relived, resuffered, and regretted again. My guests reminded me of caged animals, restless and sullen, snapping at one another over trivia.

That was the day General Koestring lost his fountain pen. Hearing angry voices from the living room, I went to investigate. The old man—Koestring was at least seventy—was on his hands and knees, looking under furniture. Scheidt and Dr. Luther were helping him, but Rintelen was sitting in an easy chair, reading, the occupation with which he passed most of his time. His nonparticipation in the search appeared to anger Koestring almost as much as the loss of his pen.

"I left it right there on the table," he was saying with extreme irritation when I came in. "Are you sure you didn't see it?"

"Will you please leave me alone?" Rintelen snapped. "For the hundredth time, I didn't see your damn pen."

"My damn pen, is it? Well, you be damned, Herr Diplomat. One can see you're not a soldier. No soldier would act this way, just sitting by when someone needs help. We soldiers fought and died while you people sat in your fancy offices and bungled us into this misery!"

"*We* soldiers, Herr Attaché?" Rintelen said icily.

"I am a soldier," Koestring said, his voice trembling with rage.

"I don't seem to recall any military attachés, or for that matter generals, serving in the front lines . . ."

I interrupted the sorry spectacle with a forced smile and some soothing words. "Gentlemen, your nerves are getting the better of you."

They apologized, half to me and half to each other. Koestring dropped into a chair. "What a rotten business it all is," he said, staring at the American guard outside the window.

I found Koestring's pen on the floor near the piano. He smiled sadly when I returned it to him. "Such small things, and what they do to us."

"It's the small things that aggravate the large," Dr. Luther said compassionately.

Koestring nodded. "One forgets who one is."

"Or one finds out," said Scheidt. "Today the whole world is being told that Germans are criminals."

"The indictment is not directed against all of the German people."

He looked at me bitterly. "I read somewhere that a people gets the government it deserves, reflecting its own needs and characteristics. I wonder if that's true."

"Nonsense," Koestring snapped. "Malicious nonsense."

"Don't you believe that the German people stand indicted?" Scheidt asked, looking at me.

"Not just indicted, but already sentenced—by the victors," Rintelen answered in my place.

"The composition of the tribunal is really hard to believe," Dr. Luther said. "That and those collective indictments against the organizations do make it look like simple vengeance."

"I submit that's just what it is," said Scheidt.

"Perhaps. Considering what happened, perhaps justice is too much to expect," Dr. Luther said with just a suggestion of sharpness.

"The idea of collective guilt bothers me," I said. "I can

90

understand it as an abstraction, but I reject it. I may be a German or a Hungarian, but I'm not Germany or Hungary. I'm at once more than that and less."

"That's because you're an artist, Countess," Rintelen said with one of his rare sad smiles. "Only the souls of artists are autonomous."

There was no irony in his remark. Rintelen loved art not as a pleasant diversion, but as a sustaining force, although this would have been difficult to tell from his clipped and reserved outward appearance. An austere-looking Westphalian, he was not an easy man to get to know or like. Most thought him suspicious and morose, but I got to know him as a decent and thoughtful man with a wide range of interests and a keen sense of the beautiful.

Like so many other potential witnesses, Rintelen stayed at the house for months without ever testifying in court. Indeed, of the five men who had arrived together, only one was called as an actual witness, and that was General Lahousen for the prosecution. Rintelen and Koestring had been requested by the defense as witnesses for Ribbentrop, but the permission to call them had been denied. This was by no means unusual. The court was never generous with the German defense and often permitted serious inequities between defense and prosecution. Since justice was so clearly on the side of the Allies, this was, and still is, difficult to understand; it did, in any case, seriously weaken the impact of the trial on many Germans.

Among my imprisoned guests, waiting and worrying took its toll. They bickered and played bridge or vented their bitterness against the trial, the party, the SS, or their erstwhile commander-in-chief. They refought old battles and renegotiated old treaties; they reviewed decisions the consequences of which could no longer be altered. They worried about their families and their own bleak futures. Each day they walked in the garden under the watchful eyes of the American guard. Koestring, who despite his age was the father of a young child, jogged half an hour each morning and afternoon wearing only his shirt and trousers, regardless of weather or plunging temperatures. Scenes such as the one over the fountain pen occurred now and then, with the barometer of irritation appearing to follow the developments at the trial. As the incredible story unfolded in all its gruesome detail, the prisoners became increasingly demoralized, more silent and separate from each other, more quarrelsome when they were together, as during the daily news broadcasts or the occasional card games.

A notable and welcome exception in this depressed company was General Hardy, who continued to cheer me in Hungarian whenever he could corner me after lunch or dinner, and Dr. Luther, who often played bridge with the German generals and Rintelen or Scheidt. Hardy did not fraternize much with the Germans but spent a good bit of time with Cuci and the children playing checkers. His greatest delight was to see the boys dress up in their Hungarian national costumes with the laced vests trimmed with national colors. Koestring and Rintelen, too, came to see the children. The old man liked to hold the baby, who pulled his white goatee, while Rintelen played on the floor with Farkas and his three-wheeled toy truck.

The one complete outsider was General Lahousen. Since that first evening I had hardly talked with him, nor, apparently, had anyone else. In the days preceding his court appearance he was picked up regularly for interrogations and seemed to be approaching a state of complete nervous exhaustion. Hollow-eyed from persistent insomnia, shadowed always by his guard, he was like a sleepwalker who could not awaken from a nightmare. He stayed in his room or walked in the garden when no one else did. When he came into the living room it was to listen to music. Then he would sit near the radio, his face buried in his hands, the nails of which were bitten to the quick. The others appeared to know about his resistance background, and I often heard the names of Admiral Canaris, Lahousen's former superior in the counterintelligence service, as well as that of Count von der Schulenburg, the last German ambassador to Russia, with whom Koestring had served and who was another of the July 1944 conspirators who ended on the Gestapo gallows. But if Lahousen avoided his fellow prisoners (as well as Dr. Luther and me), he was also avoided by them. Despite their avowed hatred for Hitler and the greater or lesser connections of some of them with factions of the German resistance, they appeared to have a curiously ambivalent attitude toward Lahousen. I do not believe that they admired him; instead, their behavior toward him expressed something between uneasiness and distaste, as if there were between them an unresolved conflict for which as yet no solution had been found.

The question of right or wrong concerning the overthrow of Hitler may appear bizarre, even monstrous to an outsider, but for a German officer that question revolved around the substance of his oath. After Hindenburg's death in 1934 all members of the German army were made to swear an oath of unconditional obedience to Hitler, who, having by now usurped all power, had made himself in that oath the symbolic embodiment of Germany.

This was not the course of events most members of the officer corps had either wished or foreseen. The army had never liked the republic born of the defeat of 1918. I could still hear my father rail against the "red traitors" who had signed the shameful treaty, the *Diktat* of Versailles. "The army was never defeated in the field—it was betrayed at home by the socialist politicians and their red rabble in the streets. . . ." The stab-in-the-back claim that did so much to kill the republic and fuel the fires of Hitler's demagogy was a myth, but a myth too readily believed by a great number of Germans who never quite recovered from the shock of the November Revolution of 1918 when Germany almost became a soviet republic. The democratic Weimar Republic that emerged from that revolution never won their trust, and between its enemies on the right and on the left was slowly destroyed. But if the anti-republican convictions of the officer corps contributed to that destruction, for most of its members the aim was not to help Hitler's rise to power. Echoing the sentiment of many of his

9 3

comrades, my father referred to the ex-corporal as an "ignorant rabble-rouser." What he longed for was the Kaiser. The overwhelming sentiment in the army was for a restoration of the monarchy. This hardly alters the fact that in lieu of a king, and for reasons of expediency, the army eventually gave its support to Hitler.

By the summer of 1934, when they stood in solemn ceremony swearing fealty to their new lord, it was too late to turn back. The power which they had thought they could use and retain control of had gained control of them instead through the most potent force it could have used, their oath. The content of this oath with its demand for personal obedience to Hitler was unknown to a majority of the officers until they were face to face with it.

As the daughter of a German officer I can appreciate what the decision to commit high treason in wartime must have cost the men who made it. The most common criticism leveled against those who did was that it would have been more honorable to resign. What these critics forgot to take into consideration was the fact that it was precisely because men like Lahousen remained in their positions that they were able to engage in active resistance, since it was their positions that gave them access to information and people. Their course of action was considerably more dangerous and courageous than comfortable retirement, or even exile.

Perhaps it was the years of tension, of living a double life, the loss of all his close associates, that contributed to the general's extreme nervous condition. Whatever the reasons, General Lahousen seemed to be slowly wasting away with a deep and secret grief. His state of mind had evidently not escaped his American interrogators, because several days before his scheduled trial appearance two American officers arrived with a dark-haired young woman, introducing her to me as a good friend of the general who had permission to visit him for three days. This, it was hoped, would help to diminish his tension so that he would be able to testify. The arrangement was unofficial; the young woman had to stay out of sight.

My first reaction was one of embarrassment, which angered me. Why should I feel embarrassment when I should have felt joy at the chance that love and warmth might have come in the person of this girl to bring relief to the unhappy man? Like the officers who had kept faith with their oath to a corrupt lord, I was placing form above substance, out of touch with the changeless vitality of the ideal beyond the artifice of the dogma; manners and law above the independent communion of conscience and God, and the death of the spirit shackled to decaying structures, giving way to monstrosity, the Germany of Hitler. I was ashamed of my embarrassment when I led the silent girl to Lahousen's room in the other house, there to wait for his return from the court. I could sense her uneasiness and would have liked to reassure her.

"I hope you will have a pleasant stay," I said with a smile, trying to communicate with my eyes what I could not put into words.

"Thank you." She returned my smile, her eyes filling with tears. For three days she stayed with the general, while his guard, who normally shared his room, slept on a chair in the hallway. Inevitably the arrangement was noticed, raised some eyebrows, and inspired some tired jokes; but when the girl had left, something of her presence remained with Lahousen, as if he had regained through her a part of himself.

Near the end of the month we had our first snow. The children were jubilantly building snowmen in the garden and having snowball fights with the American guards. As it got colder the guards built fires, while the children worried about their having to stand in the cold. Lori insisted on bringing them cups of hot tea, but Antal would occasionally pour water on them from an upstairs window, a prank most of the soldiers took more good-naturedly than Cuci.

Among my guests, though, the gloom was undiminished. One bright spot was a letter Rintelen received from his brother, bringing him the first news of his family in five months. On the same day, the atrocity films were shown in court, and in the evening we heard the report and description over the radio.

Frau Kruelle kept shaking her head, murmuring, "It can't be true, it can't be true," as if denial would wipe it out. We didn't look at each other, perhaps because we were ashamed of being German, of being human and knowing that this, too, lay within the range of human capabilities. The dreadful filmed record was to become, in time, familiar to us all.

Lahousen's court appearance was scheduled for the following day. He had been told for several days to hold himself in readiness, but since he had no proper clothing, that was easier said than done. The matter had been communicated to Captain Wulff, who was unable, however, to get anything beyond an army shirt and a pair of fatigue trousers. Since this was hardly the proper dress for so important an occasion, Frau Kruelle came to the rescue with a suit from her husband, who was, she said, about the general's height. It was a nice dark suit. We had to take it in a little to make it fit the general's gaunt frame. It was just a trifle short, but on the whole the fit was passable. The pants were ironed and Frau Kruelle starched one of her husband's shirts. Captain Wulff brought a German barber who trimmed the general's sparse fringe of hair. Throughout all the fussing Lahousen maintained a helpless, embarrassed silence.

When I came downstairs the following morning the general was already in the dining room reading a newspaper, while his guard sprawled morosely in a chair, looking sleepy.

"I got up rather early," Lahousen said. "Do I pass inspection?"

"You look just fine."

He did look well. It was not just the suit and the haircut, but a measure of composure which had grown in his demeanor since the girl had left. For the first time he appeared to be sure of himself.

As it turned out he was more than a witness for the prosecution; he was a vigorous and bitter accuser. Stating his and his now dead associates' conviction that a German victory would have been catastrophic, he revealed the full extent of the resistance activity within the *Abwehr*, from the sabotaging of orders to repeated attempts to get rid of Hitler. He described the cynicism and depravity of the regime, such as the staged "attack" by Germans in Polish uniforms on the Gleiwitz radio station, which was used by Hitler as provocation for his attack on Poland. His testimony was particularly damaging to Field-marshal Keitel (the man often nicknamed "Lakeitel" because his subservience to Hitler resembled that of a lackey), but he confirmed that some of the atrocious orders passed on from Keitel to army commanders in the field—the *Commissar Order* among others—were largely resisted and unobeyed, only to be eventually carried out by the SD or units of the SS which followed into Wehrmacht-occupied territories.

On his return Lahousen seemed calm and more communicative, answering our questions without reluctance, describing the court setting and procedures. He had been nervous in the beginning, he said, until he got used to the earphones and the different colored light signals which cued the speaker to talk faster or slower, to stop, or wait for another question. But then he had felt very calm—he had been surprised at himself. The others listened with great interest, no doubt anticipating their own appearance before the court if they were ever called.

The evening news broadcast with its trial summary was awaited with even greater than usual expectation. It was given, as always, by Gaston Oulman, a non-German commentator appointed by the military government whose obvious dislike of Germans was exceeded only by his unpopularity among them. Mr. Oulman summarized Lahousen's testimony and described its impact (which was apparently considerable) on some of the defendants. Then he proceeded to describe Lahousen himself as deathly pale, with a head like a skull, and dressed not like a general, but like a postmaster. The description was certainly uncomplimentary, but hardly justified the outrage it caused among most of the listeners. My first thought was of Lahousen. Having helped to dress him for the occasion, I felt in some way responsible for this failure of his appearance to find favor with Mr. Oulman. But Lahousen showed no visible reaction. The protests came mostly from Koestring, Rintelen, and Scheidt, who vowed to refuse to give testimony if they had to be exposed to similar taunts by the commentator. Perhaps they had lived too long with a controlled press and radio to be prepared for Mr. Oulman's unpredictable attacks (although it could not be properly said that Mr. Oulman was a representative of a free press or radio, since there was as yet no such thing in occupied Germany; as an employee of the military government he certainly appeared to work within official guidelines).

But I believe the strong reaction to Mr. Oulman's remarks had a different, more personal basis. Stripped of rank and titles, ex-servants of what may have been the most vicious regime in history, learning almost daily of more atrocities, the protesters were quite desperately trying to retain a shred of self-esteem, being at a point where ridicule could shatter them.

Mr. Oulman's voice was quite drowned out in the loud indignation of his audience. "Outrageous," "insulting," "nasty," were some of the terms applied to his commentary. Captain Wulff, who happened to come by, was besieged with complaints, which he promised to pass on to the proper authorities. He looked amused. General Lahousen, the subject of Mr. Oulman's commentary, registered no complaints with the visiting officer. When he could no longer hear the broadcast for the voices of the others, he silently left the room.

12

"*THE RASHUNS ARE COMING*, the rashuns!" yelled the tall Texan who sometimes drove the jeep that brought our food. Two of my generals were about to duck for cover, while Hoffmann turned a vivid shade of pink. I think my heart skipped several beats. "Where . . . how . . . when . . . ?"

"Why, right heah, Ma'am," he drawled, motioning with his head to the big pot he was carrying. "Your rashuns, Ma'am."

I felt relieved but rather silly. Kessler and Koestring had ventured cautiously into the doorway.

"What does he mean?"

"What Russians?"

"What's going on?"

"He doesn't mean Russians, he means rations, *Rationen*, food." The two generals looked distrustfully after the young soldier carrying the pot toward the kitchen.

"Did he do that on purpose?" Koestring wondered.

"I don't think he meant to do anything. It's just the way he talks. He's from Texas."

"Humph, a cowboy," muttered Koestring.

I followed the Texan into the kitchen, where he was having a chat in sign language and pidgin German with Frau Kirchhof, the cook.

"Versteh? Versteh?" he was saying urgently.

Frau Kirchhof looked at me and shrugged.

"Versteh what? Are the Russians still on the way?"

He looked blank.

"Never mind," I said. "What is there to *verstehen?"*

"I'd like to meet that fellow who was Hitler's friend."

"Hoffmann?"

"Yeah, that's him."

"I think he went into hiding when he heard you. Come on, I'll take you up to him."

"Did you know Hitler?" he asked as he followed me.

"No, thank God."

"He was quite a fellow."

"Yes, quite."

"Sure got rid of them Jews." After a pause, he asked, "You didn't like him?"

"No."

"Lots of people did when he was winning."

"That's true."

"It's the same everywhere. It don't matter if the guy's a ball player or a politician. Everybody likes a winner."

"That may be all right in football, but in politics?"

He dismissed my reservations with an airy wave of his hand. "Same thing."

"Is that how you decide who to vote for?"

"Same as I'd decide how to bet my money in a horse race."

"I guess Hitler would've been your man if you'd been a German."

"What do you think?" he said with a disarmingly mischievous and confidential grin.

100

I didn't tell him what I thought, but left him in the company of Hoffmann, who had recovered from his shock and with whom I felt the Texan would have instant rapport. As a German, one frequently came across this sort of thing—confidential admissions of anti-Semitism, or secret admiration of Hitler which the person doing the confiding usually presumed would immediately identify him to his German listener as a brother in spirit, even though disguised in the uniform of the conqueror. Once I asked the attending officer of the day about a certain Captain Newman who had come to see me on some official business, and got the answer—with the same confidential I-know-you-will-understand expression the Texan had worn—"He's a dirty Jew. Hitler didn't have time to get rid of them all—unfortunately."

True to my expectations, Hoffmann and the Texan appeared to hit it off famously. I could hear their laughter between Texas drawl and thick Bavarian. But downstairs the mood was its usual shade of bleakness. The two generals, Scheidt, and Dr. Luther had returned to their card game, Scheidt scowling at the sounds of hilarity from above. An American officer was waiting for me in the hall, watching the card players. I recognized him as a captain from the CIC who had come to interview me once before to inquire about the prevailing mood among my guests as well as the topics of conversations. Although the interview had been informal and I was not pressured for any particular information, I had found it distasteful. I was grateful for my job, but I resented being asked to play the spy. Perhaps I should tell him about the Texan, I thought, as I walked ahead of the captain to the as yet unoccupied dining room.

"Well," he said, smiling reassuringly. "How're things going?"

"Very well, thank you," I said, remembering my motto. "There are no problems. Everything is running smoothly."

"I know," he said with a quizzical look, "but that's not exactly what I mean."

101

I had kept my answers evasive and innocuous during our last interview, telling him that the men did a lot of worrying about their families, which was true, and that they were depressed, which was obvious. Evidently the captain felt that I had had enough time to make some more penetrating and useful observations.

"You have the chance to see and hear a great deal," he said.

"I have a great many household duties . . ."

"My dear Countess, I know you don't spend your days in the kitchen or making beds. You are in a way the liaison person between the occupants of this house and the military tribunal."

"I try my best to do my job."

He sighed. "Look, I'm not asking you to break confidences. We're trying to get a general picture about attitudes and opinions among the kind of people who are currently billeted here. I think it would be in your best interest to help us in this."

A threat, then. What did he really want? Did he think I was holding back some important information? But what was important? The criticisms of the tribunal? The occasional barbed references to certain American customs? The unspoken conflict between Lahousen and the others?

"Surely they must talk about the trial," the captain was saying. "We are particularly interested in their feelings concerning the Russians."

Considering my first experience with the CIC when I had applied for the job, the question surprised me. The subject seemed to have been taboo then. "I believe it's safe to say that no one here is very fond of the Russians."

"Do you hear any remarks concerning Russian-American relations?"

I had in fact—prognoses that the alliance wouldn't hold, that a rift was inevitable because of the great differences in ideologies. This was the sort of orientation any astute observer —and I was sure that the captain was such a one—would be able to project onto most former German officials and officers.

"You said before that no one here seems very fond of the Russians. Can you be more specific?" the captain asked.

"Not really. I suppose we're all afraid of them. There've been a great many atrocities we all know about. The Russians, I guess, have as good a reason as anyone for wanting to take revenge on Germans."

"Is there talk about these atrocities?"

"Some. But they talk a lot more about the past than the present," I said, thinking of General Koestring's bitter preoccupation with the summer of '41.

"I see," said the captain. "For example . . ."

"Oh, the dreadful mistake of moving against Russia. Koestring says he and the ambassador tried to prevent it, but they weren't listened to in Berlin. From what I can gather, there was a great deal of conflict between the army and the party, but it's difficult for me to understand or remember specific details. I'm hardly qualified to report on these things, and what's more, I'm sure none of the people would mind repeating the remarks I heard for an American interrogator."

"Then you're not breaking any confidences, are you?"

I wasn't sure how he meant that. "I hope not," I said before I could catch myself.

The captain's face expressed disapproval and distrust. "You're very concerned about these people, aren't you?"

"I don't know," I said. "They're in a difficult position. I feel for them. Is that wrong?"

"I thought your husband was on a Gestapo list. Do they deserve your concern?"

"But these people had nothing to do with the Gestapo."

He shrugged. "They're all Nazis, or they couldn't have stayed in their jobs. Remember that."

It had begun to snow again. From the kitchen came the smell of dinner. Frau Kruelle came in to set the table. I was afraid. I had thought I knew what was expected of me; now I was no longer sure. Had I been hired as a spy without knowing it? I accompanied the captain out into the hall as the card players eyed us with suspicion.

"Don't look so worried," he said as if he had been reading my thoughts. "I'm not trying to hang anybody. But your evasiveness makes it appear as if you know enough to hang the lot of them."

"You must be joking."

"Only exaggerating. I want you to remember who these men are."

"But you're accusing me of having Nazi sympathies because I admitted having some concern for them. Surely you don't consider them war criminals."

"What I consider them to be is beside the point. It's important that *you* remember who they are."

"I think you're misunderstanding both my motives and my situation here. I'm not always present when conversations take place, and several times I have noticed that conversations stop when I come into the room. It's possible that these people don't even entirely trust me." The last was not invented for the benefit of the captain. I had noticed such occurrences and had drawn the logical conclusion from them. "What you feel to be an unjustified concern on my part for these people—and you may well be right—has also something to do with a distaste I feel for this procedure, for having to report on them. It makes me feel . . . ugly, somehow."

"Sometimes it's necessary to do something distasteful if we want to stay alive."

"Isn't that just the kind of argument the court rejects as defense for the Germans?"

He smiled. "That's arguable. But let's not get into it. I may be back," he said as he opened the door. "In the meantime, please remember that it's not my aim to look for incriminating material against these people here. You're afraid of the wrong thing. But don't be so protective. Remember, you're supposed to be on our side."

I hadn't thought of sides, at least not in terms of my present position. The division did not seem to me that simple. "I'm sorry if you thought I'm not. I assure you that you're mistaken. It's just difficult for me to divide people into such simple categories. We're all human, aren't we?"

"Sometimes there's a need for simple categories, Countess," the captain said almost sharply. "I understand even Himmler was kind to children, and Hitler loved animals."

When I came back into the living room, Scheidt looked at me accusingly. "I've seen him before," he said. "He must like you."

"Dinner is ready," I said exasperatedly and opened the dining room doors.

I watched Scheidt walk into the dining room, hands in his pockets, his head bent forward, and I could feel his tension. He looked as if he were about to lunge at something, or break into shouting. He had talked to me of suicide, and I worried about it. More than a month of waiting had not improved his disposition. As with so many other witnesses, the court seemed to have forgotten about him. From day to day he brooded, venting his resentment on little things, creating imaginary situations, magnifying real ones. I thought sometimes that perhaps a comfortable prison such as our witness house might be worse than a real one. Physical pain or deprivation preoccupies; it is simple and direct, affording a measure of expiation. I think Scheidt needed that. Between self-indictment and justification he seemed to be in a deadlock.

Hoffmann, of course, suffered from no such emotions. As he joined us at dinner in the best of spirits, he seemed oblivious to Scheidt's open scowl and the others' barely disguised looks of contempt. He had probably made a good deal with the Texan.

"Is the Russian invasion still on?" he quipped.

"They're sending a special task force for you, Herr Hoffmann," Scheidt muttered as he sat down opposite Lahousen, who was following the exchange with some interest.

"Why such an honor for me when there are such eminent soldiers and statesmen around?" Hoffmann countered.

"There's a rumor that it was you who persuaded Hitler to invade Russia," Koestring quipped.

"Sure," Hoffmann said, unabashed. "I even drew up the battle plans."

"It's hardly so absurd that it couldn't have been true," said Rintelen. "I mean, when you have as a foreign minister an ex-wine salesman who can't read maps, and an ex-corporal for a supreme commander, why shouldn't a photographer prepare the battle plans?"

"The joke, I'm afraid, is on us," said Scheidt.

"Why is it that while he was successful everybody thought he was a genius?" Hoffmann said. "Nothing succeeds like success, eh? It reminds me of the rats leaving the sinking ship."

"I would suggest that you reverse that metaphor," said Dr. Luther. "We're still on the ship. The biggest rat has left it—but not before trying to drown us all."

"They're at it again. How tiring," Hardy said to me in Hungarian.

It was indeed becoming a pattern. Hoffmann's devotion to Hitler, who had called the tubby, cheerful Bavarian his "oasis," had survived intact both war and defeat, and he brought to it a ready commitment that would have done honor to a knight. War crimes trial and atrocity charges notwithstanding, I had never seen Hoffmann fail to defend his dead friend against the bitter criticism that was now leveled against him.

"Perhaps if Hitler could have concentrated on fighting the war instead of his generals, we wouldn't be in this situation," Hoffmann said calmly. "There certainly isn't any more doubt now but that what happened is largely the result of sabotage."

He was looking deliberately at Lahousen, who just as deliberately ignored him.

"I move that we change the subject," Dr. Luther said, earning my gratitude.

"Why?" asked Scheidt. "I find Herr Hoffmann most entertaining, just as the *Fuehrer* did."

"I'd rather be a clown with a clear conscience than a general with a bad one," Hoffmann shot back.

"Talking about entertainment, how about some magic tricks, Herr Hoffmann?" I suggested in desperation, thinking that the captain from the CIC would have found this dinner conversation most interesting.

"I'd be delighted. I never refuse a request from a pretty lady."

We managed to finish dinner talking about Houdini, of whose performance Dr. Luther gave a lengthy description which I managed to prolong by asking as many questions as possible.

"You seem to have discovered a sudden passion for the art of magic," Scheidt said to me as we adjourned to the living room.

"It beats trading insults."

"No one can insult Hoffmann. Conversely, the real insult lies in the presumption that Hoffmann could insult either me or the generals. I do find him amusing—without his magic tricks."

I thought that one over. "I'm sorry," I said. "It was not my intention to insult you." Scheidt's brittle veneer of arrogance troubled me. It was too much like a last-ditch defense. Through the large cracks showed his despair. I knew that he needed compassion and attention, and I felt guilty for staying aloof. Yet I also knew that he would interpret any gesture of concern in the light of his own desires.

Hoffmann had got a deck of cards and started to do magic tricks interspersed with Bavarian dialect stories. He wore his usual incongruous combination of baggy, formal striped pants, topped—in lieu of a frock coat—by a vintage Bavarian jacket. He was particularly fond of startling new arrivals by unbuckling the leather strap he wore for a belt to reveal that his trousers had a waistline circumference about twice his own. Unlike most of my other guests, he was not bothered by his sudden shabbiness, but wore his motley attire with a kind of brash insolence reminiscent of some of Shakespeare's fools. He was proud of his resourcefulness. Before he had the proper identification papers to walk freely about Nuremberg, I warned him that he might be arrested if he did. He answered my warning with an impersonation of a little old man, slack faced and dull eyed, dragging one foot behind as he leaned on his stick. "And who would stop poor little old grandpa?" No one did. Hoffmann was an artist at accommodating himself to the demands of changing situations.

His little audience was beginning to chuckle. He was unquestionably funny; he had to be to get these people to laugh. They did so condescendingly at first, freely at the end. Like all great entertainers, he had the capacity to make them forget. For moments, at least, he confined them within his own limitations, which were the key to his success. He was what he was with an integrity that was at once disarming and repelling —frivolous at a time that made frivolity obscene, a *bon vivant* when life was at its harshest.

The small audience was soon augmented by my children, who had probably been alerted by Frau Kruelle. Hoffmann used Antal and Farkas as stooges, making it appear that he was pulling cards from their pockets and coins out of their ears. He made a walking stick stand by itself (with the help of two almost invisible threads), and he played an umbrella like a trombone. The children's gleeful laughter added to the performance a dimension of joyful innocence that further liberated the audience into laughter. Even Scheidt was laughing freely now. It made him look younger. It suddenly occurred to me that I had never before seen him laughing.

The euphoria ended with Hoffmann's performance. Like an entertainer stepping out of the spotlight, he lost that universal identity which had found its image in each beholder. As the laughter faded, the bond broke; the old shadows returned to familiar faces, and he became again Hoffmann, the close friend of Hitler. He lit a cigarette and sat down.

"What we all need is a bottle of *Schnaps*. That would drown our troubles."

"You're the next best thing to it, Herr Hoffmann," I said.

"I didn't know you had any troubles," said Rintelen, glancing up from his paper.

"I just don't let them get the better of me."

Kessler and Koestring were discussing an article in *Stars and Stripes*, dropped off occasionally by Captain Wulff and in great demand because it gave access to information not found in the censored German-language paper. The article was a summary of another one that had recently appeared in an American military journal criticizing the American prosecutor, Jackson, for his alleged bias against the military. It was against the Geneva Convention, the article stated, to put a soldier on trial for obeying the orders of his government. The two generals got into a lengthy discussion about the legality of the tribunal and the statutes under which it operated. Dr. Luther commented that the writer of the article probably foresaw the implications of criminal proceedings against military men, especially since Jackson had emphasized so strongly that the Nuremberg Statutes should become standards of conduct for all nations. I thought of the captain from the CIC, wondering what he would think of this agreement between German and American military men on the policies and procedures of the tribunal.

"They'll have a hard time passing this off as justice—even among their own people," Kessler said.

It was still snowing. The guard outside had a small fire; its glow and wisps of smoke reached skyward.

"It's the way it looked when the city burned," said Scheidt. "Everywhere foreign fires; all we have left is the ruins."

"Look on the bright side," Hoffmann said. "At least we can get a night's sleep now, and we were out of it before they had a chance to drop the atom bomb on us."

"They didn't need an atom bomb to kill Dresden."

"No. They needed two thousand planes and thousands of bombs to do to Dresden what they did to Hiroshima with one plane and one bomb," said Kessler.

"It's hard to believe," Koestring said, "some hundred thousand people at a single blow."

"I'm glad I wasn't the pilot. All those ghosts would come to haunt me," said Hoffmann.

"He was only following orders, like a good soldier," Rintelen said.

Through the smoky glow of the fire I watched the flakes fall, to turn into water as they touched the window. Legalities, justifications—as if war could be codified in such terms. Justice had nothing to do with war, or for that matter with survival. One survived by luck, and through cleverness, and by taking advantage of whatever resources were at hand, like Hoffmann —or myself?

It had been snowing like this when I left Hungary. On the clogged roads the refugees were moving westward, step by step, snail-like, in a dark, doomed procession. I wondered now how many had survived that cruel journey. They had traveled on foot, on wagons, on bicycles, with packs on their backs and children in their arms; but I, with my children and Cuci, using the waning power of privilege that still separated me from the people on the road, had traveled the same route in a German military vehicle. Two days before our departure I had gone to see the commanding officer of a German unit stationed in the area. I had dressed with deliberate elegance and was driven by a liveried coachman in the bishop's black coach marked with his seal and drawn by four beautiful black horses. "I am the daughter of a German officer," I had told the grim major who was the unit commander. "I demand that you provide me with means to travel to Austria." My arrogance, worn like my costume for the occasion, almost failed me when my voice began to tremble. The major was unimpressed by my act; I felt his weary gaze like an accusation. He informed me that there was no basis for my demand, that he was unable to make any commitments, but that I could come around at ten in the evening when a mail truck usually left, bound for Austria. If there was enough room he would authorize our traveling in that vehicle. We came for two evenings before we were able to get on the truck. Each time we were driven by the liveried coachman in the absurd luxury of the bishop's coach, fragment of ancient pomp and exhausted power, past the ragged columns

110

on the road. And I too was a fragment, member of a species becoming extinct. When I left the bishop's coach for the army truck, I left behind me an aspect of my life and self. But if there was loss, there was also liberation, the discovery of new powers for unfamiliar hardships, and there were moments when I felt again the sense of limitless potential I had known as a girl. I carried with me the guilt of my flight; there was neither justice nor fairness in our survival, but there was a feeling of strength in the sharp awareness that I was on my own.

Scheidt had turned on the radio for the daily trial summary. The prosecution was still presenting its case—broken treaties, acts of aggression against Austria, Czechoslovakia, Poland. There was talk of a Christmas recess. It was almost a year since I had left Hungary. I had borne a child and did not know whether my husband was dead or alive. I was on my own. I wondered whether I was also alone.

13

CHRISTMAS WAS a week away. The court was about to recess. I had no gifts for the children, but I think the only gift we all really wanted was news from their father. As for the rest, we had food and shelter, and there was no greater gift one could have asked for that bitter winter. From one of their walks Cuci and the children had brought home some branches of pine which they decorated with pine cones and stars cut from cigarette papers. A vase filled with these stood on the living room table. But there was no holiday spirit among our company— if anything, the coming of Christmas deepened the general depression. I longed for my husband, the men for their families, of whose fate they were as a whole as uncertain as I was of my husband's. The Americans, who had more reason to celebrate, embarked on a series of preholiday parties, and sometimes the sound of their merrymaking would reach us from the other houses on the street. Perhaps it was for one of these parties that our piano suddenly disappeared. In any event, a few days before Christmas a truck pulled up before the house and a half-dozen soldiers in exceedingly good spirits carried the piano out while Frau Kruelle looked on in tears and the generals in grim helplessness. For Frau Kruelle's sake I called the courthouse but was unable to get either an explanation or sympathy. Frau Kruelle retreated to her cellar to be comforted by Cuci. The incident did nothing to raise the already low spirits of the onlookers.

In the midst of our melancholy company we had two newcomers: Nikolaus von Horthy, son of the former regent of Hungary, and Bertus Gerdes, former *Gaustabsamtsleiter*, the ranking assistant to the Gauleiter of Munich and, according to his claim, a onetime protégé of Dr. Ernst Kaltenbrunner, who was currently on trial as one of the major war criminals. The notorious successor to Heydrich, Kaltenbrunner had been a deputy of Himmler and, since 1943, the head of all German security forces.

Both Horthy and Gerdes arrived around the middle of December, though under slightly different circumstances. Horthy, who was "delivered" by an American officer, had been brought in from Rome, where he had gone after his liberation from Mauthausen concentration camp. I for one was most surprised to see Horthy, since he had been believed dead by most knowledgeable people in Budapest. Both he and his father had been kidnapped by the Gestapo after Hungary's vain attempt in the fall of '44 to surrender to the swiftly advancing Russians. The Germans had forced an immediate rescission of the surrender offer, and Hungary was doomed to follow Germany into total disaster. That was the price the country paid for the old admiral's earlier dreams of glory—restoration of some of the Magyar territories lost in 1918—for which he had allied himself all too enthusiastically with the German dictator. The older Horthy had been imprisoned by the Allies and was currently being held in the Nuremberg jail. The son, however, had been known for his outspoken opposition to the Nazis, for

113

which reason it was assumed that he had been killed. As it was, he had survived Mauthausen, though the experience seemed to have found a permanent reflection in his eyes. They did not shed their sadness even when he smiled.

Bertus Gerdes arrived unescorted and without guard, presenting me with the proper papers authorizing him to stay at the witness house. Tall and extremely fair—his hair was whitish blond—he was every inch Hitler's "ideal" Aryan. His clothes, a green Bavarian jacket, work pants, and mud-caked work shoes, suggested a farmer. He had come voluntarily out of hiding to surrender to the court, an undertaking which apparently had not been easy. Arriving on a Saturday evening, he had gone straight to the Palace of Justice, where he had told an officer on duty who he was and why he had come, whereupon the officer allegedly had laughed and said, "Even if you were Hitler in person, it's Saturday night and past quitting time. Come back Monday." Only after considerable pleading was he given shelter for the night—a jail cell. In the morning he received breakfast and was told again to leave. It was not until he had created a near disturbance that he was brought before a higher ranking officer, who then referred him to the witness house.

Gerdes's story was another variation of the ignorance-betrayal-guilt theme that was to become so familiar in postwar Germany. He was probably still in his twenties. If his appearance suggested a farmer, that impression was more true than false, for his life had begun on a farm in Mecklenburg, where as a young man he had become, as he described it, an "idealistic and enthusiastic National Socialist." His enthusiasm apparently accompanied him to the war, in which he served on several fronts and was wounded no less than five times. It was during his last stay at a field hospital in 1943 that he had met Kaltenbrunner, who was making an official visit. Apparently impressed by young Gerdes's "Nordic" appearance as well as his war record, Kaltenbrunner promised Gerdes a high position with the party in Munich after his release from the hospital.

114

The promise was kept, and Gerdes went to Munich to take over his new duties as a deputy of the Gauleiter. It was there, during his Munich time, Gerdes told us, that he became increasingly disenchanted with Nazism. In the early spring of 1945 an order was issued from Kaltenbrunner's office for the destruction through poison or gas of all remaining inmates of the Dachau concentration camp, as well as the destruction of a work camp in the area through a simulated air attack. Gerdes claimed to have withheld these orders, a claim he repeated in a sworn affidavit to the court, and fled to the countryside, where he hid until the war's end.

He might have been able to hide out indefinitely. After the occupation he "passed" as an East German refugee who, like thousands of others, had no identification papers. An American officer at a control point issued him a temporary identification under the assumed name he gave. He found work with a farmer and could have remained unrecognized for years, he believed; but, as he told us, "an inner voice" urged him to come forward and report to the court what he knew about the Kaltenbrunner orders.

That at any rate was Gerdes's story. His claim was at least in part contradicted by later testimony in which another witness alleged that the order for the destruction of Dachau and the work camp did come down from the Gauleiter's office but was not carried out. However, Gerdes was not implicated in that testimony, and it is possible that the order had been reissued after Gerdes's disappearance. Whatever the truth of the matter, Gerdes was evidently believed by his American interrogators, who showed their favor through generous gifts of cigarettes and chocolate bars and by permitting him to stay at the witness house without restriction or guard.

By contrast, most of the other witnesses did not accept Gerdes with sympathy. The two generals, as well as Rintelen and Scheidt, especially treated him with the same contempt they usually reserved for Hoffmann. They also did not seem to believe his story. Not that they challenged him or asked probing questions; they merely listened in hostile silence, their faces expressing what they would not put into words. "A likely story," they seemed to think. "An arch-Nazi trying to maneuver himself out of trouble."

I too was skeptical about Gerdes. To this day I have no knowledge of what things he did or did not do. At the end of his stay he left in an American military vehicle to be taken to some internment camp, there to face possible charges for his membership in criminal organizations. But if it can be said that there is at least some evidence of a person's character in his face and manner, then this evidence made a good case for Gerdes's veracity. If this viewpoint should be considered naïve, it was shared, at least at that time, by his American interrogators. Gerdes had about him a kind of innocence that seemed to render him vulnerable to betrayal. He was awkward, friendly, and open, and his eyes still expressed trust. He seemed to have a compulsion to talk about "his disillusionment," as if he were trying to come to terms with the monstrousness lying within what he called "the betrayal of his ideals," and his voluntary appearance in Nuremberg had about it something of the aura of a pilgrimage, an act of expiation. He was conscious of his own sin in having been an instrument of evil, and though he often protested his ignorance of Nazi reality prior to 1943, he never protested his innocence.

"I think people who live on farms have a greater love for their country than city people," I remember his saying one evening after dinner, when we were all gathered, as usual, in the living room. "There was a song we sang when I was a boy. I remember how much it moved me . . . you know . . ." He sang softly:

> Earth creates the new,
> Earth takes back the old.
> Holy German earth
> Us alone preserve;
> From you we were born;
> To you we belong . . .

Scheidt made a grimace of distaste. Koestring and Kessler looked uncomfortable and embarrassed. Rintelen determinedly kept his eyes on his book, and in the brief silence we could hear the sound of Lahousen biting his nails.

"I don't think I ever heard it," said Hoffmann, who also had little affection for Gerdes, since Gerdes insisted that the Kaltenbrunner orders he had destroyed had originated with Hitler, while Hoffmann staunchly maintained that Hitler was ignorant of concentration camp atrocities, which he blamed on a diabolical conspiracy between Bormann and Himmler.

"I suppose love of country is more defined for people who live on farms," I said, mostly to fill the silence and ease the embarrassed tension, but Gerdes was still absorbed in the words of his song.

He nodded. "For us, 'holy German earth' was a reality, and we did feel that we belonged to it and that we owed our lives to it. For us the song was real."

"If German earth is holy, it must be for all the innocent victims who are buried in it," Horthy said in his quiet, melancholy way. "Half of it must be ashes."

He had been held alone in a cell near the crematorium in Mauthausen. Day and night the smoke had poured from the chimneys.

"I pity your poor earth," he said softly.

"I tried to save the hundred and twenty thousand who were in Bavaria," Gerdes said. "Can you imagine . . . they wanted them all killed. . . ."

Just a day or so before at the trial, the nightmare of the Warsaw ghetto had been recounted by the prosecution. The documentation had come from an SS report. Some 60,000 Jews had been killed in that single action. There had been more horrors on the prosecution's calendar: the notorious SD commandoes in the East, murdering Jews and commissars, patriots and recalcitrant peasants, the terrible, merciless mass executions. Kaltenbrunner was the head of the SS and the SD; he was the deputy of Himmler. I looked at Gerdes and shuddered. I could not allow myself to think of him in that context; just

117

to have been associated with Kaltenbrunner was enough to make my blood run cold. Was it possible that he could have been ignorant of such enormity? Did he deserve to be judged apart from his mentor?

"Could the order have come as such a surprise to you after the long persecutions of the Jews, the deportations, the hate propaganda in the *Stuermer?*" I asked.

"I never met a Jew in my life, and I never saw the *Stuermer* before my Munich days."

"You must have led a sheltered life," Scheidt said with an undertone of exasperation of which Gerdes took no discernible notice. The general contempt and skepticism shown him by the majority of his listeners had no apparent effect on him, and I doubt that in his preoccupation with his own inner conflicts he was even aware of them.

"We know what we want to know," Dr. Luther said sadly.

"And what is safe to know," Scheidt added.

"Yes," said Gerdes. "One makes compromises. One suppresses suspicions. In Munich I saw what the party really was —a nest of intriguers and degenerates. But it's not so easy to give up one's faith. I really believed in National Socialism."

What compromises? He played with one of the Christmas stars my children had made. His face expressed sorrow: a clear strong face; but I could still see the faces in the cattle cars. There had been guards with machine guns riding on the platforms between cars, strong, well-grown young men, but I had not seen their faces. Were they country boys, too, dumbly and coldly following orders? Had their nerve ends been cut? Were they deaf and blind? What compromises? Now I wondered for whom he now felt sorrow: for himself, betrayed, or for the victims of the murderous system he had served so long and with such devotion. Both, if he was human, and his face told me that he was. Five times wounded in battle; he might have died with his illusions intact. Would the 120,000 then have been saved?

"I'm glad I came here," Gerdes said. "The more I heard after it was all over, the more I knew I had to come."

118

"The more I heard after it was all over, the more I felt like crawling into a hole in the ground," said Scheidt.

"I tried that, but it didn't work," Gerdes said quietly. He nodded as if in reaffirmation. "I'm glad I came," he said again.

The trial recessed on December 21. On Christmas Eve, Cuci, the children, and I went to Mass at a church in Erlenstegen. We had a good dinner—turkey with the unfamiliar cranberry sauce, fruit cake, and nuts. But there was little conversation.

Later Captain Wulff and a Private Sonnenfeld, who at times also took care of our needs, came by with some cigarettes, a bottle of whiskey, and an unexpected surprise: a large cardboard box filled with confiscated war toys—little soldiers and armored vehicles, trucks and cannons, a tiny Wehrmacht made out of tin. I did not like war toys any better than the Allied authorities who had forbidden their sale. But the power of my convictions was no match for my children's enthusiasm and joy. Private Sonnenfeld, who according to Wulff was a "Berlin Jew" and who, like Wulff, spoke fluent German, helped set up the armies. The sailors and Luftwaffe soldiers were to be the Americans; the Wehrmacht kept its own identity. Before long the war was on again on our living room floor. The opposing forces were massed at the generals' feet, Farkas's Americans driving Antal's and Lori's Germans under the sofa. When Captain Wulff reinforced the losing side, Private Sonnenfeld came to the aid of Farkas's army. Antal's and Lori's Germans regrouped behind the sofa, then proceeded to counterattack past General Koestring's boots, charging at the Americans across the living room rug. Farkas and Antal both announced that they were generals. Lori, who was not granted a military rank because she was a girl, withdrew from the battle sulking. The game was getting exceedingly noisy. Antal especially boomed and howled with boundless four-year-old enthusiasm. Both Cuci and I tried to interfere, but Captain Wulff shouted at me from across the room, "It's Christmas, Countess, let 'em have fun." Drinking their whiskey, my guests watched in solemn silence.

119

The game grew wilder. Private Sonnenfeld, who was apparently beginning to feel the effects of his Christmas whiskey, cheered on his "Americans." "Let 'em have it, boys; get the bastards!"

"Cut it out, Sonnenfeld," Wulff shouted at him.

The boys were manipulating their soldiers into hand-to-hand combat. Some broken bits of tiny bayonets, a tin arm, some wheels lay on the sidelines. Antal was crying and yelling "unfair." Captain Wulff helped me and Cuci to separate the tired "generals," both of whom claimed victory and had to be forcibly removed to bed. The real generals were contemplating the scene of devastation at their feet, the little tin bodies scattered in all directions, lying beside the overturned guns and tanks and the trucks with their wheels turned to the ceiling. General Kessler picked up one of the little airmen and examined it in the palm of his hand. *"Oberleutnant,"* he said. *"He* still has his insignia."

General Koestring reached under the sofa for some scattered Wehrmacht soldiers and set them gently on the table under the decorated branches.

"Don't resurrect the dead," said Scheidt. "They're better off where they are."

"Let's clean up the casualties," Captain Wulff said cheerfully, scooping up the dead armies and their equipment. "Lots of good battles left in them yet."

Sonnenfeld and I helped, but I felt desolate inside. I had always felt that war to many was a game, but the awareness caused me special pain tonight, perhaps because it was Christmas, the season of "peace and good will to men" that was always promised but never came. Flags, parades, bands, decorated uniforms and shining swords, the polished blade of the ax wrapped in sensuous silk, dark romance of bloodshed. No, the game was too popular to ever lose its fascination; transcending grievances and causes, it was an end in itself. My father had taken great pleasure in telling us how his regiment had faced its French counterpart for weeks across a tranquil summer countryside somewhere in Belgium. He had passed his time painting landscapes with cannons in them. In one of the pictures the regimental mascot, a little monkey, perched jauntily on the cannon, wearing a soldier's cap. The "enemy" soldiers had exchanged wines and cigarettes across their lines and got to know each other so well that my father's regiment was transferred before it saw any action in that sector, an order my father bitterly resented, since in his opinion their fraternization would not in the least have impaired their readiness to do battle with each other. Despite the solicitude of its many masters, the monkey died of pneumonia that winter in my father's arms. Its tender masters, however, went on to dispense and receive death in the manner of their calling, obedient to the rules of their game.

I would have liked to throw away the box and its contents, but I didn't. It was winter. The children were often restless and bored. The immediate needs took precedence over the larger implications.

"Don't look so unhappy, Countess," said Captain Wulff. "The war is back in the box—at least while the generals are sleeping."

"Tonight is supposed to be a celebration of peace."

"There is peace, Countess," Wulff said with quiet emphasis.

I thought of the people shivering in the ruins of Nuremberg, of my missing husband, of the millions dispossessed like us.

"I can't find it, Captain," I said.

14

THE LAST FEW DAYS of the old year were dark and short. Captain Wulff had got me permission to call Budapest to see if I could get any information about my husband. Of the three numbers I gave the operator, two were out of service; the third was answered by a stranger. The operator then connected me with an agency of the Russian military government which answered curtly and told me nothing. My uncertainty would have to accompany me into the new year. Was it possible that I should never know? He could lie dead somewhere in an unmarked grave and I should never know.

When I was sixteen I had tried to find words for an ever-growing consciousness of strength and will, an energy of which I was at once source and expression. Each page of my diary held the intensity of my desires, the presumption of my challenge. I felt as powerful as life itself. Had this power been no more than an illusion, something to be smiled at in retrospect as a "developmental phase"? Sometimes I would smile indulgently across the years at the girl who had written so fervently in those pages; but I also looked to her now for strength, my thoughts returning again and again to her boundless faith that she could bend life to her will, bear all it had in store, and see without flinching all it had to show.

Perhaps her faith had been in the power of art to create order, impose control, as God was said to have created the universe out of primal chaos. But no—she had been too intuitive for that. Later, perhaps, after she had shared Hans Castorp's frozen dream on the snowy slopes of Mann's *Magic Mountain* where Castorp had dreamed the beauty of the dancers and the purity of their dance in clear, unshadowed light, even as in the darkness of the temple the ancient blood sacrifice was running its course, counterimage of the dance. He had known then that the dance and the blood sacrifice were linked inexorably and that there was no more to know. No Manichean divisions, but dissonance as the echo of harmony, war as the long shadow of peace. How had Castorp found solace in such knowledge? It wasn't knowledge at all, but the acceptance of limitation, a relinquishing of the will. Had that young girl's strength been diminished when she had realized that? The power of art was but to codify the confusion of experience, to illuminate the mysterious patterns of countless interactions. Hans Castorp went off to the war that was gathering as inevitably as night or thunder, and he could not have halted its coming any more than he could have stopped the blood sacrifice in the temple of his dream. The bishop had raised his crucifix and the young priests had knelt in prayer, but the cattle cars had kept on moving inexorably to their final destination. One could have stood in the path of the train. Was martyrdom an exercise of will or despair? It would have slowed the train for minutes perhaps. But that was not the crucial question. The faith of the sixteen-year-old in her own potent will would not have questioned the potency of her act; and, multiplied a millionfold, could not such faith have stopped the trains? Our energies were turned toward survival, and a part of our spirit withered in the process.

New Year's Eve came with a feeling of exhaustion. The year died like an invalid after a long illness. After the children went to bed, the house was unaccustomedly quiet. Most of my guests had taken advantage of a special permission to spend the evening at the nearby inn, *Zum Stern.* It had little more to offer than watery beer, but it did at least provide a change of scenery. Since the beginning of the great trial the *Stern* had become a kind of gathering place for Germans who were in Nuremberg on trial business. This included defense attorneys and their assistants, as well as free witnesses.

A tablet above the door of the *Stern* showed that this was not the first time the modest old inn had provided the setting for historical drama. According to the sign, three hundred years earlier King Gustav Adolf of Sweden had rested there on his way south to meet Wallenstein and the Habsburg armies. Then, too, Germany had lain devastated. A different war, a different cause; only the suffering remained the same.

> *Deine Mutter ist in Pommernland*
> *Und Pommernland ist abgebrannt*
> *Schlaf Kindchen, schlaf. . . .*

What should I sing my children? Your father is in Hungary, and Hungary is devastated?

Only two more hours in the bleak year that had brought us this late and grudging peace. From the street came the occasional shouting and singing of celebrating soldiers. A jeep brought guests to an American party at a house nearby. Music spilled briefly through an open door; a girl's laughter. Silence again.

One year ago this day in Gyoer I had listened to the bishop's New Year's prayers. "May the year of our Lord, 1945, bring us the peace we long for. . . ." He had given the traditional New Year's feast. In the great hall of the bishop's castle, tall candles had flickered in the massive silver candelabra, and

124

the crystal had trembled with the impact of Russian artillery shells nearby. Still, the company, made up mostly of the area's landed gentry, had been elegant and gay. Attended by liveried servants, we dined on whole roasted suckling pigs and fine old wines. After the prayers the guests had toasted the new year. I had felt more absurd than afraid. The scene had about it something familiar. Above all, it had to be played with style. We would go down in full evening dress with our rank and manners intact. *Noblesse oblige.* From the peasant revolts to the Paris Bastille the scenario showed little variation. I seemed to be cast into a role without a choice. Was I no more than the name I bore, a stitch in the dense pattern of time?

"You, too, were born naked," a workman had told me when I was about fourteen. He had meant it as a threat, but he didn't frighten me. I would be at home where I chose, among equal spirits, not bound by name or class, and there was nothing in my childhood or youth that caused me to doubt the validity of that belief.

Our family was of modest means. My father had his small officer's pension, an old name, and the family seat on *Burg Ranis* which, if not rich in treasure, was rich in legends. A thousand years old, it rose from a strategic mountain peak in Thuringia, its romanesque spires and massive walls appearing to be an extension of the mountain itself. Beneath the castle, reaching deep into the interior of the mountain, was a huge cave rich in fossils and Stone Age artifacts. In May lilacs bloomed along the ancient gray walls of the castle and along the steep mountain-side in white and pinks and lavenders, decorating the rocky slope as for some secret, lavish celebration.

Like the farmers in the valley, we weathered the hard times of inflation and depression by helping ourselves to the bounty of the forest. My father hunted; we children picked berries and mushrooms and worked in the garden. My sisters and I helped the cook, and my mother taught us how to sew. My father drank his beer at the village inn and talked with the farmers about weather and crops or the sorry state of the country since the Kaiser was gone. But he also played host to the scientists who came repeatedly to explore the cave in the mountainside beneath the castle, and he was himself quite knowledgeable in the fields of anthropology and geology. My mother was an artist whose oil paintings had been shown in several cities. She was vivacious and versatile, as competent in the management of a tight household as she was accomplished as a painter. From her wide circle of friends we had many visitors—other painters, musicians, poets. By the light of evening fires I listened endlessly to their debates and recitals. My life beckoned to me. I dreamed of challenges and triumphs.

The world into which I followed my husband was too circumscribed for such extravagant ambitions. Here the pulse of the ancient Catholic Empire was beating still, and its vacant throne governed by divine decree. Time was patterned like a ritual dance in which the dancers were no longer conscious of their steps.

Sepsiköröspatak, my husband's ancestral seat near Kronstadt in Transylvania, was seven hundred years old. From the main building two wings extended to form a u-shaped open square designed in the manner of a formal garden with islands of shrubs and flowers. The effect was one of warmth and welcome; I thought of the two extended wings as outstretched arms about to close into an embrace. At my arrival the entrance was garlanded with flowers; children welcomed me with songs and more flowers; servants curtsied and village dignitaries kissed my hand. But that warm embrace was also a vise. It held me fast within its rigid circumference and prescribed the steps assigned me in the ancient dance. My excursions into the village were circumscribed with formality, my person effecting as automatic a response of humility and respect as did a church or the statue of a saint, and even as those things of stone were once the expression of a passion now hardened into form, so did I feel myself grow rigid around the volatile core of my being, as if I were covered with hardening clay. My attempts to reach beyond the facade of ritual were rebuffed. When I tried to make friends with the cook, she seemed to turn into stone; when I tried to practice my faulty Hungarian on a gardener to learn about the cultivation of certain vegetables in the region, his face turned red; he stammered, tipped his hat, and fled. My contact with the people then was restricted to receiving their grave and mysterious homage, standing at the gate of the castle on special feast days, watching them bend their knees and kiss my hand. I looked into their silent faces to find the meaning of the ritual, but they told me nothing—no glimmer of feeling crossed the barrier, and I wondered what passions lay stored beneath their impassive features. Had I seen a moment's revelation of contempt and hate in the cook's face, or was it the imagination of my guilt? And the boy, that half-grown boy of twelve or thirteen, who like a shadow appeared in our bedroom at dawn to light the fire—what was it like to get up when it was still night to light the fires in the master's house? "Do you wish to take his bread from him?" my husband had asked with an indulgent smile when I brought the matter up. One morning when my eyes met the boy's, I smiled at him. He stood transfixed; I could feel more than see his gaze, an intense compound of fear and hate. My husband took no notice of the cook or the gardener or the boy who made the fire, nor did he smell the faint odor of decay that hung over all. He had seen his father ride with the Empress of Austria; waiting for the restoration of his own lord, he rehearsed the retreat from the emperor, walking backwards with measured steps, head and shoulders bent forward in a slight bow.

Perhaps my guilt was as presumptuous as my idea of freedom. Where was that freedom of my naked birth in which I had so firmly believed? Freedom, too, had to see its image in the faces of others. My husband, kind, courtly, and full of tender adoration, could love me only in the manner of his breeding. In the hierarchies of his loves I was assigned my rightful place; after God, emperor, and country there was the waiting mold I was to fill with my living form, with the warm substance of my life. And yet his love was real and great, pressing against the narrow boundaries of his freedom. He could no more have moved beyond those boundaries than the peasants who had knelt to kiss my hand on feast days. Perhaps he was dead now, dead among strangers, without love, or ceremony. One year without a word. What had been the last word? I couldn't remember; only the feeling of loss, the image of his face shadowed and drawn in the half light of the carriage lantern; the breath of the horses white in the icy dark.

At the bishop's New Year's feast we had raised our glasses in a toast to our unborn child. We had both watched the candle flames flicker and the wine in our glasses ripple from the impact of a shell exploding nearby. I wondered whether he knew that this feast marked the end of that past to which he was bound, his face turned toward his emperor, his back toward the murderous passage of time. I could visualize the stony faces of our peasants among the masses of the Red Army. No hands across the barriers, only the deadly reach of a gun barrel exploding centuries of stored-up hate. The scenario had been written at the beginning of time: the growth and decline of power; decay and the violence of change. My husband was a just man, but he had effected no justice in an order governed by antique decree. The bishop was kind and pious, but he had effected no piety where faith had become formalism. What was a bishop doing in a castle? The bishop was a baron, and the baron was a bishop. In castles and cathedrals the pure faith had died.

In the light of the waning candles the bishop had raised his glass to me and wished me a happy and blessed new year. He was a handsome man with a kind, even noble face. His cellars and outbuildings were filled with refugees. He ministered to all with energy and generosity. Still, none of them was present in this splendid hall unless he wore the servant's livery. No hands across the barriers, even in the final hours. I had wondered where Christ would have dined this night had he come threadbare and barefoot to ask for shelter and food. When I asked the bishop, his smile expressed melancholy and indulgence of my simplicity.

"He would receive what He requested," he said.

"But He would not be with us."

"He is with whoever chooses Him."

"That's not what I mean."

"I know. But there is no other answer."

I wondered whether he was right. A kind man; a practical man; a pious realist.

"The social structure is a part of reality. Are we not told that there are hierarchies even in heaven?"

He had helped us and others hide our valuables—some of the family silver, some jewelry—in a nearby monastery. Although it had been considered the safest hiding place, it was almost the first that was totally plundered when the Red Army reached the area in late March. Some days later Russian troops had entered Gyoer. A detachment came to the castle. When the bishop, surrounded by his staff, came to greet them, he was shot point blank by a Russian soldier. I heard of the bishop's death from a refugee in Czechoslovakia. My husband, who had been present at the shooting, was not hurt. With others he carried the wounded man on a stretcher to the hospital. Some of the Russian soldiers had knelt to kiss the bishop's ring; others had tried to steal it. No hands across the barriers. The Russian authorities condemned the killing. The bishop had died on Good Friday. A good man—a rich man—a generous man—a baron—a bishop. What rank among men had Christ held?

It was midnight. The year had passed and this war had ended, as that other war three hundred years before had ended, in exhaustion and devastation. I went to see Cuci and Frau Kruelle in the kitchen. We embraced and cried. I kissed my sleeping children and went to bed with a heavy heart.

15

THE FIRST FEW WEEKS of the new year turned out to be so quiet that I began to fear anew for my job. Early in January the generals, as well as Rintelen and Scheidt, had been transferred to another detention facility. Since Dr. Luther and Bertus Gerdes had left us shortly after Christmas, my only remaining guest was Hoffmann. There were no more guards before our door. We had heard rumors that the witness houses were to be closed. From the window of my warm room I looked across the frozen heath and was afraid. Somewhere beyond were the ruins of Nuremberg—hunger, cold, homelessness. I felt as if that winter out there were closing in on us.

Hoffmann, the eternal optimist, tried to cheer me up by characteristically tying my fortunes to his own.

"They can't close this place as long as I'm here," he said, "and I'm not nearly finished with my job."

I had long suspected that Hoffmann was working on the

sorting of his archives the way Penelope had worked on her weaving, and that Hoffmann's employers, like Penelope's suitors, would have to wait indefinitely for him to finish. His business of selling autographed caricatures to American soldiers was as brisk as ever, and his spirits were correspondingly high. What never ceased to amaze me was that he appeared to be so completely untouched by the trial itself, despite the fact that his son-in-law was one of those sitting in the dock. Even on the day (about the middle of January) when the special charges against von Schirach were read in court, Hoffmann showed no visible reaction. These harsh realities seemed to exist beyond the boundaries of his concerns, as if nature had rendered him unable to either understand or experience them. Thus his memory of the twelve-year Nazi nightmare was crammed full of spicy anecdotes and sentimental tales about his friendship with Hitler. There was Hitler selecting a school for one of Hoffmann's children; Frau Hoffmann selecting Hitler's ties; Hitler visiting the Hoffmann family at Christmas; Eva Braun (who had once worked for Hoffmann and who appears to have been his mistress first) raving about Hitler's prowess as a lover to an unbelieving Hoffmann. Against the reality of devastation and horror, Hoffmann's characterization of Hitler was bizarre; he came across as a mixture of doting rich uncle, red-hot lover (Eva had once attempted suicide over him; an earlier girl friend had gone through with it), and benevolent despot.

Still, talking with Hoffmann was fascinating, particularly since he illustrated his stories with candid photos, many of which had never been published. He was particularly proud of one, a picture of himself with Stalin, the two of them smiling at each other over their raised glasses and Molotov smiling in the background. The picture had been taken when Hoffmann accompanied Ribbentrop to Moscow in '39 for the signing of the Russo-German pact. One of Hoffmann's accompanying photographers had snapped the picture, and, as Hoffmann recounted the incident, Stalin had made a gesture of annoyance,

131

whereupon Hoffmann had immediately offered him the film so that he could have it destroyed. But Stalin had graciously given the film back to Hoffmann, exacting from him only the promise not to publish the picture, a promise which had apparently caused Hoffmann some difficulty to keep. After the German attack on Russia, Goebbels, who had heard of the forbidden picture, pressured Hitler for its release, presumably so that it could be doctored and used as propaganda material. However, Hoffmann had prevailed with Hitler, a fact which even at this late date filled him with considerable pride.

"I had given Stalin my word of honor. Hitler supported me completely."

"Wouldn't it have been nice if Hitler had been equally steadfast in observing the treaty he made with Stalin?"

Hoffmann shrugged. "Those are matters of state. I know nothing about politics. Maybe if Hitler hadn't attacked, Stalin would have." He talked nonchalantly, as if he were describing a boxing match. "Let me tell you, though, Hitler had the greatest admiration for Stalin. He told me that he thought Stalin was a great man. On the photographs we brought back he ordered those which showed Stalin holding a cigarette to be retouched. For some reason he felt that it was demeaning for a great man to be seen smoking in public."

Hitler appeared to have had a number of very definite ideas about what was suitable for "a great man." He was appalled, Hoffmann told me, at a published photo of Mussolini in bathing trunks frolicking somewhere on the Italian Riviera, and he frowned equally on the Italian dictator's rather open alliance with his mistress, Clara Petacci. By contrast, Hitler's own relationship with Eva Braun was held in strictest secrecy; she was never seen with him in public. Hoffmann, however, had a number of pictures of her taken at the Berghof, Hitler's mountain retreat in Berchtesgaden. They showed a slender girl with a smiling, rather pretty face. There was little else one could say from the picture; the face was not memorable, though the features were even and pleasant. What struck me chiefly was

132

the gaiety of her eyes and the openness of her smile, perhaps because they seemed so incongruous when matched to her lover's and eventual husband's character. Next to Hitler I could imagine only someone like Lady Macbeth. Hoffmann did not think much of Eva, describing her as flighty and flirtatious, a "shop girl type" who had to be taught by his wife how to dress. The girl in the pictures he showed me looked elegant enough in flowing, décolleté evening gowns being serenaded in one of the photos by smiling, admiring young men in black uniforms who appeared to be members of an SS orchestra. In another picture the happily smiling Eva was being whirled in a dance by her brother-in-law, SS General Fegelein, Himmler's liaison at the *Fuehrer's* headquarters. Being thus favored did not prevent Fegelein from being executed for desertion in the very final days of the war. But Hoffmann didn't give me much time to muse over the brassy glamor and bloody demise of Nazi high society, or to decide whether to ascribe Eva's elegance to her own good taste or to Mrs. Hoffmann's. He had something better to show me.

From the lower recesses of his trunk, hidden beneath piles of paper and knots of dirty socks, he produced two most undistinctive water color landscapes.

"What do you say to that?" he asked triumphantly.

Since I couldn't think of anything to say, I looked at him blankly, wondering what he was up to. We had at times discussed painting—he was knowledgeable enough to know that what he was showing me lacked any distinction.

He grinned broadly. "Guess who?"

I shrugged. "How would I know?"

"They were painted by a good friend of mine."

"You don't mean . . ."

He nodded, still grinning. "That's right, they're Hitler's. They show another side of his personality, don't they?"

I examined them more closely. "Such as . . ."

"Calm, gentle."

I looked at him incredulously, which seemed to annoy him.

"Look at the paintings," he said impatiently. "Don't they express those qualities?"

One landscape showed a wall, something that appeared to be a part of an antique ruin, against a very pale blue sky, pale green fields and forests with some equally pallid yellow here and there. The overall design was clumsy, the colors not so much soft as timid. The whole picture looked watery, washed out, and lifeless. The other picture was similar in color and design.

"I don't know what qualities they express outside of being just plain dreadful."

"He was a better draftsman than painter," Hoffmann said, "but I'm not trying to prove that he was a great artist, just that there was another side to his character."

"Gentle and calm," I said, feeling like Alice in Wonderland. "Yes."

"Next you'll be telling me that he was a lamb in a wolf's pelt."

"That's not a bad way of putting it. You forget that I knew him well. He was capable of great affection, especially for children and animals. You know he never touched meat. I think what turned him most against Goering was the fact that he hunted."

"Too bad we weren't all rabbits or deer; there wouldn't have been any concentration camps or war."

"Hitler didn't know anything about the camps. They were Himmler's business, and he made sure that there weren't too many people who knew about his business."

Some recent trial testimony passed through my mind. SS General Ohlendorf testifying about the activities of the special SD commandoes, the *Einsatzgruppen,* in Russia—some 90,000 people, Jews and Communist functionaries, "destroyed" by his group alone on direct orders from Hitler through Himmler. SS *Haupsturmfuehrer* Wisliceny testifying about the "Final Solution" for which the orders had come to his chief, Adolf Eichmann, from Hitler through Himmler. But there was certainly

134

no point in arguing with Hoffmann. His steadfast defense of his monstrous "friend" in the face of everything should have been by now familiar enough to me not to cause surprise; still, I could never listen to him without a pervasive sense of unreality. There were times when I suspected that the whole thing was some sort of pose struck for profit, for how could he profit from his friendship with Hitler if he denounced him? And yet, I sensed that this was too logical an assumption to be true; it may have been part of the truth, but not all of it. As a matter of fact, the more illogical it seemed, the more I became convinced that Hoffmann's devotion to Hitler was genuine; it had to be genuine because it was incongruous. Like one of the seemingly mismatched details on a surrealist canvas, it fell into place: beer garden hilarity and rubber truncheons, the charmingly frivolous Eva Braun dancing and smiling beside a mass grave, the timid pastels of the clumsy water colors eclipsed in the orgiastic red of a bloody tidal wave, the dictator himself of doubtful identity, flickering, shifting, changing appearances—buffoon and demon, tramp and imperial lord, semiliterate oaf and satanic genius. Yes, Hoffmann's devotion to Hitler was genuine. Why should not the devil's best friend be a buffoon? It was the link between horror and hilarity that the authors of ancient morality plays had wisely recognized when they cast the devil in the role of the buffoon. Only virtue had triumphed in the old plays; they had laughed their devils off the stage.

"The trouble is that now that the war is lost they hold Hitler responsible for everything, but no head of state knows everything that goes on in his government," Hoffmann said. "Bormann saw to it that Hitler didn't hear of anything Bormann didn't want him to hear. In the end he even succeeded in keeping me away from Hitler by telling him I had typhus! Imagine!"

"And Hitler believed him?"

"He was very afraid of illness and immediately ordered me into isolation, calling in the best available specialist in communicable diseases. They took every possible test. I never saw anyone look so hard for germs—any germs. I suppose they were afraid to tell Bormann and Hitler that I wasn't sick after all. Finally I got worried that if the doctors didn't find something, they'd see to it that I'd get something, and I skipped to Vienna."

Another scene from a farce.

"I would say you acted prudently."

"But you see, it wasn't Hitler I was afraid of. He wouldn't have known. But Bormann would have been only too glad to be rid of me. You see, everything changed after Stalingrad. Hitler changed. He became less trusting, even with me. But you must remember that my friendship with him goes back to the early twenties. Later, after he took power, he would still come to my apartment late at night. 'Hoffmann,' he'd say to me, 'you're the only person who doesn't oppress me; you're my oasis.' We would sit before the fire and talk about mutual acquaintances of the early Munich days, or I would tell him some of the latest jokes and stories making the rounds of the cabarets. He'd listen with his eyes closed, smiling now and then, and finally falling asleep."

"How touching."

Hoffmann retrieved his pictures with an expression of resentment. "You're unjust, Countess. *You* didn't know him. None of the people who pass judgment now knew him the way I did."

As Alice had found out, it isn't easy to argue with a mad hatter. I therefore left my slightly mad photographer alone with his grudge. He would be over it by dinnertime. I could not get angry with Hoffmann, only exasperated; it was just too difficult to take him seriously. Sometimes, though, I wished that I had some of his limitless capacity for optimism. If it is true that good fortune smiles on those who believe in it, then Hoffmann was a good case in point, for he was able to turn just about any situation to his advantage.

My faith in my own fortunes was not nearly so great, which is why—despite Hoffmann's optimistic assessments—I kept on worrying about my job. But that fear was soon to be superseded by another, even more immediate one. I was visited by a major who had never had any official business connected with the witness houses but who had sometimes accompanied people who did. On those occasions he had shown a most unwelcome interest in me, repeatedly asking me for dates despite my consistent, though polite, refusals. Although I found his attentions annoying, I wouldn't have dared to be rude. I could not afford an enemy of his rank.

This time, though, he had evidently not come to ask me for a date. His face looked serious, showing concern, as he told me that he knew about an imminent concerted drive to get all foreign nationals repatriated by a certain spring deadline. Although repatriation had been going on all along, this intensification, he claimed, was due to Russian pressure to get East Europeans now in the west into Russian-held territories. Now, as before, the thought of being sent back terrified me, a fact of which the major took due notice. He vividly outlined the difficulties of the situation facing us and then offered his help. He thought that there might be something he could do; he would make a few calls. Why didn't I come to his office that evening about six? If I hadn't been so totally preoccupied with my fear, I might have suspected the major's motives and at least tried to call Captain Wulff to verify the matter. But I could think of nothing but the impending danger and the offer of help. So I entrusted the care and feeding of Hoffmann, currently still my only guest, temporarily to Frau Kruelle and set out for the major's office, which was nearby in a house similar to ours.

As I walked the short distance I thought of a year ago when I had gone to the grim German major in Hungary to demand help for the same reason, and of the straight-faced American officer in Czechoslovakia before whom I had passed out presenting the same petition. The same fear was like a gag in my throat when I knocked on the door of the house. He opened it himself, smiling too enthusiastically, I thought. The house was an office of some sort, but all the downstairs rooms ap-

peared deserted. I knew enough about the army to miss someone in charge of quarters, a noncom or an enlisted man. But I
was given no time to dwell on my suspicion. The major hastened to escort me upstairs, where he had his residence and
where it seemed as deserted as downstairs. In his room a table
was set for two; on a dresser were several bottles of wine and
whiskey. The major closed the door, locked it, and secured the
key in his trouser pocket, while I stood in the middle of the
room, too dumfounded to stop him.

"A little privacy," he said with a self-satisfied grin, hitting
his trouser pocket. "Now let's have a drink, okay?"

He was short but of fairly strong build, with a ruddy, gen-
erally pleasant face. I was measuring my chances against him,
recognizing only now that he was already drunk. He was quite
steady on his feet; it was apparent only in the bleary geniality
of his eyes. Handing me a glass, he pulled me down on the
couch beside him and put his arm around me. As calmly as I
could I lifted his arm off my shoulder and said firmly, "Please
unlock the door."

He grinned suggestively. "We need privacy."

I rose. "Not for what I came for."

For some reason he laughed out loud. "Oh yes we do," he
said, pulling me with some violence back down on the couch.
Trying to gain time, I fielded his increasingly aggressive ad-
vances by complaining that he had spilled my drink and that
I was hungry. He hurried to oblige, pouring me half a glass of
whiskey over ice. "Drink. It'll relax you."

While he was busy opening a can of Spam and a can of
peanuts, I poured the whiskey behind the couch. I knew that
above all I had to remain calm if I wanted to get out of this
situation without being seriously compromised. If I raised a
fuss to get help, would I be believed as to the reasons that had
brought me to the major's room? It occurred to me that I might
try to stall him until he was so drunk that he'd fall asleep or
pass out, so that I could get the key out of his pocket. The idea
was as revolting as the situation, but at least it was a plan of

138

action. I sat down at the table and started to eat peanuts, raising my empty glass. He grinned, obviously pleased. Refilling both our glasses, he said, "Relaxing, ain't it?"

I raised the glass to my lips, pretending to drink, gagging on the taste and smell. "Come on," he said, "down the hatch, like the last one."

"Listen," I said, pretending to hear something. "There's someone on the stairs, I think."

Moving less steadily than before, he went to investigate, putting his ear against the door. I poured my drink under the table, wondering how long I could keep this up and how much more he could take before he'd be where I needed him. I felt more anger and revulsion now than fear, but most of all I felt betrayed. Each act of kindness in this dreadful time transcended the limits of impact to become a symbol and affirmation of kindness itself. So the major's cheap little double-cross, too, loomed larger than its tawdry intent, for it upheld the principles of violence and treachery, the essential premises of war. What I was faced with was a slightly more civilized form of rape than the one I had so desperately been trying to escape. The Russians did the same with less fuss.

"Nothing," he said, returning on an uneven course. "You're hearing things." I was pleased to hear his speech becoming slurred. "Good girl," he said, refilling my empty glass. Looking at me, he shook his head. "How come you're not drunk?"

I smiled at him, raising my glass, inviting him to drink with me, which diverted him enough to blearily return my smile, give himself a refill, and raise his glass in return, saying, "Down the hatch."

I tried to empty my glass on the floor the moment his head was tilted back in drinking, but I wasn't fast enough; he'd seen me. Despite his drunkenness my plan was evidently instantly apparent to him, for he lunged at me across the table, letting go with a string of obscenities.

There was nothing left to do. I screamed, which made him laugh.

139

"There's no one here. You can scream from now till dooms-day. But if you want to play hard to get, okay, let's play."

He came after me, tearing the sleeve of my dress. Quite desperate now, I ran for the window, smashing it with my fists. The tall panes shattered violently, glass spilling into the garden below and admitting the bitter cold of the winter night into the room. I didn't know at that moment what I intended to do, though I might have jumped through the ragged glass, dagger-like framing the opening.

"You're bleeding," he said, sounding no longer slurred.

I hadn't noticed. Walking silently and steadily to the door, he reached in to his pocket for the key and opened it. His eyes expressed a mixture of resentment and remorse. I picked up my coat. As I walked past him he reached into his pocket and pulled out a handkerchief which he held out to me. I wrapped it around my left hand, which was cut worst.

"Wait," he said. Getting another handkerchief from a drawer, he bound up my right hand and helped me on with my coat.

I staggered downstairs. In the garden I vomited, but some-how I was able to get home. Cuci cried when she washed and dressed the cuts. I did not have to tell her what had happened; she read it in my face. That night I clung to the memory of my husband's love to heal the sickness I felt. Whether he was dead or alive, it was all I had to sustain me.

16

*T*HERE WERE no immediate repercussions. When I finally had the good sense to check with Captain Wulff on the deportation matter, he told me that systematic repatriation had been taking place all along, but that he didn't think I'd have to worry as long as I was employed by the military government. On the question of whether or not the witness houses were to be closed, he said that he hadn't heard any such thing, but that in the army such matters were always unpredictable—not a very reassuring answer. I felt somewhat better when Horthy returned for a brief stay near the end of the month. At least it seemed that we were still on the map. Unfortunately, though, my only two guests were on strained relations. Horthy, like so many others, had an acute dislike for Hoffmann and avoided him as much as possible. Under present circumstances, however, that was difficult. Hoffmann, resenting what he called young Horthy's baseless pretensions of superiority, needled him by reminiscing quite unabashedly about the cordial relations between Hitler and Horthy's father, the old admiral, who with many other top-ranking military figures was still imprisoned in a Nuremberg jail. The contrast between his father's and Hoffmann's present status did nothing, of course, to improve young Horthy's disposition, and he glowered in silence through Hoffmann's descriptions of state visits ("Marvelous photographs. I have them right here in my archives"), state banquets ("Even on such occasions Hitler only ate his vegetarian dishes"), a hunting party arranged by Goering ("Hitler, of course, took no part in that").

The second day of Horthy's stay I took Hoffmann aside and requested him to stop irritating Horthy in this manner. He professed surprise.

"Why should he be irritated? I'm saying nothing but nice things about his father. I could add that the old man was as vain as a peacock and acted like a king—all he lacked was a crown. You know that piece of Czechoslovakia Hitler gave to him in 1938? Well, they tell me he entered it like some conquering hero all dressed up in a fancy uniform and riding a white horse. I'd like to have a picture of *that* to show young Mr. Horthy. They were all happy to pick up the crumbs Hitler threw them when he was powerful. Now, of course, they have all suddenly turned into victims."

"Not so suddenly. Horthy was in Mauthausen. I believe his father was interned, too."

Hoffmann shrugged. "What did they expect Hitler to do? All the rats were leaving the sinking ship."

I wasn't going to argue *that* point again with Hoffmann, so there the matter rested. Since it was doubtful that he would honor my request, my only alternative was to try to outtalk him at dinner time, a formidable feat which had been only rarely accomplished by others, but which I had as yet never attempted. My efforts in this direction met with limited success, but they were so transparent that they amused the antagonists and so diffused the situation. As it was, Horthy left us again some days later. He was to be in and out for the next several months.

The early part of February remained quiet. We had a few very transient visitors who, because of their brief stays, remained as good as anonymous to me. Around the middle of the month, however, a more memorable guest arrived, although not memorable in conventional terms. Erna Michaela Ross, a lady of ample, rather masculine proportions with a handshake and a voice to match, was neither famous nor infamous; she had in fact no discoverable connection to anything that might have caused her to be brought to Nuremberg, and for the several weeks of her stay a number of court officials attempted unsuccessfully to discover why indeed she was in Nuremberg. Fraulein Ross especially tried very hard to find the mysterious missing link that bound her to these awesome proceedings. She earnestly searched her past, rummaging through countless nonevents in an exceedingly uneventful life. In the process of this she became one of those remarkable people who could outtalk Hoffmann; but he nevertheless grew fond of her, since she also listened with boundless admiration to his Hitler stories.

The most memorable event in Fraulein Ross's life turned out to be the Russian entry into Berlin, with its subsequent wave of Russian rape, a wave which also passed her by. She told the story of her adventures with such great animation and obvious fascination for gory details that over the weeks of her stay with us she became the object of much rather callous hilarity among subsequent male guests who in time referred to her as "the old maid who didn't quite make it with the Russians." New arrivals were quickly coached to encourage her into telling her "horrendous experiences during the fall of Berlin," and since she was a great talker and thoroughly enjoyed all the unaccustomed attention, she was always happy to oblige. With each telling the stories grew, sprouting new and lurid details.

I was struck how again and again the horrible and the

143

ludicrous merged into a perspective evoking neither horror nor laughter, only an appalling sense of absurdity. The same qualities that had kept Fraulein Ross from the experience of tenderness had also shielded her from violence, and she seemed to regret the loss of both. She had lived on the fourth floor, but the Russians had stopped on the third. She had heard the screams of the women below, the strange language in husky male voices, the raucous laughter, the boots trampling up and down the stairs. How had she waited? With fear and anticipation turning into relief and regret?

Pleasure in violence, the ethos of war. Disruption of the commonplace. Bloody adventures turning into romantic memories; the moment of violence becoming the moment of glory, focal point of a monotone, one slashing splash of bloody color on a canvas of gray. I remembered our local unit of the *Stahlhelm* gathering on national holidays to be reviewed by my father, who was their commander. They stood at attention before the tavern in their well-pressed uniforms, brave veterans of a lost war, lost glory, but, alas, no lost illusions.

Past the middle of February we were again moderately busy. Scheidt was returned. He greeted me awkwardly, his eyes expressing that same unhappy intensity, mingling apology and accusation, that had so often unnerved me before. He held my hand a bit too long and said he was glad to be back. For the time being at least the increase of activity made me forget my job worries. I also barely thought any more of my unhappy experience with the drunken major. When I got a call one morning to hold myself in readiness for a CIC interrogation, I thought little of it and assumed that it was a routine interview, although I had never before received prior notification.

My first inkling that this one was different came when I realized that I was to be brought to the agency's headquarters in Nuremberg. A staff car picked me up. On my arrival I was taken to a room where two officers appeared to be waiting for me. What struck me at once was the grimness of their demeanor. I was offered no chair, but left standing, awkward and

144

afraid now, in the middle of the room. Their grim silence seemed endless and heavy with accusation. What had I done? I began to feel unsteady on my feet.

"May I sit down?"

One of them, a captain, motioned gravely to a chair. I sat down and waited. The other officer was a major who was busy studying some papers on his desk.

"You are the wife of Count Hugo Kalnoky," he said finally without looking up. I wasn't sure whether he was asking me or telling me.

"Yes," I said, surprised at the smallness of my voice. I *sounded* guilty, because I was afraid. It occurred to me that their procedure was clumsy. If they intimidated a person in this manner from the outset, how would they be able to tell whether the fear so generated was a response to the intimidation or a sign of guilt?

Another possibility suddenly struck me and with it a fear so intense that I gasped. "Oh, my God, he's dead," I cried. "You've found out that he's dead." The power of my fear convinced me of its reality. I broke down and cried.

Feeling a hand on my shoulder, I saw the captain standing over me, looking disturbed and rather perplexed; so did the major, who said uncertainly, "Please calm yourself."

"Please tell me the truth. What has happened to my husband?"

The captain and the major exchanged glances. "We know very little about your husband. That's why we asked you here," the major said at last.

"He's not dead?"

"Why do you think he's dead?"

"I've had no news for over a year. The Red Cross seems unable to locate him or get any information about him."

"I'm sorry," the major said with a probing look.

"We did not mean to upset you so. However, the question has been raised as to why you chose to come to Germany alone, leaving your husband behind in Hungary."

I was so relieved that I barely heard the last question. The

145

old uncertainty was like joyful news compared to the awful certainty of that moment. When I didn't answer right away, the major repeated the question.

"Why did you come to Germany alone?"

"I thought I gave the reasons during my first interview."

"You claim your husband stayed behind because he feared arrest by the Gestapo."

"Yes."

"Did your husband fear the Russians, as you claim you did?"

"We all feared the Russians. We still do. On my first interview I was told not to talk about that."

The two men exchanged another glance.

"Do you speak Russian?" the major asked then.

"No," I answered somewhat startled, but beginning to get the drift of things.

"But you speak Hungarian?"

"Yes."

"Do you understand Russian?"

"I neither speak nor understand it. How would I be able to understand it if I can't speak it?"

"It's similar to Hungarian, isn't it?"

I wondered how in their positions they could afford to be so ignorant. "There is no similarity I know of."

"Then how did you talk to a Russian official on the phone last December?"

I looked at him blankly. "I don't believe I understand."

"Let me refresh your memory. On December 30 of last year, with the help of Captain Wulff, you made a call to Budapest. After trying several numbers you had the call switched to a Soviet intelligence branch, where you talked with a Russian official by the name of . . . what was his name again?"

They couldn't be serious. Was I really suspected of being a Russian spy? "I haven't the faintest idea who I talked to, and I don't know what Russian authority I had on the phone. I told the operator that I was looking for my husband who was missing, and she connected me with that office."

146

"You're expecting us to believe that the operator connected you with Russian intelligence without your asking?"

"If, as you say, I talked to Russian intelligence, that's exactly what happened."

"If you don't speak Russian, how were you able to talk to a Russian?"

"Because, whoever he was, he spoke fluent Hungarian."

The major looked nonplussed. That possibility had evidently not occurred to him. "Is it not unusual to inquire in this manner for a missing relative?" he asked then.

"Why? I called what was formerly my home, as well as a relative's house, and when I didn't get an answer at either number, I asked the operator for help."

"I see . . ."

"I've tried for months to get some news through the Red Cross. Is it so difficult to understand that I would try through another channel? I was very grateful to Captain Wulff for making it possible, even if it was unsuccessful."

The major looked at me long and probingly, tapping his pencil. I noticed that the captain was making notes.

"Am I accused of being a Russian spy on the basis of that phone call?"

"No accusation has been made against you. You're jumping to conclusions."

"Rather an obvious conclusion, isn't it?"

"That depends. In our business obvious conclusions are suspect."

"Then why would you have such a ridiculous suspicion on the basis of one phone call?"

"Perhaps our suspicions are based on more than that."

"What else?"

"Is it not true that you have tried very strenuously to avoid repatriation?"

"That makes me a spy?"

"Well, wouldn't it be more natural for you to want to return to Hungary if you really wanted to locate your husband?"

I was incredulous. "Major, I fled from the Russians like

147

millions of others. Any woman who'd return voluntarily to the East would have to be insane." Quite suddenly then the entire thing fell into place for me. I looked at the still red scars on my hands where the glass had cut them. "Did he tell you how his window was broken?"

The major looked at me questioningly.

"What did he tell you?"

He did not answer immediately but tapped his pencil and pondered the papers on his desk. The captain was watching him expectantly.

"You're referring to Major P.?" he asked at last.

"Yes."

"Supposing *you* tell us what happened between you and Major P."

I had told no one about that awful evening, not even Cuci. For Frau Kruelle, Hoffmann, and Captain Wulff I had invented an explanation about the cuts. As an employee of the court, and more specifically, the American military, the thought of making accusations against an American officer frightened me. The major would, of course, deny everything I said. God only knew what lies he had already told them. It was obvious that he was trying to get revenge, but God, what for? Despite my efforts to control myself, my eyes were filling up again with tears.

"Would you like a cigarette?" asked the major, sounding more gentle.

I nodded. He offered me the pack and a light. "I'm sorry," I said. "It's just such an unfair contest. He's trying to get back at me."

"For what?"

I told them of the major's offer of help and the subsequent events at his billet, showing them the scars on my hands. The captain was making notes; the interrogating major tapped his pencil and drew on his cigarette, watching me closely. I could tell nothing from their faces, but in recounting the story of that sordid evening, I felt so humiliated that I was sure they didn't

148

believe me. I felt bitter and defeated and still had to struggle against tears, which angered me, because it looked as if I were looking for their pity.

The major offered me another cigarette. "I think we've covered all we need," he said. "I'll call for a car now to take you back."

"Do I still have my job?"

He hesitated. "We have no jurisdiction in this matter. We investigate the charge that was brought against you and send the report on to the office that employs you."

My worst fears were confirmed. Innocent or guilty, I had been involved in something irregular—besides, who was I to contest the word of an American officer?

"For the time being, consider this as no more than an interrogation. If you told us the truth I don't see why you should have to worry."

"The truth, Major, has to be believed."

"It will be believed, Countess." I thought there was encouragement in his smile, or was it just wishful thinking?

Minutes later I was on my way back to Erlenstegen, through the early dark and damp cold of the winter afternoon, past the emaciated, ragged people clearing rubble or collecting debris for fuel, directing occasional dull, bitter glances at the passing jeep. How inviting and secure the house looked after Nuremberg; how tenuous was my hold on it. I tried not to think of what would happen to us if I lost my job. Repatriation seemed inevitable, though I thought I would die first. My mood on my return was close to despair. If there was one thing I wasn't looking for, it was more complications; but that is exactly what was waiting for me.

In the hall I met Scheidt, who appeared to be on his way out. His expression was agitated. He looked at me with momentary confusion as if he weren't quite sure of who I was.

"I must introduce you to my wife," he murmured, motioning vaguely toward the living room, but then he ran out of the house—next door, I presumed, since his room was there. He

149

couldn't have gone anywhere else; his movements were restricted. Or could he? We had no guards now. But he hadn't worn a coat. I wondered if I would be held responsible if he ran away.

Mrs. Scheidt, looking poised and serious, sat in a chair by the window. I was not in the mood to meet anyone and would have ducked upstairs to my room if she hadn't seen me. As it was, I had no choice but to go in and greet her. She was a small, dark, rather attractive woman who smiled sparsely and looked me over with coolly probing eyes as she offered me her hand. There was in her look something offensive and accusing, but her voice was calmly casual when she showed me written permission to visit her husband.

"I see that you are not staying with us overnight."

Again that strangely charged look. "No. I did not receive permission for that."

"I'm sorry. We do have enough room. Your husband's room has two beds." Her expression remained unchanged. I thought I understood its implication and felt angered.

"You are not Hungarian, are you?" she asked suddenly.

"No. My husband is."

"You are German?"

"Yes."

"Your husband is not here with you?"

"No, unfortunately." I felt as if I were back before the CIC.

"Yes, separation is difficult, isn't it?" she said pointedly.

"The war does such things to all of us."

Scheidt returned carrying some papers. He had the same distraught expression as before, but she looked at him calmly.

"You have met, I presume?" he said awkwardly.

"Yes." The coldness of my voice made him look at me sharply and with distress.

"You were in error, dear; the Countess is German," said Mrs. Scheidt.

"As German as you are Hungarian," Scheidt countered harshly.

150

"Which means completely," she snapped.

I excused myself and left them alone. I was too weary to be outraged at Mrs. Scheidt's unspoken allusions; the whole day had left me feeling numb. I could think of little else than the pending CIC report, and at dinner I barely noticed that Mrs. Scheidt had left.

"You are preoccupied," Scheidt said to me later in the living room, drawing me aside.

"I suppose I am. I'm sorry your wife couldn't stay."

"Why do you say that? I know she has offended you."

"Yes."

"I'm afraid you'll be even more offended when I tell you what she intends to do."

"I don't understand . . ."

"She is suing me for divorce, naming you as corespondent."

I wasn't sure whether I ought to laugh or cry. "I hope this is some sort of bad joke."

"I wish it were. You see, the point is she's looking for a reason. You're the only woman I've been in contact with since I was in prison. I think she took one look at you and decided you're it."

"You mean it's only a pretext—or does she really believe it?"

"Perhaps a mixture of both. In any case, after she saw you she convinced herself of the reality of her suspicions."

I tried to remember the morning. This day had started ordinarily enough. The laundry had come back; one of the cots in the other house had broken down; there was a stopped-up sink in the kitchen which Frau Kruelle blamed on the cook. Two people in the other house had left this morning; three more had been checked in. Things were humming. I was busy and, temporarily at least, had given up worrying about my job.

"This doesn't seem to be my day," I said.

"The funny thing is that if it were up to me she would have reason," said Scheidt.

"But she doesn't," I said vehemently.

151

"Yes. Considering my feelings for you, that's the irony of it."

"Please, that's almost in bad taste." I needed to be alone. As I turned to walk away, he grabbed my wrist and held me back, almost harshly. His face was flushed; his eyes had darkened with angry emotion.

"Since when are honest feelings in bad taste?"

"I'm not questioning your honesty, only your judgment."

"Your problem is that you're so afraid."

"And yours that you're so desperate."

He let go of my arm. "Yes."

It was my turn to stop him from walking away. Despite my exasperation, his very real unhappiness moved me, and his clear, strong affection, though beyond a chance of fulfillment, fell into the balance against the humiliation and sordidness of my encounter with the drunken American.

"Look, it's true that I'm afraid. I can't afford to be desperate; there's too much at stake. I need this job. It's all that stands between my family and disaster. Do you realize that what your wife is planning to do could cost me my job, not to speak of my reputation?"

He shook his head wearily. "No, I hadn't." Facing the solid dark outside the window, he closed his eyes as if to reinforce the darkness. He rested his forehead against the pane and was silent for a while. "I don't think I can make it," he said finally. "I can't take it any longer."

"You've lost your perspective."

"Why not? I've lost everything else."

I thought of the miserable people I had seen that afternoon sifting the rubble of Nuremberg. "I can think of many thousands who are infinitely worse off than you."

"Is that supposed to be a comfort?"

"I'm sorry. That's not what I meant. But you do have a lot to be grateful for compared to them."

"The conqueror's charity," he said with quiet bitterness. Then, raising his voice, "Don't you think I see them? I would rather share their misery than sit in this glorified prison."

152

The guest house.

Heinrich Hoffmann in his photographic archives at the Palace of Justice.

Sketch of a monk by Heinrich Hoffmann.

General Koestring, the
last German military
attaché in Moscow.

Above: *Rudolph Diels, founder of the Gestapo.*
(Photograph by Heinrich Hoffmann.)

Right: *Elmar Streicher, son of Julius Streicher,*
who was hanged at Nuremberg.

Willy Messerschmitt, airplane designer.

Poetic tribute to Countess Kalnoky from Karl Haushofer, a professor of geopolitics.

Poetic tribute to Countess Kalnoky from Hans Luther, former ambassador to Washington and former chancellor of the Weimar Republic.

Guest book signatures of General Reinhard, commander of the Berlin garrison in the revolution of November 1918, and Henrietta von Schirach, wife of Baldur von Schirach, a war criminal and a former German youth leader.

The conversation had stopped at the other side of the room and people were looking our way. Scheidt sat down, leaned back, and closed his eyes again. I had noticed that he did this often, or else covered his face with his hands.

"I'm suffocating inside," he said softly. "All I wanted from you was a breath of clean, fresh air."

"I give what I can."

"I'm sorry," he said after a moment. "The last thing you need is more problems, and that's all I ever seem to bring you."

"Don't hold yourself responsible for your wife's decision."

"You know that I'll do all in my power to prevent her from drawing you into this."

"Yes. I don't know anyway how she could use such a completely unsupported allegation as grounds. You can't use a suspicion for a reason in such a matter, can you?"

"I don't believe so."

Still, I worried. Mrs. Scheidt's threat was after all no more absurd than the drunken major's charge that I was a spy. What worried me most was the possibility of her allegations coming to the attention of the CIC, in which case I was sure—the truth of the matter notwithstanding—that it would give me the coup de grâce.

I lived through two weeks of tense uncertainty during which I expected each phone call, each ring of the doorbell, to seal my fate. But this fate turned out to be again much kinder than I had dared to expect. What finally came was an order charging me to bar all unauthorized military personnel from entering the witness house. I never saw or heard about the drunken major again. "The truth will be believed," the CIC major had said, and they *had* believed me. There was something restorative in that. As for Mrs. Scheidt, she was evidently persuaded in time that she would need proof of her allegations if they were to serve as grounds for her divorce. When Scheidt left permanently some weeks later, the matter between them remained unresolved.

17

MARCH OF '46 did come in like a lion, though the threat of heavy weather was less meteorological than political. What the defeated Germans had only dared to whisper about became a roar that echoed across Europe on the voice of Sir Winston Churchill: "An iron curtain has descended across the continent. Behind that line lie all the capitals and ancient states of Central and Eastern Europe, Warsaw, Berlin, Prague, Vienna, Budapest . . ." What to so many of us had become a grim new fact of life had finally been publicly acknowledged, and with it the serious rift among the former allies.

Some people feared an imminent outbreak of war, with Germany becoming the battleground. In any case, for a time there was talk of little else. Among Germans the trial lost even more of its credibility. Churchill's open charge of Russian imperialism—"a growing challenge and peril to Christian civilization"—was taken to support the contention of many Germans that at least one of the powers sitting in judgment at Nuremberg was itself guilty of some of the crimes with which Germany was being charged. Still, the trial ran its course with apparent solidarity among the prosecuting powers. By early March the prosecution had finished the presentation of its case, and the defense began its superhuman task of trying to counter the dreadful charges.

At the witness houses the pace of activity picked up steadily. Diels was returned, less sternly guarded than the first time by an officer of the CIC with whom he seemed to be on cordial terms. The conditions of his internment were to be the same as before: he was still under room arrest. The renewed prospect of being locked up by me caused Diels, as well as the accompanying officer, considerable amusement, with Diels referring to me as "his favorite jailer," and adding that he would gladly be my prisoner voluntarily. Ludicrous as the situation was, I did not find it amusing. The thought of having to play again the role of jailer was distinctly depressing. Once had been more than enough.

I installed the former Gestapo chief in his old room, a fact he noted with appreciation. Since he had seen so much of it, he remarked ruefully, he had really grown fond of it. He also gleefully anticipated Hoffmann's return from work and his subsequent discovery that his favorite room—he had long tried to get it for himself—was again occupied. With typical Hoffmann logic the photographer argued that since he was the senior guest the room should really belong to him, and since I could not possibly counter Hoffmann's logic, I merely bantered with him on the subject, promising him the room on the condition that he tidy up his present one to Frau Kruelle's satisfaction. My real reason for withholding the room from Hoffmann was that its size made it more suitable for two occupants than one, a consideration I waived in Diels's case to compensate for the restrictions of his internment.

Hoffmann's reaction lived up to Diels's expectations. He seemed to be as hurt as he was angry when, upon discovering

155

who was once again his neighbor, he shouted at Diels's locked door that it evidently still paid to have been in the Gestapo, whereupon Diels countered with malice that it didn't pay nearly so well as Hitler's friendship.

"You didn't do so bad yourself with Hermann," Hoffmann yelled, his Bavarian dialect thickening with his anger.

"Goering never made me a millionaire."

"You didn't have the talent."

"Now there's a joke."

"I'm used to envy," Hoffmann said archly.

"Don't flatter yourself."

"I'd rather be accused of having made money than of having founded the Gestapo. No one seems to feel it's necessary to lock *me* up," Hoffmann said and, in the full consciousness of his virtue and consequent freedom, marched jauntily off to dinner, giving me no more than a reproachful glance.

Despite his avowed contempt for Hoffmann, Diels was still angry when I brought him his dinner.

"There's justice for you," he fumed. "The parasites go free. For that fellow the Third Reich was one giant goldmine. I know he's a multimillionaire. God alone knows how much he's got stashed away in Swiss banks."

"I guess making money isn't considered a crime. He always maintains that he had nothing to do with politics and doesn't understand it."

Diels laughed contemptuously. "He knew enough about politics to stay away from it, but not so far that he couldn't grow rich on it." He began to pace with some agitation. "What bothers me is the standards by which the judgments are being made. Men like that," he motioned vaguely in the direction of Hoffmann's room, "who never did anything that wasn't in their own interest are going free. Then there are the others who did a lot of brave shouting against the regime from the safe distance of exile. They're coming back now like great conquering heroes, while those of us who stayed and fought the regime from within are in prison."

156

This, as I would find out, was one of Diels's favorite themes
—the patriotism and incorruptibility of the German *Beamtentum,*
that bureaucratic elite whose tradition of efficiency and absolute loyalty to the state reached from the Prussian Sparta of the
Great Elector to the Kaiser's, and finally Hitler's Reich. A good
official to Diels was much like a soldier—he would not desert
his post under political pressure any more than would a soldier
under fire; for Diels, resignation was equal to desertion. The
people who had remained in their posts, Diels claimed, had
done more to curb Hitler's revolution than all of the resistance
put together. When I asked him why in that case Nazism had
become so powerful in Germany, he evaded a direct answer
but cited instead a number of examples where local officials
had effectively modified decrees from Berlin and fought
against party domination.

It was impossible to listen to Diels's loyalty-versus-deser-
tion argument without strongly suspecting that it served as
convenient self-justification. He was aware of that ambivalence and appeared to be greatly bothered by it. To prove his
claims as genuine he told of numerous incidents in which he
had fought the party bureaucracy during his tenure as *Regierungs-President* in Cologne, as well as of his conflicts with Goering, Hitler, and the SA during his brief career as Gestapo chief.
I had no way of knowing at the time how much of what he told
me was true. Later assessments of him vary according to the
observer's position, although the fact that he did bring about
a Christmas amnesty for political prisoners in '33, as well as his
actions against the SA while still chief of the Gestapo, have
been confirmed as a matter of record. In addition he claimed
to have helped a number of people either to leave the country
or to evade Nazi terror, and it was one of these people, so Diels
told me, who was currently repaying him by speaking in
Diels's behalf and making it possible for him to be held at the
witness house instead of prison. The person in question was
Dr. Robert Kempner, a former official in the Prussian Ministry
of the Interior, whom Diels had helped to escape from Nazi

Germany and who had now returned as a member of the American prosecution at the war crimes trial.

But despite the positive things that could evidently be said in Diels's behalf, I found it difficult not to feel suspicious of a man who had been a protégé of Goering. What bothered me particularly about Diels was his insistent self-justification. He absolved himself of any guilt by citing his actions against the regime, by the appearance of his name on numerous Gestapo death lists, and by his eventual imprisonment under sentence of death. But by early 1945 even Goering was under Hitler's death sentence, and thousands of once ardent supporters of the *Fuehrer* had long since perished by his decree. It was the ravenous nature of revolution to devour its own. Had not Robespierre died under the guillotine? There was nothing unusual about the makers of terror becoming its victims, and it hardly absolved them of their share of guilt. The credit for Diels's proceeding against SA excesses had to be balanced against the very considerable contribution he had made to the consolidation of the regime's power. Even his apparent courage had to be measured against the power of his patron's protection. What made an unequivocal assessment of Diels's past so difficult was the question of whether he had ever really risked anything for his recognition that the regime he had helped to power was corrupt. His claim of having fought against party encroachment while running an orderly administration in Cologne had a plaintive, hollow ring; it reminded me of another government official's justification before the Nuremberg court, where he had been called to account for a proposal he had authored recommending the sterilization of all Jews in his area. He told the court that he had hoped by this measure to save them from deportation to the death camps and thus at least save their lives. He probably told the truth; within the Kafkaesque dimensions of Nazi Germany such acts may have been considered humanitarian.

It was against this macabre reality that Diels's arguments about the traditions of the German civil service sounded obscene. Like the army's adherence to its oath, the kind of tradition Diels talked of had become an end in itself, as if loyalty, obedience, and patriotism could be isolated from their object. Of those few who had in fact retained their posts only for the purpose of working against the regime, most were dead. Diels had survived, and though in the end it had been by mere good fortune, he had also shown a remarkable talent for political adaptation and survival throughout his career. That he had left some exceedingly unpleasant memories for some people was to become evident to me shortly.

Among a number of interesting new guests who arrived during March was Carl Severing, the Social Democratic Minister of the Interior of Prussia until 1932. A man in his seventies, he was rather short and of slight build, with a shock of snow-white hair above a prominently high forehead and lively, bright eyes that could deal glances as witheringly sardonic as some of his remarks. A lifelong Social Democrat, Severing had behind him a long career in the union movement and the political leadership of his party, the party that had launched the German Republic. Like Friedrich Ebert, the first chancellor of that republic, Severing had come from a working class background, at the time a comparative rarity in German politics. A combination of incisive intelligence and robust practicality had won him the respect (if not always the good will) of his often aristocratic ministerial colleagues and the career professionals whose chief he was in the Interior Ministry, one of whom was Rudolf Diels.

My first indication that the two men knew each other and that Severing had a distinct animosity toward Diels came shortly after Diels's return when they met by chance in the upstairs hallway. Diels was on his way down to meet a CIC officer who was waiting for him outside in a jeep. Having unlocked Diels's door earlier to permit him to keep his appointment, I was not present at the beginning of the argument between him and Severing, but hearing their raised voices, I arrived in the middle of it. Though it was difficult for me to

159

understand the particulars, I gathered that Severing, who was doing most of the talking, was accusing Diels of having betrayed him.

"It should hardly matter to you what I think, Herr Diels," Severing was saying icily when I arrived.

"Your opinion and judgment have always meant a great deal to me, Herr Minister."

"After you stab me in the back you would have me believe that you did it for the loftiest of reasons."

"Your accusation is as unfair as it is offensive, sir."

"So was your action. So is everything that has happened since. I'm glad to know, however, that my country is in ashes for a high moral purpose."

"Your country is my country too, Herr Minister. Might it be just possible that we both did our duty as we saw it?"

"No," Severing snapped. "Justify yourself to your interrogators, Herr Diels—I believe they are waiting for you—but don't try to justify yourself to me."

With that Severing walked away. Diels, obviously shaken, made a halfhearted attempt to detain him, but then turned and rushed grimly down the stairs to the waiting jeep.

Later, in the living room, Severing apologized to me for the scene.

"It's against my best principles to lose my temper like that, but I'm afraid seeing Dr. Diels does not improve my disposition."

"You won't see much of him. He is mostly in his room."

"He is restricted?"

"Yes."

"I didn't expect to see him here. I met him in that other place, you know, where I was billeted the first night, a real detention facility with guards and locks. He was terribly solicitous for my health because I had been given an unheated room, or should I say cell? I'm sure he thinks it very callous of me not to appreciate his concern for either my health or good opinion."

160

"He seemed quite upset."

"Of course. He's concerned about his position now. They all are. There's no one like an old-line Nazi when it comes to dressing up treachery as patriotism, but Diels must really be an artist at it, or he wouldn't be here, would he?"

"From what I understand, someone is repaying him a kindness."

Severing acknowledged this with a doubtful glance. "I'm glad to hear it," he said sarcastically.

I was naturally curious about Severing's great bitterness toward Diels, but I didn't feel free to ask him about it straight out.

"I had never heard about Diels until he was brought here," I said, "but a number of people have told me since that he tried to hold the SA in check while he headed the Gestapo."

Severing smiled bitterly. "That was a little late; don't you agree? You may be too young to remember," he added gallantly, "but the Brownshirts had shown themselves for what they were a long time before they took over."

"I do remember. They came to my wedding."

He looked at me questioningly. "Uninvited, I presume?"

"Yes. Although by that time they had already taken over. It was in '34. They burst into the courtyard screaming 'out with foreigners and Jews.' There were about a hundred of them."

I remembered the crushing sound of boots with flower garlands trampled under foot, the brutal, hate-filled faces of the invaders, the fear-stricken faces of the guests. My father managed to contain them, perhaps because he had been the commander of the *Stahlhelm*—there were many former *Stahlhelm* members in the SA. They had left, shouting obscenities and threats, but we had escaped serious physical violence. The Brownshirts and the courtyard strewn with my trampled wedding flowers were the last, ominous impressions I took with me from my homeland.

"Well, then, you understand what I mean," Severing said. "Why didn't Dr. Diels decide earlier that the SA needed checking? First he helps to set the monster free, and then he goes around claiming credit for having saved some of its victims."

"I suppose that's a fair assessment. Have you known him long?"

"He was on my staff at the Ministry."

"Oh, I understand."

"I doubt it," Severing said, "but if long stories about political intrigues don't bore you, I'll tell you my reason for my grudge against Diels."

I hastened to assure him of my interest.

"Do you know what happened on the twentieth of July, 1932?" he asked then.

"No, not offhand."

"It was the day when the last remnant of democratic government in Germany disappeared. Dr. Diels's contribution to the events of that day was by no means insignificant."

The events Severing proceeded to describe culminated in the forced resignation, under threat of violence, of the last elected government of Prussia, the largest of the German *Lander*. For Severing, who had been a member of that government, the memory of that July 20, just a few months before the beginning of the Hitler catastrophe, was as bitter as that same date (curiously profound coincidence!), exactly twelve years later, was to become for the few surviving anti-Hitler conspirators. The coup—for although there were pretensions to legality, it would be difficult to describe it in any other way—was engineered by Chancellor Franz von Papen (in 1945 one of the defendants at Nuremberg). But the particular developments leading to the ouster had their background in the long-standing, gradual deterioration of democratic government in the republic, which, for some time prior to von Papen's chancellorship, had been governed under the emergency provision of the Weimar Constitution giving the president the power to rule by decree. President Hindenburg, then in his eighties, was feeble and reportedly senile, no more than a revered name behind which those who wished to usurp power could

162

manipulate and intrigue. Von Papen, an ultraconservative with ties both to the landed aristocracy and to big industry, was one of the last chancellors to head the dying republic. Without backing in the Reichstag, or even in his own party, he was maneuvered into the chancellorship through the efforts of the men around the aged president, a number of whom had been for some time collaborating with Hitler.

Immediately after taking office in June 1932, von Papen dissolved the Reichstag, set new elections for the end of July, and lifted a ban on the SA which had been instituted as a safety measure by the previous government. The direct result of this was an unprecedented wave of violence as the unmuzzled Brownshirts did their electioneering in the form of pitched battles with the Communists. But while the rabble was raising havoc in the streets, von Papen prepared his own low blow against what little was left of constitutional government in Germany. Exploiting the crisis he and his fellow intriguers had helped to aggravate, he invaded the last stronghold of the Social Democrats by seizing power in Prussia.

It was in this undertaking that Diels appears to have played an active part. Even under the emergency provision of the constitution a pretext was needed to justify such extraordinary measures, and von Papen found it in a manner cynical enough to have done honor to the Nazis who were waiting behind him in the wings. After having first destroyed the safeguards against violence on a national level, he charged the elected government of Prussia with being unable to preserve the civil order. Added to this "reason" was another equally as spurious: a report concerning itself with an allegedly impending alliance between the Social Democrats and Communists was interpreted by the rightists for their purposes of the moment as nothing less than a Marxist conspiracy against the state. The report, which was almost certainly transmitted to the Papen government through Diels, was about a meeting between a close Severing associate and two Communist deputies. In this meeting, at which Diels was present, Severing's associate allegedly solicited the cooperation of the Communists to strengthen the anti-Nazi forces in Prussia. Although on the face of it this may appear to have been a reasonable move, in terms of the political realities of the times it seems highly unlikely that it was ever made. The Communists were after all as much the sworn enemies of the republic as were the Nazis, and while the two factions fought each other bitterly and brutally in the streets, their deputies frequently made common cause in the legislatures against the Socialists and center parties. If a Communist had a greater enemy than a Nazi, it was bound to be a Social Democrat.

Whatever the exact purpose of the meeting may have been, Diels's version differed sharply from that of Severing's associate given in a later proceeding before a federal court concerning itself with the legality of von Papen's action in Prussia. Diels was widely accused of treachery for breaking the confidence of his superiors when he submitted the report in question, while those who disbelieved his version of the meeting accused him of perjury as well.

Nor did Severing escape criticism for his role in these events, most particularly the charge that he and his associates had yielded without resistance to von Papen's demands. Because he was the head of the most powerful police force in Germany and a representative of the equally powerful Social Democratic trade unions, some of Severing's critics argued that he should have used the Prussian police to protect his government, or called a general strike, as the Social Democrats had successfully done in 1920 to counter another rightist coup.

This criticism was to become a factor even in the war crimes trial when it was brought up by Rudolf Dix, the attorney for Schacht, in his closing brief. By offering no resistance to von Papen's coup, Dix argued, Severing and his colleagues had contributed as much to Hitler's eventual take-over as had Schacht. Severing was, of course, incensed over Dix's charges, which received a good deal of attention in the press. He answered sharply in an open letter, his defense being, briefly, that

164

the political and economic situation in Germany in 1932 would have made a general strike enormously dangerous, even with the support of the Prussian police. Six million people were unemployed; the tensions of political polarization had almost reached a breaking point. Calling a general strike, Severing argued, would have precipitated a blood bath and full-scale civil war. Instead of preventing the Nazis from seizing power, as his critics claimed, it would have swept them into power only sooner.

What upset Severing especially was the allegation by some of his critics that he had lacked the courage to act more decisively. As proof to the contrary he cited his attempt on January 30, 1933, the day Hitler became chancellor, to contact General von Hammerstein, the commander-in-chief of the army, who had once assured him that he would not tolerate Hitler's takeover. The purpose of the attempted contact, which Hammerstein evaded, was to assure the general of labor support if he would move against Hitler. But the general was otherwise occupied; like too many of his colleagues he was—however reluctantly—cooperating with the new regime. Later Hammerstein became a confirmed opponent of Hitler and an active member of the military resistance. By contrast, Severing's opposition to Hitler never varied, from the time when as a Prussian minister he moved to curb the excesses of the SA, to the moment in March 1933 when he spoke his last word as a freely elected Reichstag deputy—an impotent but spirited "no" to the Nazis. The occasion was a vote on the so-called Enabling Act. Requiring constitutional change and therefore a two-thirds majority, the act was to be the legal basis on which Hitler would assume dictatorial powers.

Severing vividly described to me the Berlin scene, the streets seething with brown and black uniforms and resounding with the shouts of the storm troopers. On his arrival for the opening of the Reichstag session he was promptly arrested. Pressure from his colleagues got him released to participate in the vote on the Enabling Act, probably because Goering, who

165

was president of the Reichstag, knew that he had his two-thirds majority in any case. The convenient Reichstag fire a month before, which (although this has never been satisfactorily proven) had been almost certainly engineered by the Nazis with a dimwitted Communist pyromaniac as their tool, gave the new Nazi government the needed pretext to suspend all civil liberties. Goering seized the chance he had been waiting for to ban the Communists from further participation in the Reichstag and, with the help of his Gestapo chief, Diels, arrested thousands of them as well. For hours before the voting the halls and stairways of the building, and the streets leading to it, had been lined with the Brownshirts, shouting in unison, "We demand full power!" Those who were known to be of the opposition ran a gauntlet of jeers and threats. The act was adopted by a vote of 441 to 94. All of the "no" votes came from the Social Democrats. In time some would pay for such defiance with their lives, some with prison or exile, all with harassment.

Severing himself survived the Nazi years with the help of many friends and former associates who remained in the service of the new regime but did not lose their humanity in the process. His name, appearing repeatedly on arrest lists, was quietly overlooked or removed. He was warned about impending SA raids and, during periods of extreme crisis, sheltered by friends in their homes. He had not joined the resistance, although he was asked to participate in the forming of a new government in the event of a successful coup, an offer he declined. The groups who had joined to purge Hitler were the same, Severing felt, as had originally helped him to power—the military and the conservative nationalists. He strongly objected, for example, to the name of Schacht on the list of people who were to compose the projected new government, but above all he disliked the idea of a military coup, because he had no faith in the political acumen of generals.

Severing and I became good friends. His vitality and optimism buoyed my spirits. He was like a long-overdue antidote to the prevalent mood of gloom. While most of my other guests nursed their despair, Severing's mind and energies, despite his age, were already turned toward reconstruction. The Social Democratic party was beginning to emerge from its long political exile, and Severing was fully involved in the efforts to rebuild it. He was always busy, mostly with correspondence. Occasionally I helped him. He had little patience with people like Scheidt who allowed themselves to be immobilized by their depression.

"Despair is a luxury and a waste of energy," he once told me. "I've learned long ago that I can't afford it."

I learned it, too, not least from his example. Often in the months and years ahead I leaned on the memory of that remarkable old man.

18

*S*PRING, always welcome, was doubly so that year. For the Germans in the shattered cities it meant relief at last from the misery of a heatless winter; for my children it meant leaving behind their cramped quarters and restricted life at the witness house for long hours of freedom on the greening heath. This happened just in time, because March and April turned out to be increasingly busy months, with both houses frequently filled to capacity. For the most part the new guests stayed only briefly. They were chiefly technical experts who either filed affidavits or interpreted data in German documents that were to be introduced as evidence. A few testified in court, such as several former directors of the Reichsbank who had been called as defense witnesses for Dr. Schacht.

But we were also accumulating a few more long-term occupants, among them a Vice-Admiral Lohmann, who could recite in detail, so it seemed, the vital statistics of every ship ever built in the German navy, and a Dr. Skubl, whose recitations were decidedly more poetic than the admiral's—he was a practicing poet as well as a former police chief, a combination which probably could happen only in Vienna. Diminutive, his marvelously expressive face dominated by a large downward curve of nose and two emphatic curves of shaggy gray brows moving in a choreography of accents with his recitations, our poetic police chief soon replaced Hoffmann as the star attraction at our after-dinner gatherings. Dr. Skubl's poetry was quite good—lyrical, with a gentle touch of irony. Although sometimes it would stray into the sentimental, it was a welcome relief after a steady diet of "Tales of Hoffmann," magic tricks, and Fraulein Ross's—yes, she was still with us—graphic portrayal of "the rape of Berlin." (More than a month after her arrival in Nuremberg, the army bureaucracy was evidently still trying to unravel the mystery of her presence here.)

But if Hoffmann gave up the spotlight, it was never willingly. Trying to regain it, if only for a moment, he managed on the first night of Dr. Skubl's debut as our poet laureate to insult him with a compliment. Skubl's poetry, Hoffmann said, reminded him of his son-in-law's, Baldur von Schirach. Unfortunately, Schirach, who had once published a volume of romantic poems, was not only known as a terrible poet, but had been Gauleiter of Vienna as well, two factors which would make him hardly popular with an Austrian poet-patriot who had spent the past seven years in the "protective" custody of the Gestapo. Dr. Skubl's reaction to Hoffmann's faux pas (one was never sure whether Hoffmann knew what he was doing) was a strained smile and a curtailed performance. Severing tried to save the situation by quickly commenting that he heard echoes of Hofmannsthal in Skubl's poetry, a genuine compliment which restored the offended poet's smile to graciousness.

Another new guest, a fragile-looking, sad-eyed lady, often appeared to be on the verge of tears, but, I suspected, not in response to Dr. Skubl's poetry. Luise Funk was the wife of the former Economics Minister and Reichsbank president, Dr. Walter Funk, who in 1937 succeeded Schacht as head of the German economy and was currently (with Schacht) one of the defendants in Nuremberg. Frau Funk looked dazed; she seemed unable to understand what was happening to her. Like several other defendants' wives, she had been briefly imprisoned. She complained a great deal about headaches, insomnia, indigestion, and unjust charges against her husband. It was interesting that attacks on her husband's character and appearance seemed to upset her even more than the charges in the indictment "which could be countered." Causing her particular bitterness and pain was a description of her husband as a "notorious homosexual" in a book just published in Switzerland by Hans Bernd Gisevius, a member of the German resistance who was soon to be himself a guest at the witness house. "How is it possible that people are permitted to write such things?" she asked me indignantly. I remembered the similar outrage of my guests when Gaston Oulman, the radio commentator, had attacked Lahousen's appearance. This sensitivity to personal humiliation seemed to be a common attribute, emanating from the stripped uniforms and second-hand clothing, the loss of title and position, the enforced dependency. Because they were thrown back on their naked selves, an attack on character or appearance became an attack on the last outpost of their lives.

I tried to feel sympathetic toward Frau Funk but found it difficult. She reminded me of a troublesome patient in a hospital who, having no greater illness or pain than anyone else, was still convinced that her suffering exceeded that of all others. Not that her distress wasn't real—after all, her husband was on trial for his life—but it seemed to be experienced in isolation, as if there were no shattered world around us, no trauma of gas ovens and mass graves. Perhaps it was natural not wanting to face such horrors, especially when one's husband stood accused of participation in their commitment. It could not have been easy to be the wife of a Nuremberg defendant. In addition to the ordinary hardships of survival, which were in themselves considerable, these women had to face the hate and contempt directed at them from both the victors and their own embittered countrymen, for whom the wives and next of kin too often became scapegoats.

Nevertheless, my feelings toward Frau Funk remained ambivalent. I could not help but compare her to Frau Jodl, who seemed to have turned the measure of her unhappiness into a determination to help her husband's defense, taking personal abuse and hardship in stride. When Frau Funk left after a stay of less than a week, I was not sorry to see her go. Her self-indulgent suffering had been distinctly irritating.

There were several other departures around the same time which caused me quite the opposite reaction. Our literary evenings broke off when both Skubl and Severing were informed by the court that they would not be needed in the immediate future and were advised to return home until further notice. I had grown fond of both men, and our farewells were warm and a little sad. But another goodbye a few days later was to be infinitely harder. Scheidt, who except for one short period had been with us since November, left permanently in early April. Many of my guests had taken from me their toll of emotional energy, but none more so than Scheidt. There was little said in our parting. I was glad that we were not alone. Still, his face, expressing a mixture of bitterness, sorrow, and affection, told me all that remained unsaid. My feelings, too, were painful and uncertain. I had behaved correctly, but was there enough kindness in that? I had never been really sure of my own true response to his great need for solace and affection. He left me with a sense of failure.

Diels remained behind, as well as Hoffmann, the admiral, and Fraulein Ross, who still occasionally searched her memory for some forgotten friend or relative whose position or actions might provide the link for her presence in Nuremberg. If she had forgotten the person in question, she worried, how would she be able to testify about him or her? We managed to restore her peace of mind by convincing her that lapse of memory was no crime.

If Fraulein Ross and many of my other guests worried too much, I had never seen so much as a ripple in Hoffmann's peace of mind. I could not remember his showing any particular concern about anything, his son-in-law's trial and eventual fate or his daughter's imprisonment, though in the latter case he had expressed great delight at the news of her release. But, as I was soon to discover, even Hoffmann had a weak spot in his psyche.

I had noticed that on occasion his normally white hair would suddenly turn blue. This was usually on evenings when he planned to visit the nearby inn, *Zum Stern*, which had become quite a gathering place for Germans connected with the war crimes trial. Frau Kruelle and I had made the parallel discovery of a noticeable decline in our laundry bluing, upon which circumstantial evidence we decided that Hoffmann had a girl friend for whom he was trying to glamorize himself.

We never met the girl friend, if there was one, but we did meet Frau Hoffmann, who arrived one fine spring day in a large car driven by a handsome civilian. Though Hoffmann had mentioned that his wife planned to visit him and that he had received permission to have her stay with him, her arrival was a surprise, but she was even more so. Some twenty years younger than her husband, with a shapely figure, dark brown hair, and a pretty, doll-like face, she was hardly the kind of wife one expected alongside a man nearing seventy, although her lively, gay personality was well matched to his. They appeared to have only one real difference. Frau Hoffmann did not share her husband's loyalty or love for his late friend Hitler. She had never joined the party, she told me, and had tried to curb Hoffmann's enthusiasm, but to no avail. Her regrets did not appear, however, to be a matter of conscience. The Hoffmanns owned a considerable amount of property, among other holdings a lovely estate in Bavaria which she now feared she would lose, merely, she said, because she was the wife of

Heinrich Hoffmann. Still, she was proud both to be the step-mother (Hoffmann's first wife had died) of Henrietta von Schirach and of the latter's marriage to the handsome youth leader. "A magnificent couple. Have you ever met my daughter?" When I answered in the negative, she assured me that I would soon have the privilege, since Henrietta would also be in Nuremberg in the near future, to be near her husband and visit with her father.

Frau Hoffmann managed to accomplish in one day what Frau Kruelle had been unable to do in six months—tidy up Hoffmann's room. She also darned his socks, sewed on his buttons, and took in his wraparound pants. ("Would you believe it, they once fit him?") Since she could not eat with us, she dined on a variety of exotic delicacies of which she seemed to have an abundance—sardines and corned beef, chocolate and cookies.

On the second day of her stay with us the handsome civilian who had brought her came to call on her and invited her to come for a ride, a matter which seemed to cause Hoffmann more pride than distress, because at dinner he spoke of nothing else but his wife's useful contact with this gentleman of undetermined nationality, who appeared, however, to have some connection with the military government. It was he who had helped spirit Frau Hoffmann out of Austria, saving her the hardship of being processed by hostile Austrian authorities and returned to Germany with the usual overcrowded refugee transport. What rated with Hoffmann was his wife's finesse, just about equal to his own, in escaping the deprivations common to the time. He appraised her skill like a fine art, and perhaps it was.

Frau Hoffmann appeared to have returned quite late from her sojourn with the handsome foreigner, for she was still wearing her street dress when she knocked on my door well past midnight. She spoke with extreme agitation.

"Please come . . . something has happened . . . my husband . . ." She broke off, stifling a sob.

173

Grabbing my robe, I followed her. Hoffmann was on the floor beside the bed, his face blue and distorted. Wrapped around his neck and fastened to the bedpost was a narrow leather belt; on the table stood an empty bottle of cognac.

"A knife . . . scissors . . ." I hissed, somehow remembering to keep my voice down. Avoiding trouble, running things smoothly had almost become a reflex with me. Frau Hoffmann sobbed quietly and fumbled in a drawer. "Hurry!"

She had found a pair of scissors, but she was trembling so hard she could barely hand them to me. I felt nauseated and my hands were trembling, too, when I put the scissors to the belt which, fortunately, was well worn and therefore rather soft. Still, at that moment the scissors seemed incredibly dull and the leather incredibly tough. When I had finally managed to make an incision, the belt broke under Hoffmann's weight and he slumped sideways against the door. We tried to lift him on to the bed, but finally gave up and settled for stretching him out on the floor with a pillow under his head. His breath gained strength in uneven gasps, rattling and rasping in broken rhythms like the sound of an engine on the verge of breaking down. I checked his pulse; it was weak but seemed to be holding steady.

"Perhaps he should have a doctor," I said, though I was by no means anxious to have to call the courthouse.

"No," she said urgently. "He seems all right now. It would make a lot of trouble."

"Perhaps we could avoid telling what he did. . . ." But we were both looking at the ugly depression of bluish red that marked Hoffmann's neck like a collar where the belt had been.

"He'll be all right," Frau Hoffmann said again, much calmer now. "I don't know what got into him. He had a little too much to drink, as you can see. The cognac was a gift from my friend. He had almost finished it when I came home. Then he started to complain about how late it was and worked himself up into some sort of jealousy fit. He was talking such abusive nonsense —he'd never done anything like this before—I just left him

174

and went to the bathroom. When I came back, I found him, you know how . . ."

Hoffmann's breathing had become steady, if still noisy. He had also begun to snore. I was fairly sure now that the worst he would end up with was a hangover. When I got up to leave, Frau Hoffmann stretched out her hand imploringly. "Please . . . stay awhile . . . I don't want to be alone with him." The tension and late hour made her look older, exposing lines and shadows on her face, but it was still a doll's face, the summary of its age in surface cracks and fading color. I stayed with her until dawn, listening to melancholy reminiscences and Hoffmann's snoring. When I finally went to bed, the birds were chirping loudly outside my window, drowning out the echo of this sordid night.

19

"You look as though you've had a rough night" was Diels's uncomplimentary greeting when I brought him his breakfast. I hadn't spent much time before the mirror that morning, and if I looked as bad as I felt I should have been quite a sight indeed.

"I had a toothache," I said, which was only half a lie, since my teeth, as a common consequence of dietary deficiencies, had been giving me a good bit of trouble lately.

"I'm sorry you're bothered again," Diels said. "But I don't believe you're the only one who had a bad night. You should have heard the commotion next door."

I thought we had been quiet and had hoped that Diels, who was the only one else on that floor, had slept through whatever noise there was. Obviously I had been wrong.

"Frau Hoffmann told me that her husband was sick last night. I don't believe he is going to the courthouse today."

176

Diels nodded with an ironic smile. "I'd like a bottle of Hoffmann's sickness. I wouldn't even mind the hangover."

I was relieved that Diels presumed to have found the answer. No one, it occurred to me, would ever suspect what really happened. Indeed, if I hadn't seen it myself, I would not have believed that Hoffmann had actually tried to kill himself. The irony of it struck me only now. How often had I worried about possible suicide attempts by such people as Haushofer, Lahousen, and Scheidt, but the idea of Hoffmann ever choosing such a course of action would have struck me as ludicrous, and somehow it still did, even after the fact. Had it been merely an act of drunken lunacy? Now I remembered his exhausted face as he slept, laboring to breathe. The initial distortion caused by the strangulation was gone, but he had still looked altered. As if liberated by his drunkenness, new sensibilities had revealed themselves in his face. The joker had turned solemn; beneath the dead grin lived bitterness and disgust.

"On second thought, it must be quite depressing to get drunk like that, all alone."

"I don't know. I haven't tried it."

He laughed. "I wouldn't recommend it to a lady, though it might cure your toothache."

"With a hangover."

"Leave the hangovers to Hoffmann. But you ought to come to one of the gatherings at the Faber-Castells'. They're really quite pleasant. It would give you a change of scenery. I assure you, it does wonders for one's perspective."

He spoke no doubt from personal experience. There had been some drastic changes in the manner of his internment. Although he was ostensibly still under room arrest, he now spent very little time in his room. Most often he was picked up early in the day, always by the same CIC officer, the one who had brought him. They usually drove to the nearby castle of Count Faber-Castell, the pencil magnate, which had become a gathering place for people attached to the military tribunal from both the allied and the German side. I was not sure

177

whether or not the castle or parts of it had been requisitioned, since the family of the count still lived there and often played host to parties of quite diverse composition. Not infrequently Diels stayed at the Faber-Castells' overnight. When he was home he still took his meals alone, but to my great relief, his door remained unlocked.

"You know that you have a standing invitation," Diels said. "Remember, even you need a night out once in a while."

A night out was the last thing on my mind right then; a good night's sleep would have sounded a lot more enticing. The standing invitation he had referred to came from the Countess Faber-Castell, who occasionally visited Diels when the latter was not visiting the castle. An elegant and very attractive blonde whom Diels described as a good friend, she would drop in during the mornings to hold prolonged tête-à-têtes with my erstwhile prisoner. This morning, however, it seemed to be Diels's turn to do the honors, which meant that he would be out probably till dinnertime, or perhaps overnight, a fact for which I had reason to be grateful.

The new guest who arrived in the evening introduced himself as Dr. Gisevius. He seemed to be in his early forties, rather tall and exceedingly self-assured. His clothes and bearing suggested that he came from abroad; he did not share the look of defeat. But Hans Bernd Gisevius was German. His name was familiar to me because his book, *To the Bitter End* (in which, Frau Funk had alleged, he had slandered her husband), had just been published in Switzerland and had attracted widespread attention in the press. Gisevius had started his career in the Gestapo. Later he had become a member of Admiral Canaris's *Abwehr,* the heart of the German resistance, the story of which was told in his book. But if "the bitter end" had left its mark on most German faces, it appeared to have given Gisevius only the title for his book. There was in his self-assurance a distinct note of arrogance. He had come from Switzerland where he had fled after the failure of the July 1944 coup on Hitler, and he left no doubt in anyone's mind that he was annoyed at having been called back to Germany as a witness.

I was just about to show my new guest to a room in the other house when Frau Kruelle came from the kitchen to ask me whether I expected Dr. Diels back for dinner. I noticed that Gisevius gave a start. When I looked at him his face was suddenly altered with hate. He almost growled, "Goering's lackey?"

Frau Kruelle gave me an unhappy look and retreated to the kitchen.

"Dr. Diels is staying with us," I said in a noncommittal tone.

"How nice for Dr. Diels," Gisevius said icily. "Couldn't they find a vacant jail cell for him?"

"May I show you your room?" I asked, anxious to change the subject and to get Gisevius out of the house before he would run into Diels who might return at any time.

"Is Dr. Diels on this floor?" Gisevius asked when I took him upstairs in the other house.

"No. He lives in the main house."

He sat down on the bed. "Has he been here long?"

"Fairly long."

He shook his head. "Incredible. And what do you think of the founding father of the Gestapo?" he asked a moment later. "Or didn't you know?"

"I know."

"I'll finish that man once and for all. I'll finish him," he said more to himself than to me.

As I turned to go, he asked me to wait for a minute. He lifted his suitcase onto the bed and rummaged through it until he found a copy of his book. "In case you're interested in Dr. Diels's career you might find this fascinating."

"May I keep it?"

"Certainly. I won't be here long enough for you to finish it—at least I hope I won't."

"It sometimes takes more time than people anticipate."

He nodded. "I won't object too much if I can be of help to my old friend Schacht—and perhaps put Diels where he belongs. Curious practice, isn't it, that indicts a man like Schacht for war crimes and permits the likes of Diels to walk about freely and live in comfort?"

"He's not exactly free," I said lamely, as if I were responsible for Diels's advantageous life-style.

But Gisevius went on as if he hadn't heard me. "Schacht worked against the regime. He spent time in a concentration camp, and now they put *him* on *trial.*"

"Diels was in prison, too. I believe he was arrested in '44 on Himmler's orders," I said, wondering a moment later why I felt obliged to defend him. There was something in Gisevius's manner that made me feel resentful. He seemed too convinced of his own virtue. I did not like Diels's self-righteousness any better, but I knew that it was an expression of his self-doubt.

"Too bad his old Gestapo friends didn't finish him off," Gisevius said. "But of course they only killed the wrong people."

I wondered if that referred to Dr. Schacht, too, but said nothing.

After thanking him for the book, I told him that dinner was about to be served, and returned to the main house, glad that there was at least no chance for the two men to meet at the dinner table. I had often been exasperated by the curious arrangements concerning Diels. If he could have visitors and go to parties, it seemed absurd that his meals had to be brought to him. Today, though, I was more than grateful for the arrangement. There was still a chance that he could run into Gisevius on the street or in the downstairs hall. I could do little to prevent such a chance meeting, but once Diels was back in his room I resolved to warn him and thus help avoid a confrontation.

In the hall I met Hoffmann. He was wearing a scarf tucked into his shirt collar, but except for the dark circles under his eyes, his face revealed nothing of the night before. The joker was again in control.

"I guess I overdid it a bit last night," he said with an apologetic grin." "Haven't had a cognac like that in years."

I wondered whether he knew or remembered what he had

180

done, or if he didn't, whether his wife had told him. He made no mention of it then or later, and neither did I.

"How do you feel now?" I asked.

"Oh, fine, fine . . . thank you . . . I'm hungry."

My son Farkas was standing by the living room doorway, and Hoffmann turned to ruffle his hair as he passed. Then, as if on a sudden impulse, Hoffmann grabbed his big black umbrella hanging on the coat rack.

"Come on, Farkas, let's have a parade!" he cried and began to march around the hall, imitating a trombone with the umbrella. Farkas dashed into the kitchen and returned with two pot lids which he turned into cymbals. As my other children ran in to join in the commotion, I sat down on the stairs and held my ears shut, while Frau Kruelle, the cook, Cuci, and several guests watched with expressions ranging from annoyance to amusement. Antal, my younger son, evidently not wishing to be outdone by his brother, pulled Cuci's umbrella from the coat rack and imitated Hoffmann. A moment later he decided to open the umbrella and waved it up and down as he marched.

When Hoffmann caught sight of the open umbrella, he cried out, "Don't! Shut that thing, shut it!" and fled up the stairs, almost stepping on me in his haste. His face expressed real panic. Upstairs his door slammed shut.

The children looked puzzled and disappointed; the onlookers dispersed, shaking their heads. I went upstairs and knocked on Hoffmann's door. It was a while before he answered. He was alone, his wife having gone out in the afternoon (by herself this time). His face wore the expression I had seen on it the night before. His eyes had a vacant look.

"Are you all right?" I asked.

He nodded and sat down on the bed. "I suppose you think I'm pretty silly."

"I think you're pretty superstitious."

"It's the actor in me. You know, rabbit's feet, and that sort of thing."

Gradually his expression returned to normal, his smile

181

flickering on and off like a lamp on a loose connection. "My nerves are a bit on edge yet from last night."

"A good night's sleep and you'll be your old self again."

He nodded, eager to accept the reassurance. How odd, I thought, that I should be trying to cheer up Hoffmann.

"What I need is a good dinner," he said. "There's nothing more depressing than an empty stomach."

At table he did seem back to normal, treating the matter as a joke. The curious interlude had made me forget my fears concerning a chance meeting between Diels and Gisevius, until the latter's rather solemn face reminded me. Diels had not yet returned. There remained a chance that if Gisevius joined the usual after-dinner gathering in the living room, he would see Diels come home. I was still debating how to avoid this when I heard a key being turned in the front door. I jumped up too abruptly, catching a suspicious glance from Gisevius as I excused myself.

It was Diels.

"Am I too late for dinner?" he asked.

I almost pushed him up the stairs, which seemed to cause him considerable amusement. "I haven't been treated this roughly by a lady since the time I was being hidden from an unexpected husband."

Instead of an explanation I went to my room and got Gisevius's book.

"I thought I'd warn you that he's here. Frankly, I'd like to avoid any more clashes."

"I assure you that I wouldn't dignify him with an argument. How does he even know I'm here?"

"Your name was mentioned by chance."

Diels opened the book. "May I borrow it?"

"Yes."

If he had no intention of dignifying Gisevius with an argument, Diels nevertheless proceeded to give his undivided attention to his enemy's book in which he was already engrossed when I brought his dinner. He must have read most of the

182

night, because at breakfast the circles under his eyes were as large and as dark as mine and Hoffmann's the night before. He looked rumpled and was unshaven. I wondered whether he had slept at all.

"It looks as though this time you're the one who had the rough night."

He looked at me grimly. "It isn't every day that one finds oneself so hideously slandered."

"You've finished the book?"

"No. But you can have it back. I've made some notes in the margins. I hope you don't mind."

For the next few days I spent whatever time I could spare reading Gisevius's book. The author himself, to my considerable relief, had been transferred to different quarters the morning after his arrival. In many ways, I found, the book resembled his personality, self-assured and self-important, dogmatic in its assertions. It was also fascinating, full of strong hates and equally strong loyalties, tracing the tangled lines of countless intrigues and conspiracies that made up the ill-fated history of the German resistance. Diels had good reason to be upset, for he was accused by Gisevius of everything from blackmail to fraud and murder. The charge that most outraged Diels was his alleged complicity in the SA's reign of terror immediately following Hitler's assumption of power, a charge which Diels not only vigorously denied, but of which he was later exonerated.

A case in point to illustrate the murky and sinister nature of the controversy between the two men was the issue of "protective custody," which meant arrest without warrant of persons who were politically suspect. Gisevius charged that Diels had used this manner of detention to facilitate SA access to political prisoners who were then invariably murdered. Diels claimed to have used protective custody for exactly the opposite reasons—namely, to protect potential SA victims, who more often than not were dragged out of their homes, kidnapped off the streets, and not infrequently seized in armed raids on police jails. Quite often, so Diels told me, potential victims requested to be put under protective police custody to escape the SA.

Many events during the first year of the regime—a year often referred to as "The Second Revolution"—support Diels's contention of an ongoing struggle between the regular police forces and the revolutionary SA. Not least among these events were Diels's police raids on SA bunkers and concentration camps, his successful realization of a Christmas amnesty for political prisoners, and a number of criminal proceedings he initiated against individual SA members. Even if Diels's record of involvement in this bloody period is by no means entirely clear, from what I can gather, he was not so odious a figure as Gisevius painted in his book. But then the mutual antagonism of the two men appeared to have its origin less in the issue of Diels's alleged misdeeds than in a larger conflict of which both became a part. Diels had briefly been Gisevius's superior in the early Gestapo. In the power struggle between Goering and Himmler for control of the Prussian police, Gisevius and Diels had been on opposite sides, which does not mean that Gisevius either was, or became, a loyal follower of Himmler. In 1933 this sinister little man with the pince-nez had not yet attained his later fame, even as the Gestapo had yet to earn its reputation. Instead, Gisevius's course of action appears to have been dictated by an acute dislike for Goering, whom he blamed, with probable justification, for the Reichstag fire, and Diels, whom he blamed (among a lot of other things) for having helped to cover up the crime. A conservative nationalist who claimed to have lost faith in the regime almost immediately— and this seems to be borne out by his record—Gisevius evidently felt that any change in the agency he was working for would have to be a change for the better. The change, of course, did come about, though hardly for the better. By that time, though, neither Gisevius nor Diels was any longer with the Gestapo.

Gisevius had held a number of other government positions, evidently using all of them as a cover for his resistance activity.

In time he became a member of the *Abwehr* circle around Canaris and General Oster, under whose auspices he contacted Allen Dulles of the OSS in Switzerland to inform him of the plans of the German resistance.

In between my own reading sessions I lent Gisevius's book to Diels so that he could finish it. The notes in the margins were profuse, especially in the early chapters. Such comments as "outrageous, false, ridiculous," as well as numerous exclamation and question marks abounded. But Diels wasn't doing all his writing in the margins; he was also making copious notes on a pad. When I asked him whether he intended to write a rebuttal, he looked mysterious and said "perhaps." Later I learned that a manuscript belonging to Diels had been confiscated in Switzerland by the British War Crimes Division of the Nuremberg tribunal. He never talked to me about this, nor about another manuscript he still had hidden in the garden of his home and which eventually was also found and confiscated by the occupiers. Perhaps he did not trust my ability to keep such secrets from the CIC, which would have been, much as I detested being pumped for information, a fairly reasonable assumption. He did ask me, though, to keep for him the voluminous notes he had made in his room, which I was ready to do if for no other reason than curiosity, being quite unaware at the time of their evident interest to the Allied authorities. As it was, the manuscript was still in his room when he was picked up unexpectedly, and it was promptly confiscated.

Diels finally managed to get into print in 1950, using a lot less space to denounce Gisevius than the latter had used on him. Whether his reason was that he would not "dignify" Gisevius with a count-by-count rebuttal, or whether he had none for some of the charges, I do not know. What I did know after I finished Gisevius's book was that my strenuous efforts to prevent a meeting between the two antagonists had been more than justified.

20

GISEVIUS TESTIFIED in late April, creating the expected sensation. Among my guests, reactions varied considerably, with two of the most interested spectators at opposite ends of the spectrum. Like other defense witnesses before him, Gisevius turned out instead to be quite a star for the prosecution, inflicting particular damage on Goering, Keitel, and other members of the General Staff. As he had promised, he did not forget Diels. I don't know whether he "finished" Diels, but he seemed to be trying his best. Needless to say, Diels was in a dark mood. He tried to divert himself with a collection of mosses he had begun to cultivate in a planter on his balcony. Horticulture was his hobby, and he was fond of giving Frau Kruelle unsolicited tips on her garden now that spring was here. He studied the mosses with a magnifying glass and, equally unsolicited, lectured me repeatedly and in great detail on their structures.

On Elizabeth Struenck, who joined us briefly around that

time, Gisevius's testimony had quite a different effect. Small, frail, and for the most part silent, she listened with great intensity and absorption to the radio reports. At the mention of certain names she bowed her head and looked at the clenched fists in her lap. The names belonged to the dead of the German opposition, one of whom was her husband.

Both Struencks had belonged to the *Abwehr* circle of the resistance, their Berlin apartment serving as a frequent meeting place. In early 1943, however, the Gestapo had begun closing in on some of the conspirators. The *Abwehr* was reorganized, and both Admiral Canaris, its commander, and General Oster, his Chief of Staff, were relieved of their posts. Gisevius, threatened with arrest, escaped to Switzerland, where he stayed in contact with the new commander of the greatly diminished *Abwehr,* who turned out, however, to be as staunch an oppositionist as his predecessors. The courier between Berlin and Gisevius, who was then establishing contact with Allen Dulles, was Theodor Struenck. In the summer of 1944 Gisevius returned clandestinely to Germany for the planned coup, and after its failure he fled Berlin with the Struencks. Only he had reached the safety of Switzerland. Struenck died on the gallows; his wife spent months in Gestapo custody, escaping death only because time ran out for the oppressors.

Compared to Frau Struenck's silence, Diels's protests against Gisevius's alleged slander, justified though they might have been, had for me an increasingly irritating quality. In fairness to Diels it must be said that there was no one then except himself to refute Gisevius's charges, and since I had no way of knowing whether they were true or false, they did make me feel uneasy in his company. But that was not the only reason for my irritation. I could not help comparing Diels and Gisevius, Diels and the Struencks. For all his overriding self-assurance and possible self-aggrandizement, Gisevius had actively fought the regime. The claim so often made by Diels (curious at best for a man who had been a relative and protégé of Goering) that he had remained in government service to

187

fight the regime from within was put to shame by people like Lahousen and Gisevius and all the dead members of the resistance who had done the same, but turned what sounded like a pretext, or at best a rearguard action with minimum risk, into a front-line position that cost most of them their lives.

Something else, not directly related to Diels, intensified my feelings in the matter. In the middle of April, Rudolf Hoess, the former commandant of Auschwitz, testified before the war crimes tribunal. We had seen the pictures and read the statistics, but there was another dimension in the quiet recital of that colorless little man who seemed to have been miscast in his role as monster: he narrowed the limits of possible perspectives on the immediate past. Not that Diels had had anything to do with Auschwitz—he certainly had not; but Hoess, who had, did not suffice, nor did the upward chain of command. The monstrosity of Auschwitz loomed like a culmination above all that had occurred in those last dozen years, and transcended all mitigating considerations. Whatever common failings and stupidities had once combined to build Hitler's hellish empire, their combined toll rendered worthless the value of intent. The mystery of collective guilt lay in that, in the lethal sum of petty biases and concerns, and acts neither venal nor virtuous.

There was little discussion about the Hoess testimony; its impact was paralyzing. The gatekeeper of Hell had delivered his report and then told us that he had been in our employ. The fact of his being was at once absolute and incomprehensible, like a vision from the apocalypse.

It was a different matter when Gisevius took the stand. Measurable by mortal standards, his charges and assertions became the subject of considerable controversy. His accuracy in regard to certain events was being questioned, as was his own role in some of these events, as well as his connection with American intelligence. To some people his portrayal of Schacht as an oppositionist came as a surprise, Schacht having been known as one of Hitler's earliest and most ardent supporters. Even more eyebrows were raised at the naming of a high Gestapo official, Arthur Nebe, as an important resistance fighter. Nebe, chief of the German Criminal Police, had indeed died on the Gestapo gallows following the July attempt on Hitler (ironically, he had headed the criminal investigation of the coup before his own involvement was discovered); but at least some of my guests also remembered Nebe as the commander of an *Einsatzgruppe* in occupied Russia, engaged, as were all other of these notorious units, in the systematic destruction of Jews. Diels especially challenged Gisevius's portrayal of Nebe, whom he knew from his own Gestapo days and whom he accused of having collaborated, with Gisevius's help, with Himmler and Heydrich in the battle over control of the secret police.

Diels's neighbor, Hoffmann, got no small pleasure out of the former's discomfiture over Gisevius's charges. Now that the weather was nice he had even more reason to envy Diels his room, which had a balcony, and when the former Gestapo chief watered his mosses, Hoffmann would occasionally stick his head out of his window and heckle Diels with mock sympathy. He berated Gisevius's "slander" and its possible consequences for Diels, since no one would believe a former boss of the Gestapo and personal friend, even relative, of Goering, against a real live celebrity from the resistance. He, Hoffmann, was in a similar position, he said; because of his friendship with Hitler everyone automatically assumed that he was aware of everything that had happened in and outside Germany, when Hitler himself hadn't known half the things they were bringing up at this trial. Diels's response was to schedule his watering chores during Hoffmann's work hours.

But Hoffmann was in any case soon diverted by an eagerly anticipated event, his daughter's arrival in Nuremberg. Henrietta von Schirach lived up to her father's and stepmother's description: an exceedingly attractive young woman with a fine figure, a soft, rather round face, and thick, dark brown hair that glowed with reddish highlights. Her appearance gained an aura of fragility through the pastels she chose for her dresses

189

—I never saw her wear any strong colors—and the softness of her voice. Her elegance and poise could not conceal her agitation, which broke beyond containment in her eyes and hands; her hands especially seemed never still, brushing aside a strand of hair, twisting a glove or the handle of a purse. But if in personality she differed considerably from her parents, she was, excepting her brief period of internment, equally successful in circumventing the deprivations and physical hardships of postwar life. While her husband sat in the prisoners' dock to be judged by the victors, she was amply provided with all the amenities the victors had to offer, and during her brief but frequent visits to her father—an American officer would usually wait for her outside in a car—she rarely came without a gift of cigarettes or liquor. All the Hoffmanns, it seemed, had a talent for making "the right connections"; but surely their greatest accomplishment was that their "wrong connections" never interfered with their "right" ones.

That was hardly the case for most other people. Luise Funk came to my mind. All the wrong connections were catching up with her husband, such as the SS vaults in the Reichsbank stuffed with booty from death camp victims—cash and jewelry and the gold from their teeth. When the vaults had threatened to burst, much of the jewelry was disposed of through state-owned stores. Dr. Funk denied, the prosecution affirmed with documents and affidavits. Frau Funk had also submitted an affidavit for her husband. He had angrily protested to Goebbels, she wrote, about the events of the *Krystall Nacht*, the "Night of Crystal," November 9, 1938, when synagogues had burned and shop windows had been broken all over Germany in violent anti-Jewish demonstrations, organized in response to the murder by a Jew of a German embassy secretary in Paris. Frau Funk was loyal to her husband; her husband had been loyal to his *Fuehrer*. He had protested in 1938; but the vaults of the Reichsbank were filled with the loot from Auschwitz and Treblinka. Dr. Funk said he had not known about the death camps. I wondered whether Frau Funk had done her

190

Christmas shopping in the stores handling the SS loot. How many such fiendish connections? Little girls smiling in Christmas joy at lockets torn from the necks of murdered children. . . . Was there guilt in that?

The trial inched through May and June. On the heath the nightingales courted so loudly that they kept me awake at night; in the witness houses things got so busy that I could barely catch my breath during the day. Of the long-term occupants Fraulein Ross had finally departed as mysteriously as she had arrived, being none the wiser as to the reason for her Nuremberg sojourn. But the admiral was still with us, holding numerous conferences with the attorneys for Raeder. From among the old acquaintances Severing returned in May, Skubl in June. A Fraulein Krueger, who had been a secretary to Martin Bormann, stayed with us briefly. She was young, pretty, and in excellent spirits. With the court she filed an affidavit that Bormann, who was being tried in absentia, was dead. She herself had been present in the bunker under the Reich chancellery when the Russians had entered Berlin. Bormann, she claimed, had been killed while fleeing the bunker. Hoffmann, who hated Bormann (it was Bormann who had told Hitler that Hoffmann had typhus to keep him away from the *Fuehrer*), tried to draw her out about certain of her former boss's actions and his relationship with Hitler, but Fraulein Krueger, though always friendly, was most unresponsive. The one topic of conversation she avoided was her erstwhile employer.

"He's got her trained like a poodle" was Hoffmann's disgusted assessment of her. But he consoled himself with the thought that at least it hadn't been the *Fuehrer* who had played him the dirty trick.

"He did, you know, play tricks on people. You'd never believe what he did to Putzi Hanfstaengl. Did you know that Hanfstaengl was one of his oldest friends? He knew Hitler almost as long as I . . ."

I did know about Hanfstaengl. The son of a Munich art publisher, he had been one of Hitler's earliest and staunchest

191

supporters. As Hoffmann went on to relate the story, the trick Hitler had played on Hanfstaengl involved an alleged secret mission for which he had been "chosen." It was during the time of the Spanish Civil War. Hanfstaengl was told that a plane was waiting for him and was given sealed orders which he was instructed not to open until after he had been in the air for one hour. When the required time had passed and Hanfstaengl opened his "orders," he learned that he was being dropped behind the red lines in Spain with the instructions to establish "peace feelers" with the Communists. Some hours later the plane dropped Hanfstaengl in a dark meadow and immediately took off again. The poor fellow stumbled along in a dead fright until he came to a village that didn't look particularly Spanish. From an open window he heard voices speaking in German and realized that he had been the butt of a bad joke. Apparently he wasn't amused, because he left Germany never to return.

"I got in touch with him, trying to get him to change his mind about leaving Germany. After all, it was only a joke," Hoffmann said.

"I guess it didn't appeal to his sense of humor."

"He was lucky it wasn't worse. I think Goebbels had proposed to let him jump with a parachute."

"And you still think that's funny?"

"Well, Hitler vetoed that. What they did in the end was really quite harmless."

"That's a matter of opinion, to say the least."

Hoffmann shrugged. "Not everyone laughs at the same jokes. Didn't you ever play a trick on anyone?"

Hitler had been, of course, the master of tricks, most of them unfunny. One by one they were being unpacked at the trial, the audacities, the treacheries, the brutalities. There was little consolation in the fact that he had had some competition from Moscow. Two examples surfaced at the trial, the first over the strenuous objection of General Rudenko, the Russian prosecutor—namely, the secret agreement on the partition of

Poland which had been a part of the Nazi-Soviet nonaggression pact; the other was the massacre of Polish officers and soldiers at Katyn.

The secret protocol was brought to the court's attention in the form of an affidavit by a German diplomat which was, however, not admitted into evidence, presumably because of Russian pressure. It did nevertheless become a *cause célèbre* for the German defense and formed a substantial part in the testimony of one of my guests at the time, Baron Ernst von Weizsaecker, who had been First Secretary of the German Foreign Office and the last German ambassador to the Vatican. A seasoned diplomat, he had an obvious distaste for the minister and government he had served (Ribbentrop had tried to prevent his appearance as a witness), but like so many others, he *had* served. I could not help but wonder whether he had felt the same distaste when he had assisted in the division of Poland between the two stalking predators, or did the language of diplomacy soften such bloody realities? He seemed a decent, cultured man; he took a great liking to my children and wrote a line from Goethe's *Iphigenie* into my guest book. Even while he served the regime, he had cooperated with the resistance. Here, too, the pattern seemed to be endlessly repeated, service and opposition canceling each other out.

Weizsaecker had a curious reaction when he heard parts of his testimony on the evening broadcast. He turned pale and was visibly shaken. "It doesn't sound like me," he said. "I have the feeling that I'm listening to someone else."

Perhaps he wished that he were, for he was soon to go on trial himself on charges all too similar to the ones for which his despised former chief was shortly to hang.

The massacre at Katyn was one of the charges brought by the Soviet prosecution. Culpability was assigned to none of the major defendants specifically; instead the commander of a German regiment stationed in the area, a Colonel Ahrens, was charged with this atrocity involving the murder of approximately 11,000 Polish prisoners of war, the majority of whom

193

were officers. The bodies were discovered by members of Colonel Ahrens's regiment in 1943 when wolves dug open some of the graves. An investigation by an international team of experts, including members of neutral countries, was launched shortly after with great fanfare by the German government. The commission's findings, based on forensic examinations, clothing, diaries, and the ages of the trees planted on the graves, established that the men had been dead since the winter of 1940 when the area had still been under Russian control, not the summer of 1941, when the Germans had arrived. Even the Polish government-in-exile did not blame the Germans for this atrocity; nevertheless, the charges were brought in Nuremberg by the very people who, according to all available facts, had committed the crime.

To the Russians, Colonel Ahrens, who stayed with us during part of June, was a wanted war criminal; in the American zone he was no longer even a prisoner of war. An attractive, personable man with slightly graying hair, Ahrens spent a great deal of time playing with my children, while worrying about and longing for his own somewhere in the Russian zone. Because of the Russian charges against him, he feared greatly for the safety of his family.

Like so many of my other guests, Colonel Ahrens occasionally went to the *Stern* in the evening for companionship and beer. On one such occasion he noticed two men at a nearby table who appeared to be watching him. Since he had never seen them before, he unobtrusively asked the proprietor whether he knew them. Ahrens was told that the men were strangers and spoke with an accent, apparently Polish or Russian. The proprietor presumed them to be displaced persons, of whom thousands were still in Germany. Ahrens, taking no chances, decided to find out who they were. He took his hat, paid his bill, and walked out of the front door. Once outside, he ran quickly around the building, reentering it through the back door. The two strangers had also quickly paid their bills and left after Ahrens. Watching them through a window, the proprietor had seen them stand undecidedly for a while, looking about, until they finally walked away.

That night Ahrens returned to the witness house with a safety escort of half a dozen companions, not all of whom were billeted with us. He reported the incident to the American authorities and was requested not to leave the house again until after he had completed his testimony. It was during this period, too, that Russian jeeps began to cruise along our street. Sometimes they would stop before the house for a time with their motors racing. The purpose of these attempts to intimidate Ahrens has never been clear to me. Since it was the Russians who had brought the charges against Ahrens and his regiment, they could not logically have tried to prevent him from testifying. Did they expect through such pressure to change his testimony? Especially mysterious was the incident at the *Stern.* I suspected that the Russians wanted Ahrens, presumably to try him before a Russian military court; but any kidnap attempt would have made more sense after Ahrens's testimony than before, since the removal of a witness would immediately indicate that someone was afraid of what he might say.

"I don't really care to find out what they're trying to do," Ahrens said. "In fact, I hope I never do."

He prepared himself for his court appearance by drawing a map of Katyn forest, located not far from Smolensk. A small castle had been staff headquarters for his communications unit. He was careful to give an overview of the operational setup. His regiment had been a technical unit. They had never held any prisoners of war. As he absorbed himself in his work, the past returned. It had been a good unit, decent men. Many were dead now. They deserved a better memory than being saddled with the butchery of Katyn. He asked me to assist him in finishing his map by using my water colors to shade the various areas according to his directions. Green for the forest, blue for the river, amber for the little castle.

"The army was decent. But we're being blamed for what

the SS did, and the SD. The dirt is rubbing off. The army fought fair and clean."

Scheidt had said the same, and Kessler and Koestring and Rintelen. The soldiers had fought fair and clean and died bravely. Islands of decency. And the people had worked and starved and died in their shattered cities.

The massacre of Katyn did not belong on Colonel Ahrens's neat little map—green for the forest, blue for the river, amber for the little castle. They had not murdered the Polish prisoners that lay beneath the forest's green canopy. They had done their duty well and honorably while Hoess stoked the ovens of Auschwitz. They had not obeyed the *Commissar Order*. They had looked away while the legions of the Death's Head did their bloody job.

Colonal Ahrens gave his testimony and left the witness house. The massacre of Katyn was not mentioned again during the trial, nor did it appear anywhere in the final verdict. Within the long catalogue of crimes it was barely missed.

21

TOGETHER with the individual defendants, a number of organizations had also been named in the original indictment, among them the SA, SS, Gestapo, the OKW (High Command of the Wehrmacht), the General Staff, and certain ranks of party membership. Under a law of the Allied Control Council for Germany, membership in these organizations constituted a crime. In a country as rigidly controlled and organized as Nazi Germany had been, the implications were enormous, the possible interpretations confusing. The organizations were mass-based; the number of possible defendants ran into the hundreds of thousands. Often membership in the SS or the party had been the price for success in business or government service. Ribbentrop, for example, had summarily enrolled his entire Foreign Office in the SS, and such men as Weizsaecker had ended up as "decorative" SS members, inactive but with suitably high rank. In the early thirties membership in the SA had often meant the difference between a job and unemployment; barely a dozen years later it meant criminal indictment. As one weary veteran of the political wars confided in me, "First you join the KPD (Communist Party), and the SA gets after you; you join the SA, and the SS starts giving you trouble. I stopped joining, and now they're still trying to hang me."

The last was a considerable exaggeration. Although the law prescribed possible penalties up to death, no one was ever hanged for being merely a member of a criminal organization; tens of thousands were, however, eventually tried before military tribunals in the various zones, and later before German courts acting under military government authorization and direction.

In July of 1946, though, the defense had just begun to present its case in behalf of the organizations (a task, needless to say, of enormous difficulty), and for some weeks prior to that we were filled to the rafters. Not all the witnesses had belonged to the organizations that were on trial. They represented a variety of groups, from churches to defunct veterans' organizations. But we also had our share of small party functionaries, police officials, and SA leaders. Few if any of these people testified in court, but many were interrogated instead, or gave sworn depositions before officers of the tribunal commissioned for this purpose.

The states of mind of my latest guests varied according to their past and their prospects for the future. For some, defeat and occupation meant liberty and a grim satisfaction; for others, bewilderment and fear. There were an engineer and a farmer who had been at Dachau; a Communist from the Rhineland who had survived Hitler's horrors through silence, cunning, and his needed skill as a mechanic; a onetime *Obersturmfuehrer* of the mounted SA; an intimidated *Ortsbauernfuehrer* (a rural district party representative) who had not been allowed to change his muddy clothes or shoes when the Americans came to get him while he was hoeing his sugar beets, and who appeared to be more troubled by this flaw in his appearance than by his prospective interrogation. The church was represented by two Catholic priests, an official from the Lutheran Church, and several Jehovah's Witnesses. All of the latter had been in concentration camps, belonging to a sect that had suffered under Nazi persecution almost as atrociously as the Jews. A former Wehrmacht colonel who had prevented the SS executions of British prisoners taken by his unit and an ancient general who had commanded the Berlin garrison during the Spartacist uprisings in 1918 rounded out the company.

In the dining room we had added two tables to the large one we had, arranging them in horseshoe fashion. With our motley company assembled we looked rather like a parody of a state banquet. But the state was dead. Most of the company was preoccupied with postmortems. Over the corpse old conflicts flickered in glares exchanged across these tables set with the conqueror's bread. The general talked with veneration of Bismarck and the Kaiser and with wrath about Hitler's destruction of their work. The colonel nodded agreement, Hoffmann protested, and our lone Communist respectfully reminded the general that the Kaiser, too, had made and lost a war, which made the old man shout in a red rage about strikes, subversion, and the undefeated glory of the Imperial army. The SA leader in a curious switch of party lines came to the aid of the Communist (who did not seem to appreciate the support), declaring his distaste for the Kaiser's army in which he had served as a corporal, like his *Fuehrer*. He described the despotism of the officers and explained that he had been attracted to the SA by its "democratic structure."

"We too believed in socialism," he told the Communist with an earnest expression. The engineer from Dachau turned his pale, tense face to the earnest SA man and told him in a voice that was too quiet that he had been a socialist and that in 1934 the "democratic and socialistic SA" had first broken into his home, beaten him, and dragged him to one of their infamous bunkers. Hoffmann's remark that such incidents had been the reason for the *Fuehrer*'s severe punishment of the SA during the Roehm purge earned him a nasty glance from the SA leader. But Hoffmann seemed more interested in the Rhineland Communist, whose presence appeared to offend him. When he had seen the fellow's signature and affiliation in my guest book, he had said to me in a reproving tone, "That's going a bit far, don't you think?"

"For a man who drank with Molotov and Stalin, your reaction is rather strange."

"That's different," he had said. "That was on a different level."

Since Hoffmann's logic usually evaded me, I hadn't pursued the subject then; now I wished that I hadn't brought it up, because Hoffmann, undaunted by the SA leader's irate expression, proceeded to first agree with him on the socialistic aspirations of the SA which, he said, had been shared by Hitler, and then went on to tell the unhappy Communist, and whoever else cared to listen, the tale of his Moscow visit, not forgetting a description of his report to Hitler about Stalin, and the former's great admiration for the Russian dictator. The reaction was unexpected. The poor Communist merely winced, but a lady Jehovah's Witness set out to prove at length and with numerous quotes from the Scriptures that all these events of the immediate past had been prophesied in the Bible, that the end of the world was imminent, and that the Nuremberg war crimes trial was the prelude to the Last Judgment. This left even Hoffmann speechless and got us safely through coffee.

In the living room the company usually divided into two groups, with the old general who told stories of the Imperial army the focal point of one, and Hoffmann of the other. It occurred to me that perhaps I should make a similar division, but along political lines, in the dining room, and so break up the volatile horseshoe arrangement into compatible groups. It was something to think about.

Having no particular affinity with either group, the farmer who had been at Dachau preferred to sit by himself on the sidelines darning my children's socks, smiling now and then as he appeared to be listening with half an ear to the old general's tales. The farmer had requested the socks. He liked to darn, he said, because it calmed his nerves. Not that they appeared in need of calming. Unlike the engineer with his haunted, haggard look, the farmer had not been visibly marked by Dachau. His ruddy, ever smiling face seemed to know neither horror nor bitterness. I once ventured to ask him how he managed to be so cheerful after so terrible an experience.

"I was on a good block, and I did a lot of mending and such things for the guards," was all he said, nor did he ever tell me what had earned him his term at the concentration camp. It was obvious that he had found a way to survive the experience intact. Had it been luck, ingenuity, or collaboration? Either way, who was I to judge? No moral precept was ever more than a figure of speech, the unexacting habit of quiet times, until it had been lost or achieved in the crucible of such a trial, until the choice was burdened with sacrifice of life or conscience.

However the farmer had lived through Dachau, he was reluctant to talk about it; instead he was intent on savoring the food, the clean linen, the comforts of a bath or a chair in the sun. He insisted that the morning grapefruit juice was made from lemons since he had never heard of grapefruits, and he wanted to know what recipe we used to "bake" the cornflakes. His darns were little works of art, dense without irritating thickness, patterned of small, patient stitches.

"I shall have you declared indispensable," I said to him one evening, watching him thread a needle at arm's length.

He broke into a delighted smile. "It's always better to be indispensable than superfluous," he said. He drew an even web of stitches, the needle moving swiftly and expertly in his stubby, hairy, lightly freckled hands. The ragged edges grew smooth; slowly the tear was mending. Behind us the old general's listeners were laughing. I thought I had heard the story somewhere before. Was it one of the tales my father had told his *Stahlhelm* friends in the village inn? Over the wounds a web of scars, pain spun into tales of glory. Would this war produce

201

a crop of such stories to be told by some aging soldier in beer halls after parades? Why was it that so many men found the vitality of life only in the midst of death? But this war had been different. Or had it? The Wehrmacht colonel was applauding. He had a kind, weathered face, creased in the pattern of an easy smile. This morning I had heard him talk with an American major who had come to take him to the courthouse where the colonel was to be interrogated about the British prisoners he had saved from the SS. But the two men didn't talk about that. Their animated and genial conversation—the German spoke excellent English—revolved around the technical details of a particular operation in which they both, so they discovered with great delight, had participated on opposite sides. With fascination they listened to each other's descriptions of strategies, their faces expressing satisfaction or the kind of half-serious exasperation and disappointment people show sometimes when they have just realized that they made the wrong move in a game. It was clear that they liked each other ever more as they talked, and that they thought they had both played a good game. Later they would tell about this meeting to their friends and families with due admiration for each other's skill and sportsmanship, the way my father had talked about the French on the other side of the trenches with whom he had exchanged gifts of wine and cigarettes. The colonel had played with admirable sportsmanship. He had saved the British prisoners from the SS outlaws at great risk to himself.

"There is no question in my mind as to the criminality of the SS," he told me after his return from the courthouse. "The important thing is that the army's name is cleared."

Five new guests arrived in early July. The first thing that struck me about them was their frailty; they looked like convalescents from a long illness, fragile and brittle, with pale, translucent skin. This appearance of invalidism which they had in common did on first encounter blot out their individual characteristics. It was as if a common experience had equalized them, annulled their former identities, and turned them into reflections of this experience. This was certainly not the first time I had had former concentration camp inmates as my guests—even at that moment the farmer and the engineer from Dachau were still with us—but never before had I seen the story of their ordeals written so succinctly in their faces. Four of the five men were Polish Jews, survivors of Treblinka and Maidanek; the fifth was a German who had spent time in several concentration camps, the last of which had been Mauthausen. The American lieutenant accompanying the arrivals informed me of these particulars in a hushed, awed voice, requesting that all care should be taken to ensure their comfort.

As I showed them to their rooms I had some difficulty retaining my composure. I felt the rise of the familiar anxiety, the tension that was a permanent inhabitant of this incredible house. How often had I faced the task of having to reconcile the irreconcilable? Enough antagonists in the late drama had faced each other across their plates of American hash observing a bitter truce, but the idea of seating these five men at the same table with the former SA leader, the party functionaries, and Hoffmann had in it something indecent. I decided to do immediately what I had considered doing for some days, namely, changing the table arrangement in the dining room. I had wanted to wait until some of the current people left to be less obtrusive about it, but the way things stood now, it would have to be done without further delay. I knew I could not shield the concentration camp people from the party men and Hoffmann. Sooner or later—in the living room after dinner, in the garden, in the hallway—they would meet and discover their respective identities; but at least they would have the choice then to quietly shun each other instead of being held captive at the same dinner table. Initial separation, it appeared to me, was the only way to avoid a potentially painful and embarrassing scene.

I showed my new guests the bathroom, told them that dinner would be at six, and bade them to make themselves at home. Why was it so difficult to talk to them? My anxiety gave my voice an extra measure of concern. It was too solicitous, but my solicitation stigmatized them. I thought about it later. The effect on me of what they had suffered was sacramental; it isolated them and absolved them of the guilt that had become a part of the atmosphere we breathed. Martyrdom cleanses. One speaks of martyrs softly and with reverence, but, in degrees, the guilt for their suffering was the burden we bore.

I hurried to the dining room to rearrange the tables, saving the smallest one for my new guests and deciding to share it with them. It was about half an hour before dinner and I was placing the cutlery on the tables when Hoffmann, having just returned from the courthouse, sauntered into the dining room.

"*Gruess Gott,* dear lady, and what are you up to?"

I had often wondered how he had been able to stop saying "Heil Hitler!" after having used it for more than ten years for all and sundry occasions, but then no one had a more Darwinian capacity to adapt to new circumstances than Hoffmann.

He watched me for a while. "I see you've rearranged the tables. No more family style?"

"We've got some new people. This arrangement yields more seating space."

This happened to be true, but Hoffmann looked doubtful and, I thought, suspicious. "I don't really think so," he said. "But you're the hostess. Are we going to be seated differently tonight?"

"I certainly wouldn't expect you to give up your seat at the main table after all this time, Herr Hoffmann. I think I may just sit with the new people for a while to make them feel at home."

"That's a nice gesture," he said with a satisfied smile. "We shall miss you, but we'll give you a leave of absence."

"You're very generous and I thank you." Since he still made no move to leave, I excused myself to get away from him. I was in no mood to banter with Hoffmann.

In the kitchen Frau Kirchhof, the cook, was pouring tomato

juice into those narrow, thick ugly glasses the army had provided for that purpose. Her sad red face glistened with perspiration.

"It's too hot in here, *gnae'* Frau," she protested as I helped her to fill the bread plates and load them on the serving trays. I had long noticed that my presence in the kitchen seemed to make her uncomfortable. Perhaps she thought I was spying on her. I knew that she was taking bread home and occasional odds and ends she could scrape together. She had two young sons. Her husband was missing in action. Did she think I would begrudge her her modest booty while watching Hoffmann turn such handsome profits trading on his notoriety?

I helped Frau Kruelle set the tables in the dining room with juice and bread, keeping an eye on the door for my new guests so that I would be able to show them immediately to their table. As the other people trickled in, I assigned them to their seats, explaining that our present crowded state made the change necessary. Most seemed to think no further of it, though they might have grown suspicious by the arrangement which placed Hoffmann and all the ex-party and military people at the main table, the church people, the two men from Dachau, and the Rhineland Communist at the next table, with the smallest one reserved for the new arrivals.

All went well until the new guests entered the dining room. There was a moment of recognition. I could sense it, hear it in the fading noise of conversation falling to barely a murmur. Had I shielded the newcomers by this segregation, or merely accented the polarity of the groups in this room, heightening the consciousness of each other's difference? All I had wanted was to give a discreet warning, a signal of caution, not a drawing of battle lines.

As the conversation started up again at the other tables it seemed louder and more animated than necessary, and Hoffmann's laughter sounded even more boisterous than usual. Was it all just my imagination because my own table companions were for the most part silent? Two of the Poles spoke a tolerable German. They answered my various inquiries politely but made none of their own, nor did they talk to one another. I had a chance now to observe them individually, and noticed that all but the German were rather young. Perhaps it was their gauntness that had at first hidden their youth, or perhaps it was the bitter quiet of their eyes. The youngest appeared to be in his early twenties, possibly even younger; the others might have been in their middle or late twenties. I found out that they had spent the last eight months in a relocation camp near Munich and that they hoped eventually to emigrate to Palestine.

"What about your families?" I asked. "Do they like the idea of going to a new country? Will they go with you?"

There was no answer. They glanced at each other somewhat perplexed but kept on eating. It took some moments before I realized what their silence meant. I would have liked to swallow my tongue. Could I have lived through this long war, seen all I had seen, and still ask such a question? Perhaps the horror was so incomprehensible that my mind neither understood nor accepted the inescapable logic of this horror and thus still insisted on supplying the survivors with mothers, wives, and children. The German noticed my mortification. He smiled sadly, with just the faintest trace of irony.

"My dear Countess, your question is entirely understandable and forgivable. After all, it is, or at least it used to be, customary for most people to have relatives. We tend to hold onto old customs, especially when the new ones are distasteful to us."

"I'm sorry," I said to the young Poles. "Please forgive my ignorance."

The men appeared to be studying their empty plates.

"I have a sister," the youngest one said then. "She is married to a Pole. They didn't know she was Jewish. But my parents are dead, and both of my brothers."

He had broken the silence; what followed was a roll call of their dead: grandmothers and cousins, mothers, fathers, aunts, wives, children—names, ages, towns, extermination camps, as if they wished to engrave the record in my memory. There was a compulsiveness in their recital, yet their voices were subdued, their expressions devoid of obvious emotions. The intensity was entirely subliminal, but its power cut through all those comforting emotions that cushion grief, leaving only the dimensions of the terror itself. Despite the warmth of the summer evening I felt cold, as if the chill from all those graves had reached out and touched me. There was, of course, nothing to say; words could measure neither what I felt nor what they had endured. Indeed, I was not sure that I understood what I felt. Beyond my compassion, beyond the bounds of reason loomed a kind of elementary fear as of something too monstrous to behold, the sight of which, like the sight of Medusa, would turn the beholder into stone.

My instinct to flee was accommodated by Frau Kruelle, who arrived to collect the dinner plates and serve the dessert. I excused myself from my table companions and took the tray containing small dishes with canned peaches to the main table. Why was I thinking of Frau Kirchhof's sons? There had been four large cans of peaches. Had she managed to save some of the sweet, bright fruit for her boys? I had a sudden urge to tell her that I didn't mind, that I wanted her to, that she shouldn't be afraid that I was spying on her. Why was it sometimes so difficult to communicate feelings? Was it because within a given structure of reality they didn't really count?

Hoffmann, as usual, was dominating the conversation at the main table. He spoke too loudly; the names of Hitler and von Schirach, Bormann and Goebbels seemed to fill the room. What had I really expected? That the dauntless Hoffmann would respond to a discreet warning? I knew that his loyalty to his *Fuehrer* was unconditional. I had no reason to doubt that he would take his defense of his dead friend right up to the chimneys of Auschwitz and Treblinka.

"The one who is making so much noise, who is he?" asked the German as I served him his peaches.

"His name is Hoffmann. He was Hitler's photographer. He's sorting out for the court all the photographs he took."

He made no comment but kept watching Hoffmann, who, appearing to have sensed that we were talking about him, was coming toward our table, balancing his coffee cup.

"Countess, you must do me the honor of introducing me to your new guests."

My heart was beating with apprehension as I introduced the German who had given his name as Hebert. He did not rise and Hoffmann wisely refrained from extending his hand.

"These gentlemen are Polish," I said pointedly. "I have still some difficulty remembering how to pronounce their names."

"They have numbers, dear Countess," Hebert said, but he was looking at Hoffmann. "Perhaps Herr Hoffmann would be content to know them by their numbers."

I was mortified. Already the situation had surpassed my worst fears. Hoffmann, however, remained unabashed.

"Why not? I had a sergeant in the army back in '14 who used numbers for his squad because he couldn't remember their names." He turned his broad cheerful grin on the Poles. "I shall be happy to know you by your names or your numbers."

The Poles looked back at him in silence, but they seemed more curious than offended. Hoffmann pulled a package of American cigarettes from his trouser pocket and offered it to each in turn. His generosity troubled me; it was undoubtedly a part of a strategy, though I was not entirely sure for what. Did he resent my separation of the group and was he trying to get even with me?

"May I join you for a moment?" he asked, not waiting for an answer but pulling a chair between Hebert and me, forcing us to make room for him. "How do you like our little place? Isn't it marvelous? Good food, clean rooms, and the most charming lady in the world as a hostess. What more could a man ask for?"

"You have been here a while?" Herbert asked.

"Almost a year," Hoffmann answered proudly. "I'm sorting my photographs for the court."

"One good job leads to another, eh?"

208

"Why not? I've been lucky. The camera knows no politics, but there's a lot of history in those photographs nevertheless."

"There's a lot of history that isn't in them," Hebert said. He pushed back his chair and pulled up one of his trouser legs, revealing deep, ragged-looking scars on his calf. "Like that."

Hoffmann's grimace could have indicated either distaste or exasperation. "How terrible," he said.

Hebert shrugged. "It's nothing really. We had much more spectacular attractions which in consideration of the countess I will refrain from describing in detail. But if you've considered yourself a recorder of history, I must say there's a great deal of Third Reich history you missed."

"I couldn't photograph things I didn't know about."

Hebert's harsh, deeply lined face allowed a grudging, bitter smile.

"Of course not. Nobody else knew about it; why should you? I suppose even the great *Fuehrer* himself did not know what went on in Mauthausen and Treblinka."

"Of course he didn't, or he wouldn't have permitted it," Hoffmann said earnestly, while I wished I could sink into the floor.

Hebert's expression vacillated between anger and incredulity, as if he weren't quite sure whether to be offended or amused. Deciding on the latter, he laughed. "How naïve we were. All this time we believed that nothing in the Third Reich happened without the *Fuehrer*'s omniscient knowledge."

"He didn't know about the extermination camps or atrocities; I vouch for that. He would have died of horror if he'd seen those films. He couldn't even stand the sight of blood. He hated hunting because he thought it such a cruel sport."

Hebert looked at him in growing amazement. "I think you really believe what you're saying."

"Look," Hoffmann went on persuasively, "does it seem realistic to assume that a head of state knows everything that goes on in his country? You have no idea how isolated Hitler really was. But I know. People only told him what they wanted him to know, especially Bormann and Himmler."

209

"Can you really say things like that with a straight face after all that has come out at the trial, or is this some sort of bad joke?"

Hoffmann chose to ignore Hebert's growing irritation. "Look," he said. "Don't you understand, it's convenient to blame everything on Hitler in the trial. He's dead and can't defend himself. People simply believe what they want to believe."

"Like you?"

Hoffmann shrugged. "Maybe like you."

"How so?"

"Well, you insist on believing that Hitler knew about the atrocities in the camps. But I knew Hitler as well as it was possible for any man to know him, and I tell you that he didn't know what went on inside the camps. Still you don't believe me. Now, I've never been inside a concentration camp. The first time I ever heard or saw what had taken place was in the films they showed during the trial. But you have spent time inside those camps. What if I told you that I didn't believe that those films are true or those things you say you experienced?"

"Is that what you *are* telling me?"

"Not at all. But *you* are disputing something you have no knowledge of. Because you want to believe your own version of the truth, you're calling me a liar."

"There's documented proof of my claims."

"A lot of things can be faked on film. Our newsreel people did it all the time."

Hebert scrutinized him closely. "You don't really believe that what you saw is true, do you?"

"I didn't say that. I'm only suggesting that you have no more reason to disbelieve me than I have reason to disbelieve you. I knew Hitler since 1921 and I was his friend and close associate right up to the end. If he bared his soul to anybody, he did to me."

"I didn't know he had one," said Hebert. "I hope they added another wing to Hell."

210

The Poles had been listening intently, straining to follow the conversation. "You were friends with Hitler?" one of them asked. His expression of mingled awe and revulsion reminded me of the way children look at fascinating but repugnant animals. But Hoffmann returned his gaze unabashed and with disarming friendliness.

"I often think that I may have been his best friend," he said, offering once more his package of cigarettes around the table.

"Thus a man shall be known by the company he keeps," said Hebert, taking one of Hoffmann's cigarettes, but Hoffmann ignored him, addressing only the Poles now.

"Do you believe me when I tell you that Hitler, like myself, knew nothing of the atrocities?" No one answered him, but he appeared to take their silence for assent. "As a matter of fact, I often interceded with him for people who got into trouble with the Gestapo, and he always was willing to help. You see," he said, turning to Hebert now, "I knew Hitler as a man, not just as chancellor or *Fuehrer*. I was the one who introduced him to the woman he loved. It was me he came to visit sometimes as late as three in the morning to sit by the fire and talk about the old days in Munich, and then he would laugh and finally fall asleep. He had great trouble sleeping, you know. We never talked about political matters. My home was his oasis to get away from the burdens of his office."

"You say Hitler knew nothing of Auschwitz and Treblinka?" said the Pole.

"Belsen, Dachau, Buchenwald, Theresienstadt, Mauthausen, Sachsenhausen . . ." Hebert took over the list. "I saw a map of Europe last year marked with the location of the camps. Those black dots were everywhere, covering the face of the land like a murderous rash. But they were, of course, invisible to the people who built them."

One of the Poles pulled a shabby wallet out of his coat pocket and carefully extracted a photograph, frayed around the edges and bearing the likeness of a young woman and two small children. He showed it to Hoffmann but wouldn't let him hold it.

"My wife," he said. "My children. Dead. All dead." He gestured toward his companions. "Families, all dead. Your people do terrible things and you say you not know. But you know. What you want to know you know. Is enough to know little, to know all if you wish so. Is how you think." He tapped his forehead for emphasis.

Now, I thought, even Hoffmann would know enough to be silent. I fervently wished he would be. I tried to catch his eye, but he didn't look at me; only Hebert answered my imploring glance with a small, wry smile.

Hoffmann was shaking his head mournfully. "My dear fellow, Hitler adored children. I must have taken hundreds of pictures of him with children. He was no murderer, and he was not the first head of state who was betrayed by his subordinates. Don't you see, running a government is a big operation. You've got to delegate powers. These atrocities were the brain-children of Himmler and Kaltenbrunner, Bormann and Heydrich. They were perverts."

Hoffmann argued with such earnestness and conviction that the Poles grew more and more bewildered. What amazed me about their behavior toward Hoffmann was the absence of any visible anger or hate; indeed, their only reaction toward him appeared to be incredulity.

The Poles and Hebert stayed with us for about a week. Most of the people of what Hebert dubbed "the Nazi table" appeared to be grateful for the separation at mealtimes, and at other times also avoided the guests from Treblinka and Mauthausen, though I heard the Wehrmacht colonel once talk to the Poles, expressing his great sorrow and shame over what they had suffered. They listened to him coldly and without a word turned their backs on him. But Hoffmann appeared to have a fascination for them and they for him, for he listened to their terrible tales with apparently genuine curiosity and abhorrence.

Only once did I witness a brief flare-up of anger by the

Poles. The conversation had again turned toward the argument of whether or not Hitler knew about the atrocities in the camps. When Hoffmann remained adamant in his position that Hitler was ignorant of the facts, the Poles suddenly revolted and proceeded to berate him in a mixture of Polish, German, and Yiddish. Hoffmann parried the situation with his usual expertise. He told them that their anger was justified, that it was really fruitless to argue about what Hitler knew since whether he knew or not, as head of state he probably had to be held responsible for what had happened; that all these atrocities were dreadful, and that he, Hoffmann, was truly grateful to have the opportunity to finally talk to people who had experienced all these terrible things. The Poles spared him no detail. They exposed him to the full range of the pains they had suffered, the horrors they had witnessed. The spectacle was somewhat disconcerting. Baring their griefs, they were like people exposing prized relics to nonbelievers. Before Hoffmann their suffering was divested of its dimension of tragedy, because Hoffmann could not respond to its magnitude. What was left was the sordid alone, unredeemed by that bitter compassion that is the sharing of all suffering and all guilt.

Unlike the Poles, Hebert shunned Hoffmann. In the evenings after dinner he would sit alone reading, though I did see him on occasion talk to the engineer who had been at Dachau and to the Wehrmacht colonel. But one evening, when Hoffmann was holding forth about the early days of the movement, Hebert heckled him from across the room.

"When did you join the party, Herr Hoffmann?"

"In 1921," Hoffmann answered with incongruous pride. "My card number is fifty-nine."

"But I thought you had no interest in politics?"

"I haven't. I have no interest in ideology, never read any of Rosenberg's stuff. I never even really read *Mein Kampf*. I joined the party because they were getting a lot of publicity and they wouldn't let anyone photograph Hitler. This was my chance to get in on the ground floor as their photographer. I once tried

213

to get a picture of Hitler before that but couldn't get near him because of his bodyguards."

"So you became a Nazi to further your career?"

Hoffmann shrugged. "Why not? So did millions of others, only I did it earlier."

"And that's all. No other reason?"

"I liked and admired Hitler as a man, but I really don't believe in ideology. Experience has taught me that people act in their own interest. Sometimes ideology just happens to coincide with it, but a person shouldn't need one to know what it is. The sooner one learns to look out for oneself, the better off one is."

"Now there is what I call a success story in a nutshell, uncomplicated by all those messy questions about ethics and personal integrity."

"I learned my ethics early," Hoffmann said without rancor. "There's good luck and bad. You're either on the bottom or on top. Once when I was a boy an officer offered me ten *Pfennig* to pick up his pants from a tailor and bring them to the barracks. I walked for two hours in midday heat and upon arrival received from the officer, instead of the eagerly awaited ten *Pfennig*, a slap in the face because the pants had been stained by my sweat and the flying dust of the road. That, Herr Hebert, is the ethic of real life, not of books."

"Touché," said Hebert. "Who can argue with such naked reality? All the rest is a matter of faith."

On a hazy July morning, after about a week's stay, the four Poles and Hebert signed my guest book and got ready to leave. Hebert thanked me "for your generous efforts to make our stay pleasant."

"And where are you going now?"

He shrugged wearily. "For the time being, to Frankfurt. I know a publisher there."

"Will you write a book about your experiences?"

"I don't know. Perhaps in time, if I can get them sorted out."

214

"It's not easy for you to talk about them, is it?"

"They have certain dimensions which perplex me." He looked thoughtfully at the rectangle of summer framed by the open doorway. "Do you hear that?"

"What?"

"That bird?"

"Yes."

"*. . . wie sterbend einer vorgebeugt in die feucht herwehende Maerznacht, ach, den Fruehling verliert in die Kehlen der Voegel . . .** Do you like Rilke?"

"Yes. That was Rilke?"

"From one of his elegies. I heard a bird sing like that on one of the barracks roofs, while one of my friends was being led away, just like that. Dying, bent forward, toward death. That bird's voice transfixed me; I abandoned myself to it, let it absorb my whole being. I think those were the most intensely beautiful moments I have ever experienced. Can you understand that?"

"I think so. It was the contrast."

"Yes. Stark and beautiful. Black and white, death and life. What we lived was an allegory in which the song of a bird became a miracle."

"You sound almost regretful."

"I know. I'm drawn as by a magnet back to my memories, as if I had left something behind. I've had over a year to think about it, and I still ask myself why I had to live in hell in order to see the radiance of heaven."

The sound of the approaching jeep drowned out the bird song. With a sudden impulse Hebert clasped my hand.

"Thank you for listening to me."

Moments later the jeep came to a stop in front of the gate. I accompanied the five men to the car and wished them peace and a safe journey.

---

*". . . as one dying bent forward into the damp blowing March night loses spring in the throats of birds . . ."

22

AUGUST had come again. Bobby, having passed her first birth-day, toddled happily around the garden. Did her father look at other babies the way some of my guests looked at Bobby, with affectionate sadness and longing? I did not want to be-lieve that he was dead. I only wished that hope could keep him alive. We tried to buoy each other up, those people who were in similar positions and I—and there were few who weren't. An unhappy police official from Kassel who had sent his bombed-out family to relatives in Silesia had heard nothing of them since the war's end; a woman from a church group wor-ried about a daughter and grandson somewhere in Mecklen-burg. Most others had someone missing in action, or in prison. Some had the grim certainty of death.

Throughout that summer, until the court recessed on the last day of August, the witness houses were filled with the rank and file of Hitler's Germany, its onetime supporters as well as

216

opponents and victims. In the courtroom the German attorneys battled with the issue of collective guilt in their defense of the organizations; at the witness houses the issue of punishment and collective retribution loomed larger than the reality of indirect guilt. On the witness stand the great names of the German army—von Rundstedt, von Manstein, Brauchitsch— were defending their conduct of the war; at the witness houses most people worried more about how long the Russians would hold German prisoners. Only a trickle had returned so far. They had brought back stories of hunger and hate, work and privation, death from disease and exhaustion. Pain by pain and death by death the beaten soldiers were repaying the debt, while the field marshals, stripped of braid and brass, praised their valiant spirit in the conqueror's courtroom.

But retribution was catching up with the onetime powerful, too. The German commander of Norway had been condemned to death; in Strasbourg the ex-Gauleiter of Alsace had been shot; in Poznan the former Gauleiter had been hanged before a crowd of thousands. All over Europe, Germans and their collaborators were being tried and executed, expelled, deported for forced labor, or held as prisoners of war to rebuild what the German war had destroyed. To be an attorney for a war crimes defendant was fast becoming the most thankless job in Europe. The Nuremberg attorneys were being vilified in the press, threatened with disbarment by at least one professional association, threatened with reprisals by right- and left-wing militants, and severely discriminated against by the Allied court. It was a time for vengeance, not for justice. It was a bad time to be a German, any German.

For the nameless millions huddling in the ruined cities it was difficult to understand their punishment or their crime. For them, now as before, their collective identity transcended the individual. Collective will, enforced through terror, inflamed through ignorance and hysteria, distorted in the deeds of a handful of fiends, had become the collective guilt of a nation.

In the last few weeks of the trial we were more than ever

2 1 7

brought face to face with the abysmal horrors that had been committed in the name of the German people. There were, of course, the many guests who had spent time in concentration camps; but it was a new name entered into my guest book during August that provided an even more terrifying link to the late horror. It was that of a Dr. Rascher, a physician from Munich, and it had an ominously familiar ring. My suspicions were confirmed by looking through some back copies of the newspaper trial reports. Dr. Rascher was indeed the name of the notorious doctor who had conducted unspeakably hideous "medical" experiments at Dachau, ostensibly for the benefit of the Luftwaffe. It seemed inconceivable that such a man should have been allowed to stay at the witness house. All those who had had anything to do with the concentration camps were being themselves held for trial, mostly at the camps at which they had formerly practiced their terrible trade. I vaccillated whether to call the courthouse to verify Dr. Rascher's orders, or to decide on commonsense grounds that it couldn't be *the* Dr. Rascher.

Perhaps he could sense my uneasiness, because during dinner I noticed him looking at me several times with a troubled expression. He said little and appeared to be ill at ease. I thought him to be in his late fifties or early sixties. He looked ordinary enough, sedate, neatly dressed, though with that faint shabbiness that was the mark of German appearance in 1946. I wondered whether anyone of our, since the beginning of August, rather shrunken company had recognized the name of Dr. Rascher. The farmer and engineer who had been at Dachau were no longer with us. To the best of my knowledge only one of the current crowd had been in a concentration camp; he was Otto Pelzer, a former world champion long-distance runner who had been imprisoned for his alleged homosexuality.

There was no indication that anyone knew about or had taken particular notice of the doctor. The table conversation was subdued, revolving primarily around private concerns. The mood was somber. In the waning summer, as the trial moved toward judgment, the weight of its accumulated record was like a gathered force, an oppressive presence in the sultry air. There was little concern about the probable verdicts for the main defendants. Few worried about what would happen to Goering or Hess; but a guilty verdict for the organizations would have far-reaching consequences for many thousands. Whatever might happen to the other organizations, there was no question in anyone's mind but that Himmler's network of security organs, as well as the SS, would be judged guilty. The police official from Kassel worried about his status. Since all police forces, including criminal and regular uniformed police, had been under the jurisdiction of Himmler's *Reichsicherheits-hauptamt*—the RSHA—had he been guilty of a crime for having practiced his profession? Even Hoffmann was subdued in the face of the approaching verdict. His daughter had visited him earlier in the day. When she left he had escorted her downstairs, his arm around her shoulders. Her eyes had been red from crying.

"She's overwhelmed by it all," he said after she had gone. "She thinks he will get the death sentence."

"Do you?"

He drew angrily at his cigarette. "For what?" he snapped, the cigarette bobbing. "What is the boy supposed to have done?"

"He was Gauleiter of Vienna, among other things, wasn't he?"

"Is that enough to be put to death, to have held a government post?" He shook his head glumly. "The ironic thing is that he had been pretty much out of favor with Hitler for several years. I think my influence helped to prevent his really getting into difficulties. I felt somewhat responsible for his problems, because Henrietta compounded them. She once complained to Hitler's face about a roundup of Jews for deportation which she had seen from her window in Holland. I can tell you, Hitler was so angry, I thought he would have her arrested."

219

"But you've always said that Hitler knew nothing about what was happening with the Jews and in the concentration camps. What did he say when your daughter complained, that she was lying?"

"No. He accused her of being presumptuous and sentimental."

"Well, then he knew, didn't he? After all, he gave the orders."

"He gave the orders for deportation, not for what they did at Auschwitz."

"Even after what Hoess said, that the orders came from Hitler through Himmler, you still believe he didn't know?"

The face that looked at me through the thin, curling smoke of the bobbing butt was that of the other Hoffmann, sad and sagging, but defiant. "Himmler was a fiend and a liar," he said grimly, crushing his tiny cigarette butt in the ashtray.

Today Hoffmann's grotesque loyalty was oppressing. Perhaps it was the imminence of the verdict, his daughter's red eyes, the presence of Dr. Rascher, or perhaps it was the absence of Hoffmann's grin that made his lunacy seem ominous.

After dinner I was still debating what to do about Dr. Rascher, and my uneasiness finally made me call the courthouse. Since the offices were closed after six, I got only a sergeant on night duty who said he would connect me with someone in authority if the matter was urgent. But I did not want to create a stir. Certainly I could not magnify my own uneasiness into a state of emergency. Rascher's papers were in order. I could not challenge anyone's right to stay at the witness house if he had the proper authorization.

When I returned to the living room I saw Rascher looking at me again as he had during dinner, with that same troubled expression, as if there were something he wanted to tell me but didn't quite know how to start. I decided to give him the opportunity and sat down beside him, inquiring how he had enjoyed his dinner and if he had found everything he needed in his room. Some of the tension left his face, though a wariness remained in his eyes. He praised the hospitality, the view of the heath, and said he had not expected to be so generously treated by the court.

"Not everyone is," I said, too pointedly without intending to.

"I know," he said quietly. "Perhaps they felt that I should not be held responsible for what my son is alleged to have done."

"It was your son?"

"Yes. You recognized the name all along, didn't you? Did you think I was the Dr. Rascher of Dachau?"

"I didn't quite know what to think."

"Neither do I. They've made a monster out of my son."

My face must have revealed what I did not say, that his son *was* a monster. The evidence against Dr. Rascher was his own records of his experiments—sheer exercises in sadism—as well as correspondence and the testimony of witnesses who had acted as his assistants.

"It's ironic, isn't it? They accuse him of all these terrible things, yet he was himself arrested on Himmler's orders and later killed at Dachau."

"He is dead?"

"Yes. If what they say about him is true, it's probably best."

"Had you any idea of what he was doing at Dachau?"

"Only that he was engaged in research for the Luftwaffe. It was top secret."

Human guinea pigs immersed for hours in ice water, exposed naked to the bitterest winter cold, or driven to distraction in decompression chambers. What kind of mind contrived such horrors? It was an eerie feeling to sit beside the man who had fathered such a monster, as eerie as the thought of Hitler as a baby, or small child, being lovingly rocked in his mother's arms.

"Why did they kill your son?"

"Not only him, his wife, too, but at another camp."

"His wife?"

221

"It's a very strange story and not a pretty one," Dr. Rascher said, with more sadness than bitterness.

The tale he went on to relate was as ludicrous as it was sordid. His son had married a former mistress of Heinrich Himmler, a woman some fifteen years his senior. Himmler had opposed the marriage on grounds that it would be unproductive. To prove to her former lover that she was still in her fertile prime, Frau Rascher, then in her late forties, pretended to several pregnancies, traveled to various towns with forged papers through which she obtained orphaned or abandoned infants, and then took these children home, alleging that she had given birth to them. She "bore" four children in this curious fashion before the swindle was discovered, when one of the institutions investigated Frau Rascher's claims. Himmler was infuriated; though the woman had done no harm to the children, but had been on the contrary an exemplary and loving mother, he had the Raschers arrested and eventually executed. It was like an absurd parody of a morality play. What Frau Rascher had violated was a sacrament of the holy gospel of National Socialism in which the act of breeding "the pure race" stood exalted above all else, certainly above such sentimentalities as love and kindness, and so that small area of light in their dark lives became the Raschers' capital crime, while the doctor's heinous experiments earned him only praise and honor. It had all been a parody, the whole ghastly twelve years; like the Devil's Mass of the Middle Ages, it had been a diabolical parody of a state, a diabolical parody of law and custom. The cock had crowed, the trance dispelled; of the shoddy mystique only the horror remained, and the huge legacy of sorrow.

"I don't know what they want with me," Dr. Rascher said. "They know a great deal more about my son than I do." He looked weary and worried. "It's like a nightmare you wish you could wake up from to know that it isn't really true."

His somber face showed at once his tension and his exhaustion. I wondered what he thought about the monstrous evidence against his son. Did he take refuge in disbelief? How did

222

one live with such a memory? I felt an uneasy compassion, half suppressed, like a forbidden sensation, and then the anger that had so often struck me during my tenure in this fateful house when I had noticed that my responses were governed less by the true depth of my feelings than the assumptions of convention. Should compassion be measured miserly like the dole to the deserving poor?

Rascher got up. I tried to think of something comforting to say but couldn't.

"I know it's early," he said apologetically, "but I'm quite tired."

"I hope you sleep well."

"I haven't for quite some time." He smiled ruefully. "Maybe that's why I'm so tired."

"Would you like a newspaper?"

"No, thank you. I have enough nightmares to last me for the rest of my days."

We all had. A sense of unreality prevailed. We looked at the past sketched by the trial as one might look at a surreal canvas, trying to read its meaning. Against the background of that past the present, too, was out of focus; the conventional routine of our lives at times assumed an aspect of the ludicrous. A fastidious former administrative assistant to a Gauleiter, who had been a fanatic on cleanliness, washed his only shirt and underwear every night (he hadn't been given time to pack a change), ironing them meticulously in the kitchen the following morning before breakfast, much to Frau Kruelle's annoyance. He brushed his teeth and gargled after every meal and held a handkerchief protectively near his lips when he talked to anyone. The Gauleiter was incarcerated somewhere, awaiting trial, but the ghost of his power continued to wield his assistant's toothbrush.

An elderly woman was frightened by a mouse in her room and spent the night in the living room, where I found her the following morning slumped in an easy chair and snoring vigorously. With Frau Kruelle's aid we procured a trap, a humane

223

one which would not kill the animal. The mouse was caught, admired by my children, shuddered over by the lady, and discussed over breakfast as to its future disposition. It was voted its freedom on the heath, where my children took it on their morning walk.

"I'm glad it wasn't killed," the woman said. "I'd hate to have anything die for my sake."

There was an uncertain silence, a curious telepathic silence in which the same thought seemed to occur in every mind. Someone led off with a guffaw and then our entire table burst into howling laughter. Only Dr. Rascher and the lady didn't laugh. She blushed with embarrassment and mumbled, "I don't understand."

"May the mice inherit the earth," said a professor from Cologne. "We don't deserve it."

The lady still looked blank. I remembered an incident in the cellar of the Bohemian castle where we had spent the last days of the war. An old peasant woman had been dragged in, furiously resisting this interference with her freedom. When we finally got her calmed down enough to explain to her why she had been forced into the cellar, she began to wail loudly, because, she said, no one had told her that there was a war on, and now, she feared, she had missed most of it. I had frequently thought of her with a measure of envy. Dr. Rascher left that evening as inconspicuously and somberly as he had arrived.

On August 31, after the defendants had made their final statements, the court recessed to consider its verdict. During the month-long recess the regulations concerning the strict isolation of the defendants were relaxed somewhat. For the first time since the beginning of the trial their families were permitted to visit with them briefly each day. For a while there was a rumor that the wives and children of the defendants would be given rooms at the witness houses during this period, which for many would prove to be the last time they would ever see their husbands and fathers again. I found that prospect

224

even more worrisome than the original plan of a year before, according to which the defendants' wives were to have been quartered with us. Much to my relief nothing came of this latest plan either. I was not sure how I would have coped with the emotional tension inherent in such a situation. It was enough for me to see Henrietta von Schirach grow progressively more terrified as the sentencing date approached.

One day, though, about the middle of September, a young man rang our doorbell. He carried a small, dirty suitcase tied up with string and wore muddy shoes and an ill-fitting suit over an old German army shirt. He handed me a handwritten note from an officer of the court which informed me that he was Elmar Streicher, and was allowed to stay at the house for one night.

The son of Julius Streicher, former Gauleiter of Nuremberg, publisher of the notorious anti-Semitic rag, *Der Stuermer,* and probably the most primitive and obscene of the Jew-haters among the Nazis, had come to take leave of his father. He stood before me with downcast eyes, like a schoolboy waiting to be punished. His father had strutted around Nuremberg with a riding crop, bald, thick-necked, brutal, the undisputed lord of his domain. There were reports that even his co-defendants shunned him, and there was little doubt that his sentence would be death.

Elmar Streicher said little and was difficult to talk to, appearing to be listening to the most ordinary pleasantries and communications with apprehension. He said he was working as a hired man on a nearby farm and that he had been surprised when he had been informed that he could see his father. He held himself aloof from the few other guests, as Rascher had, trying to attract the least possible attention. With a name like Streicher that wasn't easy, and there were a number of gratuitous remarks obviously aimed in young Streicher's direction, despite the fact that he did not participate in any table conversation. During the court recess these conversations inevitably turned around the imminent verdict, or the arrival and visits of a defendant's relatives which were reported on the radio and in the paper. Among the ex-officials of Nazi ministries and low-ranking representatives of party and party affiliates who now made up the bulk of my shrunken guest list, there was little compassion for the visiting families. Like those of most Germans, their own families were decimated by the war or separated by zonal borders. The people in the Nuremberg jail were the former *Bonzen*, the big shots who had lorded it over the people throughout the war, who had not done their share of suffering, whose well-deserved turn had come.

"They're taking an awful lot of time to deliberate the obvious" was one embittered remark. "You know what a German court would do today with the *Bonzen*."

"It's been more than three years since I've seen *my* son and more than a year since I've heard anything from him" was another remark obviously directed at young Streicher.

"*They* didn't have such problems. Their sons didn't get close enough to the enemy to be taken prisoner."

My attempts to change the line of conversation were only moderately successful. Hoffmann, himself now frequently the target of such jibes, made no effort at contradiction. Streicher never lifted his eyes off his plate. His painful awareness and acceptance of being the butt and outcast were evident and somehow very sad. I knew nothing about young Streicher, but as it seemed unfair to equate the elder Rascher with his son, it seemed even more so to transfer one's hatred for the depraved Streicher onto his son.

Immediately after dinner the young man headed for his room. I waylaid him in the hallway and apologized for being unable to halt the heckling at the table. He muttered something about his father, about the many terrible things he was accused of, and that much of it seemed to be true; that he had never seen eye to eye with his father and had not even belonged to the party. "But whatever they say of him, he *is* my father."

With his dirty little suitcase (he was not coming back), Streicher left the following morning and went to the courthouse to take leave of his father. Forlorn and shabby, he bore his sad legacy; there was no compassion to spare for such as him.

With mounting tension the day of the verdict moved closer. Interest in the long trial began to pick up again. The Hoffmanns did not much resemble the gregarious couple of a few weeks ago. The gravity of their son-in-law's situation, the very real possibility of his receiving the death penalty, appeared only now, as they watched their daughter grow more wan and distressed every day, to have a real impact on them.

On September 30, the court reconvened for the reading of the verdicts. The first day was given over to a summary of the charges contained in the indictment and the verdict on the indicted organizations. As expected, the Gestapo, SD, and SS were found guilty as charged; so was the Corps of Political Leaders—the top ranks of the party. Found not guilty in verdicts causing a considerable sensation were the SA and the General Staff. On the latter, the verdict, despite its rejection of the group's collective guilt, contained a scathing denunciation of the German military, and specifically announced that a number of individual members would face charges in the future.

On the second day the verdicts and sentences for the individual defendants were announced. They could be found guilty on anywhere from one to four counts specified in the indictment: conspiracy to make war; crimes against the peace; violations of the customs of war, or war crimes; and crimes against humanity.

Henrietta von Schirach had come to listen to the verdict on the radio with her parents. Her face was white and rigid, set grimly for catastrophe; her presence in the house seemed to make the very air vibrate with tension. The reading of the verdict began, the roll call of all the infamous names, signatures in blood and tears on the ruins and mass graves of Europe: Goering, Hess, Ribbentrop, Keitel, Kaltenbrunner, Streicher, Frank, Rosenberg, Funk, more than a dozen verdicts before Schirach's. Then it came; indicted on counts one and four, guilty on count four—crimes against humanity—for his part in the deportation of Viennese Jews to Poland during his tenure as Gauleiter of Vienna.

There was no reaction from Frau von Schirach; she had hardly expected a not-guilty verdict. The question of major concern was the sentence. The tension of waiting for this was prolonged till afternoon. Then came the final fateful roll call: Goering, Ribbentrop, Kaltenbrunner, Keitel, Jodl, Streicher; death sentence after death sentence. I think we all expected to hear the same for Schirach, and I was terribly afraid of the effect on his wife. But the grim scene was destined to have an unexpectedly happy ending. Schirach's sentence turned out to be twenty years in prison. His wife's cry of joy and relief resounded through the house.

"Anything, as long as he lives," she cried. "Just as long as he doesn't have to die."

Hoffmann's face was gray and solemn, an expression I was still not accustomed to seeing on him. Putting his arm around his sobbing daughter, he led her to his room.

I shared her relief, but could have shared her grief with less ambivalence. It appeared to me that the tribunal's judgment was somehow lacking in proportion. Twenty years seemed a small price for the mass deportations of Viennese Jews. On the other hand, the trial had effectively discredited a nation, perhaps justly so. But the darkest period in its history was isolated and focused on; the boil was examined without the source of infection. By and large, mitigating evidence was rejected. Defense attorneys were forbidden to mention the stupidities of Versailles, the treacheries of Stalin in the Baltic and Poland; the very real contribution of the West to the consolidation of Hitler's power.

Perhaps correctly the trial was dismissed by many Germans as a political one; perhaps it could have been nothing else. Haushofer had predicted that the tribunal would fail because the manifold process of history could not be measured by the standards we sum up as justice. In the end the victors were most lenient with some of the men who had contributed most to the catastrophe of Hitler: von Papen, maneuvering him into power, serving him faithfully even after he had Papen's closest associates murdered, went free; Schacht, arrogant and brilliant, managing the economy for Hitler's rearmament, absolved of all charges; Fritzsche, henchman of Goebbels, mouthpiece of the venal Nazi propaganda machine that had for so long suppressed all freedom of thought and speech, feeding the ignorant lies and hysteria, equally free. But the nameless millions of the nation they had helped so industriously to discredit did not go free. Summarily judged, without benefit of trial, they served their sentences of misery and death.

The trial ended in twelve death sentences, three sentences of life imprisonment, and three lesser prison terms, of which Schirach's was one. The three not-guilty verdicts were met by severe criticism from many Germans, with the result that the German civil authorities surrounded the Palace of Justice with police who promptly arrested the three men when they attempted to leave the court building. They were later tried and sentenced before German denazification courts.

It was all over then but for the grisly finale on the gallows. I thought with sorrow of Luise Jodl who had fought so gallantly to save her husband's life, of the bewildered Frau Funk, of the beaten, forlorn son of Julius Streicher. Guilty or not, they paid a part of the penalty; but the long remaining debit ledger of retribution was being filled with unfamiliar names.

23

THE EXECUTIONS were to be carried out on the fifteenth day after the sentencing. Luise Jodl had sent an appeal to Generals Eisenhower and Montgomery. Admiral Raeder was petitioning the court to change his life sentence to death by a firing squad. There was talk about the defense appealing the manner of executions for Generals Keitel and Jodl, requesting death by shooting instead of hanging. A newspaper article reminded us of the fiendish methods of Nazi executions and of the generals who were hanged after the attempt on Hitler without protest or intercession by the two generals who were now awaiting the same fate.

For Henrietta von Schirach the first joy and relief over her husband's sentence had given way to a quiet, deep depression.

"It's better than death, but it's an awful long time," Hoffmann said. "I'll have to take care of her and the children now."

He rallied all his optimism to sketch their common future.

Although he was nearly finished sorting his archives, he had been assured, so he said, of further employment by the Americans. His son, just released from an allied prison, had joined him to wind up the old assignment and help with the new one, the nature of which was not entirely clear. Young Hoffmann, in his late twenties, blond, of medium height, slim build, and with pleasant features, did not much resemble his father in personality or appearance. He was quiet, soft-spoken, and polite, and often seemed embarrassed by his father's brash manner and his notoriety, especially when the latter undertook to sketch his family's promising future for some incredulous listener. Hoffmann had told us that he expected to be given the use of an entire house like the witness house for himself and his family.

"He practically owns this one already" was the wry comment of one guest, probably referring to the fact that we already had three Hoffmanns with us, since Frau Hoffmann was on one of her frequent visits.

Hoffmann's optimism was generous enough to include me in his future projections. New trials were in preparation, he said, and he was sure that because of these, both he and I would have employment for some time to come. But my own estimation of my future was, as usual, not nearly so optimistic. I had also heard that new trials were ahead, but I had no idea whether or not the witness houses would be kept open for these. Another winter was facing us. At the Red Cross all replies to inquiries about my husband remained negative. I seemed to be back where I had been more than a year ago, but with waning hope for a reunion. At the witness houses things were much too quiet to give me confidence for the future, although the stories we had heard and read concerning more trials in Nuremberg seemed to be given credence by the return visit of Emil von Rintelen, who had been with us earlier in the year. Diels, too, returned for his third stay with us, this time without any restrictions. Two higher ranking ex-officials of the former Ministries of Agriculture and Nutrition, who were accompanied by their wives, rounded out our small circle. With less pressure on the facilities, the court had become much more lenient in giving permission for visits by spouses. Rintelen's wife, too, joined him shortly after his arrival, and Frau Hoffmann, of course, had become almost as much at home as her husband in the witness house.

On the evening of October 15, the beginning of the night that was to see the executions in the Palace of Justice, we were joined by a new guest whose brief visit would leave a long memory for at least one person in our midst. He introduced himself as Dr. Schmidt, appeared to be in his middle fifties, looked distinguished, and was very well dressed—an exceedingly rare sight among Germans at the time. But not just in dress; in bearing too he differed from the other guests as a visitor in a jail might differ from its inmates. The stigma of being German in 1946, the sense of humiliation and fear expressed in American surplus clothing, stripped uniforms, and supplicant attitudes toward the victorious foreigners, was not part of the personality Dr. Schmidt projected. Somewhat like Gisevius he exuded prestige and a kind of grim certainty. At dinner he took no part in the conversation, which revolved mostly around Goering's suicide the night before and the executions which were to take place that night. Though no one (save Hoffmann) was particularly concerned about the men who were to die tonight, the gallows in the Palace of Justice cast a shadow across our table. The gallows taking as criminals the men who had until recently governed Germany would remain the last image in the brutal saga of the Third Reich, stark symbol of a shameful past. As at a wake, the mood was subdued. For Hoffmann alone the event had a more personal quality. He had known nearly all the men who were to be executed tonight. Perhaps he was as strongly affected because he realized that, considering his close ties to Hitler, he could easily have been one of their number. What had saved him was his camera and probably his very real indifference to politics and power. He was restless; there was a fear in his eyes.

"I wonder what time they'll do it," he said.

"It's usually done after midnight," said Diels, who now took his meals with us when he was at home.

"Isn't dawn the common time?" asked one of the ministerial directors.

"Not necessarily," said Diels with professional sureness.

If Dr. Schmidt did not participate in the conversation, he did listen and observe the speakers with profound interest. A little later when the conversation had turned to the three defendants freed by the tribunal, he appeared agitated and on the verge of making a remark, especially when someone expressed the opinion that Neurath, too, should have been freed. But he controlled himself and remained grimly and somehow ominously silent. His behavior was not without effect on the other people. The conversation grew cautious, sporadic, and finally stuttered into silence. Hoffmann especially grew increasingly uncomfortable under Dr. Schmidt's inquisitorial glances. Trying without much success to don his mask of joviality, he made a halfhearted attempt to draw out the mysterious doctor.

"I understand you are from Munich, Dr. Schmidt. You know, that's my home town, too."

"It is a lot of people's," Schmidt said curtly.

"I remember there was quite a famous Dr. Schmidt at one of the hospitals. One of my friends came all the way from Berlin to have him operate on his gall bladder."

"We Schmidts are numerous," said the doctor. "You'll never know who you may find in our midst."

Hoffmann got no further than that with his inquiries, nor did anyone else get a chance to find out more about Dr. Schmidt, for he excused himself almost immediately after dinner, telling me that he still had an appointment that evening. In the hall while he waited for the car that was to pick him up, he involved me in a short conversation that could be better characterized as an interrogation, because it consisted almost solely of rapid inquiries about the witness houses. My impression that I was being interrogated was heightened by the fact that Dr. Schmidt received my answers without comment or change of expression. Sensing a definite threat, I answered cautiously and with reluctance. He wanted to know how long the houses had been used for their present purpose, how long Hoffmann and Diels had been there, whether all witnesses were permitted to bring their wives, whether the wives, too, received American rations, and so on, until to my relief a car halted before the house. Then, as the doorbell rang, he summed up his feelings in a single comment:

"I can see it still pays to have been an important Nazi. It means you don't have to starve or go through American garbage cans for food."

I had opened the door for an American colonel who greeted Dr. Schmidt seriously with a handshake and escorted him to a large black limousine, the kind used most often by high-ranking members of the tribunal.

As I listened to them driving off, I felt pretty much as if my own death warrant were in the making. I didn't know who Dr. Schmidt was, or what he could do to us, but, considering his undisguised hostility and obvious prestige with the occupiers, I was sure that he would do something. The irony was that his accusatory attitude, though threatening my family's existence, struck a familiar echo in my own feelings. I had seen generals, ambassadors, and party functionaries live in the warm comfort of the witness houses, and Hoffmann profit from his notoriety, while ordinary Germans shivered and starved in the ruins of Nuremberg. Even the people who were being executed tonight, unlike the beaten soldiers who succumbed in distant prison camps, had suffered few physical deprivations before their deaths. The arrangement was wrong and I was a part of it; but I had wanted us to survive. How often the price of survival turned out to be a battered conscience. But was not survival everybody's priority? Did I essentially differ from the mother who competed for garbage scraps and the most sheltered room in the cellar? I would have done that, too, but I would try my best to avoid having to do it. The question I had to answer to myself was how great a wrong I was thereby committing. My rationalizations bumped into too many tender spots. Everyone had wanted to survive, survive the bombing and the terror, survive by obeying, and by looking away when the trains were loaded and the ovens smoked. What the time had demanded then was martyrdom; what it demanded now was penance. We had lost our home, and perhaps our husband and father; was that not enough? With it all, homelessness was staring us again in the face. Against that threat the pangs of conscience were weak indeed.

I did not sleep much that night. It seemed no one else had been able to either, for the faces at breakfast were bleary-eyed, gray, and solemn. The absence of one person was immediately noticed. Dr. Schmidt was missing. He had been assigned a room in the other house, but no one had heard him come in.

"He might have come in very late and overslept," Frau Kruelle said and went to investigate.

But Dr. Schmidt was not in his room, nor had his bed been touched. Not knowing whether this was proper, I called the courthouse to report his absence. The answer at the other end of the wire was laconic; a tired voice muttered, "We'll check into it."

I heard nothing more about Dr. Schmidt until Rintelen confronted me with a picture in the day's paper, covering the caption with his hand. It was a photograph of several serious-faced men, one of whom I recognized immediately. When Rintelen uncovered the caption I read the names of the witnesses to the night's executions; one of them was Dr. Wilhelm Hoegner, Minister President of Bavaria, our Dr. Schmidt.

I wondered what the masquerade had been for, and why he had come to the witness house. Perhaps he had requested to see the arrangements the Americans made for some of their witnesses, having most likely heard about our operation. He had probably disapproved of it even before he came, because he had arrived as grimly as he had left. What remained to be seen now was the consequences of his incognito visit. The

Bavarian government, though operating under the control of the military government, had certain areas of jurisdiction, including the right to prosecute Germans. It was Dr. Hoegner, a Socialist and an exile during most of the Hitler years, who had led the protests against the not-guilty verdicts for Schacht, von Papen, and Fritzsche, and who had had two of them arrested after their release from allied custody. Von Papen, at last report, was still in the court building, afraid to leave.

The revelation of Dr. Schmidt's real identity had its effect on my guests, too. Diels, especially, seemed worried and preoccupied. Nearly all of them, after the Americans had done with them, would still have to face German denazification boards, which were frequently more severe in their judgment than the victors.

As it turned out, my guests' worries were more justified than mine. On the following day late in the afternoon two men in civilian clothes rang our doorbell and introduced themselves as representatives of the Bavarian criminal police with orders to wait for Heinrich Hoffmann. I verified their mission with the courthouse, from where I was told that the German authorities were within their rights in thus occupying the premises. When Hoffmann arrived a short time later he was told politely that on orders of the Bavarian government he was to be kept under police surveillance until further notice. One of the men posted himself in front of Hoffmann's door; the other moved into a small adjoining room.

Hoffmann was shaken. In an instant his expression went from amazement to despair, as if his fears, covered so carefully with the artifice of his optimism, were ready to surface at the cue they had long been expecting. But the presence of the two German police officials was oppressive not only to Hoffmann. For the others it presaged the troubles they might yet encounter. The stony face of Dr. Hoegner seemed omnipresent among us. Frequent topics of the subdued conversations were the cases of the three defendants who had been freed by the tribunal only to be rearrested on the orders of Hoegner.

"He is on a personal vendetta," was Diels's assessment of

Hoegner. "He was dissatisfied with all the sentences that weren't death. If it were up to him, half of Germany would be swinging from the gallows."

"It seems as though half of Germany was doing that in '44 without benefit of foreign judges or vengeful political exiles," I said.

Diels grimaced. "True enough, and I wasn't far from it. It's the more infuriating to have to be judged now by people who sat it all out in the safety of exile."

Hoffmann was unaccustomedly silent. The conversation was proceeding quietly in a corner of the living room; his policeman stood in the doorway, hands folded behind his back, rocking lightly on his heels. Frau Hoffmann sighed.

"Shall we never be left in peace?"

Despite the police surveillance, Hoffmann's movements were not restricted, and for a number of days one of the policemen accompanied him wherever he went, waiting for him outside the courthouse while he was at his job, waiting while he drank beer at the *Stern*, waiting outside in the rain—so Hoffmann told me gleefully—while he shared a black market goose with friends in nearby Fuerth. Within a few days Hoffmann had managed not only to get used to his shadow, but to amuse himself at the poor fellow's expense.

"What are you trying to do, kill him through exposure?" Diels muttered when Hoffmann told him of his sojourn in Fuerth.

"It's his duty to protect me, no matter what," Hoffmann said, but not with irony. His optimistic fantasy had been able to transform the policeman into a personal bodyguard ordered by high authorities to "protect" him, though he never said from what. He had been notified by the Americans, so he told me, that they could no longer supply him with living quarters, and that he should begin looking for his own. But although this ended the dream about the house that was to be put at his family's disposal, Hoffmann still managed an optimistic interpretation even for that.

"It's only for this interim period that I've been given police protection. Why would anyone want to arrest an innocent man? They're protecting me because I'm still important to them. There's a lot of work to be done in preparation for the new trials."

To whom he thought he was still important, the Germans or the Americans, was not clear to me, nor, do I think, to him. He simply clung to a last vague notion of privilege almost as a matter of faith. It had come his way for so many years, it could hardly stop now. Only when one looked at him closely, at his eyes that would no longer agree with the familiar grin, making it look more than ever like a lifeless mask, only then could one realize how desperate an effort it cost him to still believe in his own illusions. He sustained them with past glories.

"I may have been Hitler's photographer, but, I tell you, I had a thriving studio long before Hitler came to power. You have no idea how many famous people have been in front of my camera. I was still a boy when I went with my father to photograph the royal family of Bavaria. . . . Did you know that I am the only photographer who ever sent Caruso a bill?" Lloyd George was really witty; Chamberlain quiet, very reserved; Czar Nikolaus imperious and impatient; King Edward of England extremely gracious; and no one more elegant than the Duchess of Windsor. His memory was a photo album filled with smiling poses, images devoid of context. I had noticed that at times his hands trembled, spilling a bit of coffee or cigarette ashes.

"It's either old age or nerves," he acknowledged on one occasion, forcing his grin, "and I can't even blame Dr. Morell."

"Who?"

"He was Hitler's doctor. Some people swore it was Morell's injections that made Hitler the wreck he was in the end."

"Do you think it was the injections?"

Hoffmann shrugged. "They may have contributed to it, but he probably needed them." He contemplated his hands resting in his lap. "He was under terrific pressure, enough to break any man; but I've often wondered whether that doctor was Hitler's friend or enemy." He was for a long time silent, his hands now clutching his thighs, watched over by his anxious eyes. "I don't want to remember the last time I saw him. You should have seen *his* hands tremble . . . and his voice; it was almost gone. One could barely hear him."

His own voice was filled with emotion, his eyes with sorrow. It was an eerie tableau he conjured up for me: gallows, ruins, and acres of graves, and the jester mourning the expired monster. I could see the suffering tyrant at the end of his strength, at the end of his mission—a passion of sorts, a passion in reverse, a messiah of damnation—in the midst of his devoted followers sharing his final agonies. I could think of nothing to say; the processes of Hoffmann's thought remained mysterious to me. They seemed to belong to a different dimension where compassion went to the executioner instead of his victim, where creative power equaled annihilation, where nobility and elite meant the cultivation of the fiercest barbarism held dormant in the depths of human souls, where all the best qualities men could muster—courage, love, loyalty—existed and flourished in the service of evil.

He lit a cigarette, almost controlling the trembling of his hands, and glanced morosely through the rising smoke at the bored-looking policeman sitting at the other end of the room. The drawn and bitter set of his features startled me again as unaccustomed. Did it reflect sorrow for his monstrous friend, for the memory of his disintegration? Or was it the acceptance of his own reality which he could no longer subdue with illusions? Perhaps both, because Hoffmann was calm when reality caught up with him in the person of the district head of the Denazification Board, who drove up one afternoon about a week later to inform Hoffmann that he was under arrest.

"Do I have time to say goodbye to my family and pack some things?" Hoffmann asked.

The district chief offered him a cigarette. "Of course. Our methods, as you will see, differ from those of your late friend."

239

"I hope they differ from the Americans'," Hoffmann muttered. He had often complained of mistreatment in some of the American internment camps in which he had been held prior to his employment by the court.

"The Americans saw the concentration camps," said the district chief. "They might have been influenced by what they saw."

"What am I charged with?" Hoffmann asked. "Being Hitler's friend?"

"Wouldn't that be enough?" asked the district chief. "People who made friends with the devil used to be burned at the stake."

Hoffmann did not reply. He turned abruptly and went upstairs, returning shortly after with a small bag. Frau Hoffmann remained at the top of the stairs, watching silently as her husband was led outside to the waiting police car. He nodded to me in passing. Across his face flickered the shadow of his grin. Then the car door slammed behind him. The last I saw of Heinrich Hoffmann was a corner of his coat caught in the door of the car as it drove off.

24

Aɪᴛʜᴏᴜɢʜ I ᴡᴀs convinced after Hoffmann's eviction and arrest that my own eviction was not far off, November and December passed without change. The houses were less than moderately occupied. Hoffmann's son remained behind, presumably to wind up his father's job; Diels left by the end of October, Rintelen in late November. Among the guests who passed through during these two months only two stand out in my mind: Dr. Paul Schmidt—this time a genuine Dr. Schmidt—for nearly twenty-five years the chief interpreter for the German Foreign Office, and Wilhelm Messerschmitt, the man who had helped Goering build the Luftwaffe.

Dr. Schmidt's linguistic talents were reputedly unequaled, and for nearly twenty-five years he had been devoted to creating masterful translations of countless communiques, treaties, and transcripts, from the hopeful concord of Stresemann and Briand at Locarno to Hitler's ranting ultimatums. He had been present at every international conference at which Germany had been a participant, from Locarno to Munich, peace to war, serving with equal diligence the struggling republic and the brutal dictatorship. He had been at Moscow with Ribbentrop, at Berchtesgaden with Hitler and Chamberlain, in Berlin when the aged president of Czechoslovakia was brought there to seal his country's doom. After the invasion of Poland it was Dr. Schmidt who translated the final British ultimatum for Hitler and Ribbentrop. Dr. Schmidt had a remarkably kind face with small, quick eyes that expressed intelligence and warmth. It was an unusual face for a man who, at first hand, had been witness to so much treachery.

Throughout most of the trial Dr. Schmidt had been held at the Nuremberg jail, with his talents and intimate acquaintance of diplomatic history at the disposal of the tribunal. He was still working for the American investigation, apparently for the preparation of new trials, when he stayed with us at the witness house.

Messerschmitt, too, had been imprisoned until he came to us in November. Unlike Schmidt, the airplane designer was bitter against the Americans, who, he said, had been trying to pressure him into going to the United States, presumably to work for the American air force. His bitterness stemmed in particular from alleged mistreatment by American guards and was not diminished by the fact that it was through the intervention of the American air force that he had been released into the relative comfort of the witness house.

"If I ever go to America, I will go as a private person, not as a scientist," he told me. "I will not be coerced."

Though he had helped to build Hitler's air force, Messerschmitt did not consider himself a Nazi. Like many of the highly talented people who had served the regime, he rejected most of it with contempt and distaste. But the defeat of the Luftwaffe and the massive destruction of German cities appeared to have left him with an equal distaste for the conquerors. Among the people at the witness houses Messerschmitt

242

created a definite sensation, a circumstance which appeared to please him. In a small circle of intensely interested listeners he talked about the technology of space flight, rocketry, and the threats and promises of atomic energy. Although one could see then that he was in his element, his interests seemed by no means limited to things of such magnitude. Messerschmitt had asked me to get him a drawing board (which we improvised), pencils, compass, and rulers, "to occupy his mind." Once supplied with these implements, he spent much of his time in his room working on various designs—for what? Not necessarily airplanes or spaceships, but on one occasion an electric broom and on another a new kind of bed which would help to induce sleep electronically.

I used to marvel at his drawings. They were composed of lines so fine and intricately interwoven that they reminded me of spider webs. Fragile lines that could direct the construction of cities as well as the flight of the rockets that would level them. How awesome were the powers and perspectives of the human mind—analysis, pattern, construction—the dimensions of form. We were all born engineers with drawing boards in our minds, projecting cathedrals from piles of stones and bombs out of atoms. The beginning of creation was choice, form imposed on components. No spider could build a cocoon instead of a web. But from the pile of stones could be built a prison as well as a cathedral, and the atom's energy could be made to drive the generators of a city as well as blow it to bits. The beginning was choice, synonymous with thought. Faust hadn't thought of that when he brooded about the beginning of the beginning. *Im Anfang war . . . ?* In the beginning was . . . what? Word? Intellect? Strength? Action?—*Im Anfang war die Tat!* Haushofer had quoted that passage to Walsh. I remembered. "In the beginning was the act . . ." I wondered why Faust had reached that conclusion. Did God act before he thought or chose? Did God act and think and choose?

What Faust had lost faith in was his own powers. His pact had been less choice than surrender, a murder of the will to go on choosing, earning him the damnation of guilt. Would we all, like Faust, be saved through grace, forgiven for the limits of mind and courage that drove Faust to despair? Brooms and airplanes, prisons and cathedrals and the crematoria of Auschwitz—the same efficiency, the same web of thought assembling components, structuring form. Faust hadn't mentioned choice and perhaps he was right; the absence of choice explained the world much better. Did it go by default, a surrender of moral autonomy, or was that autonomy a myth? *Die Tat* was the beginning, Faust had concluded; a primal, epic burst of energy. Nothing more could be known of it. We were bound by these limits of what was knowable, and our acts occurred within these limits, each bound, like the spider's spinning of its web, by the terms of its own necessities. The choice of electric brooms over airplanes, or prisons over cathedrals was conditional; its limits were dictated, as were the words of peace and war Dr. Schmidt had so expertly translated over a quarter of a century. Perhaps the limits of mind were more awesome than its powers. God wills His goodness, Aquinas said; but this was a power he failed to grant humankind.

November passed, dark and slow. I remembered All Souls' Day in Transylvania, when the peasants set out candles on every grave and the gypsies played their violins to entertain the dead, and there were candles by every roadside for the faraway dead, for every road would sooner or later lead to their graves. Was it time for me to set out candles to light the way to my husband's grave?

I had too much time on my hands to keep my mind off my worries. I painted more and played with my children, and gave thanks for every sheltered day granted us, for winter came with exceptional harshness. As they had done the year before, the people suffered its punishment. There were no warm clothes, no fuel, and almost no food. The target ration of 1,500 calories daily was rarely met. Schools and factories closed. In the few industrial plants that remained open, workers not infrequently collapsed from hunger and exhaustion. The ragged, beaten people huddled in a few heated public places where overcrowding and lack of general hygiene spread disease like wildfire. There were at least two reports of typhus outbreaks, one in Berlin, one in Hamburg. In time the military government made available some army food stores, and several relief agencies began food programs for children, many of whom were suffering from hunger edema. Christmas came and went, barely noticed, though the bells tolled loudly across the frozen heath, across the frozen corpse of the city.

And then the year was gone, too, the second year of separation for our family. I had little hope left that my husband was still alive, and could not decide what to do with that small remnant of hope—nourish or extinguish it and face the ever-growing probability of his death. But probability was not certainty; perhaps I should never have certainty. When did probability become certainty? At the Red Cross I was told that thousands were still missing and that some were found and even reunited every day. It *did* happen. They were kind and advised me to be patient. I tried to be. For the second time I listened to the New Year's bells in the witness house, grateful for the year behind us, afraid of the one before us.

As it turned out, the year had barely moved beyond its beginning when one of the events I had feared so greatly and for so long, namely, the termination of my employment, did come about, but in a manner so totally unexpected that I was completely unprepared for it. In the late morning of a cold, clear day around the middle of January I answered the doorbell for a man wearing a brown uniform marked on the sleeve with a red cross.

It was my husband.

I had been told that it *did* happen, and it happened to us. There were, no doubt, many such moments scattered like beams of light across a dark canvas, moments of transfiguration which compressed within their brevity all the mystery and magnitude of human experience, moments of purity that rose above the wretchedness, the senselessness and sorrow, restoring meaning and form—a resurrection of sorts. No words can measure the intensity, depth, or breadth of such a moment, the shock of its joy, the harsh fervency of that first embrace.

I had never seen my husband weep, but he did when for the first time he held his youngest child. I think we were all crying —Cuci and I, and Lori, my oldest, and even Frau Kruelle. Antal, who had been only three when we had to separate, did not recognize his father and looked puzzled. It seemed difficult for him to believe that the man in the brown uniform was not just another guest.

It was difficult for me to believe, too. He was altered, his body swollen from hunger edema, his hands calloused; only his eyes had retained their warmth and glow, or perhaps they had been rekindled by this moment of our reunion. He had survived his time, his order. Was this the man who had rehearsed the retreat from his emperor's empty throne? He was not broken; he had survived, drawing his strength from his greater loves. For two years he had managed to hide his identity as a member of the aristocracy, though the new masters had readily discovered that he was not a member of the working class. They had done this by examining his hands, and, finding them lacking the marks of hard labor, they had assigned him the hardest category of work. He had dug up fields, cleared rubble, loaded freight, hauled coal, and driven a beer wagon. Like me he had been repeatedly in touch with the Red Cross, and although he was equally unable to get information about us, he was eventually offered a chance to work for the organization, largely because he spoke English and French, languages needed by members of a Hungarian Red Cross delegation that was to be sent to West Germany for the purpose of tracing certain Hungarian properties and negotiating their return with the allied occupation authorities.

It was only after he reached West Germany that he had been able to locate us. Wanting his arrival to be a surprise, he had requested the Red Cross not to notify me in advance. But what he found was a surprise as well. He had been given an

246

address; no one had told him that it was the witness house. Though pleased to find us in such good circumstances, he appeared to have mixed feelings about my position. We had both bent to the needs of survival; he was changed, but so was I. The years at Sepsiköröspatak with its lovely formal gardens and stony-faced servants seemed centuries away. I was no longer his lady, the lady whose hand the silent peasants had kissed on feast days; I was but his wife. He was no longer my lord, the lord whose gesture or glance had commanded obedience; he was only my husband. The ancient images had been smashed; beneath their fragments we had to find ourselves. That was quite literally all we had left.

For me there had been in it all a kind of liberation, a rediscovery of my own powers; for him the blow was harder. The substance of his self had been too inextricably bound to the structure that had collapsed not to have been hurt by it, and he was hurt enough never to fully recover. That he was bound by the pride of his name and the burden of a tradition that had ceased to be was not vanity, but quite the opposite. He had been trained to sublimate the needs of his self to the demands of his name from the time when as a young boy he was forced to sleep on his back with his hands above the covers, to the time when, as an impoverished young man who had not yet come into a proper inheritance, he had been forced to seek work under an assumed name; a count was unemployable. Such conventions may now seem absurd, but they were part of a functioning social order that was more often than not as rigorously enforced at the bottom as it was on the top. The rationalizations of change throw the spotlight on old forms and label them absurd, to be smiled at like the fashions of bygone decades; but as fashions reflect the spirit of a time, so its conventions may well reflect its needs. A convention becomes absurd only after it has ceased to be necessary.

We stayed together at the witness house for only another week. I notified my employers of my intention to leave and found them not at all pleased with the idea. Apparently Hoffmann had been right; the witness houses would be needed for some time to come. But my husband's plans were to go to Austria, the country of his birth, where he hoped to renew old contacts and find employment. Force of circumstances changed these plans, and our stay in Austria turned out to be brief. Our roots were severed; our lives had to be rebuilt. The promise seemed elsewhere. We applied to come to America.

What remains to be said? That we came to the United States as immigrants with nothing more than our hands and our hopes, like so many thousands before us? Let me finish there, with another beginning. It was a long journey from the feudal strictures of Sepsiköröspatak on the high and quiet plains of Transylvania to the competitive vitality, the ruthless energy of America, a journey spanning a millennium. For my husband it turned out to be too much time to carry on his back. Like some of my guests at the witness house with their stripped uniforms and suddenly meaningless titles, he remained what he had been, even while trying to become something else. As he had done during our separation in Hungary, he fought to survive the poverty, the menial work, the strains our altered circumstances imposed on our relationship, until illness took him in 1955.

The beginning and the promise belong to my children, who became citizens of the new world without bondage to the old.